W9-BGS-419

THE FUTURE UNIVERSITY

As universities increasingly engage with the world beyond the classroom and the campus, those who work within higher education are left to examine how the university's mission has changed. Official reviews and debates often forget to inquire into the purposes and responsibilities of universities, and how they are changing. Where these matters are addressed, they are rarely pursued in depth, and rarely go beyond current circumstances. Those who care about the university's role in society are left looking for a renewed sense of purpose regarding its goals and aspirations.

The Future University explores new avenues opening up to universities and tackles fundamental issues facing their development. Contributors with interdisciplinary and international perspectives imagine ways to frame the university's future. They consider the history of the university, its current status as an active player in local governments, cultures, and markets, and where these trajectories may lead.

What does it mean to be a university in the twenty-first century? What could the university become? What limitations do they face, and what opportunities might lie ahead? This volume in the International Studies in Higher Education series offers bold and imaginative possibilities.

Ronald Barnett is Emeritus Professor of Higher Education, Institute of Education, London.

International Studies in Higher Education
Series Editors:
David Palfreyman, OxCHEPS
Ted Tapper, OxCHEPS
Scott Thomas, Claremont Graduate University

The central purpose of this series is to see how different national and regional systems of higher education are responding to widely shared pressures for change. The most significant of these are: rapid expansion; reducing public funding; the increasing influence of market and global forces; and the widespread political desire to integrate higher education more closely into the wider needs of society and, more especially, the demands of the economic structure. The series will commence with an international overview of structural change in systems of higher education. It will then proceed to examine on a global front the change process in terms of topics that are both traditional (for example, institutional management and system governance) and emerging (for example, the growing influence of international organizations and the blending of academic and professional roles). At its conclusion the series will have presented, through an international perspective, both a composite overview of contemporary systems of higher education, along with the competing interpretations of the process of change.

Published titles:

Structuring Mass Higher Education
The Role of Elite Institutions
Edited by David Palfreyman and Ted Tapper

International Perspectives on the Governance of Higher Education
Steering, Policy Processes, and Outcomes
Edited by Jeroen Huisman

International Organizations and Higher Education Policy
Thinking Globally, Acting Locally?
Edited by Roberta Malee Bassett and Alma Maldonado

Academic and Professional Identities in Higher Education
The Challenges of a Diversifying Workforce
Edited by Celia Whitchurch and George Gordon

International Research Collaborations
Much to be gained, many ways to get in trouble
Melissa S. Anderson and Nicholas H. Steneck

Cross-border Partnerships in Higher Education
Strategies and Issues
Robin Sakamoto and David Chapman

Accountability in Higher Education
Global Perspectives on Trust and Power
Bjørn Stensaker and Lee Harvey

The Engaged University
International Perspectives on Civic Engagement
David Watson, Susan E. Stroud, Robert Hollister, and Elizabeth Babcock

Universities and the Public Sphere
Knowledge Creation and State Building in the Era of Globalization
Edited by Brian Pusser, Ken Kempner, Simon Marginson, and Imanol Ordorika

THE FUTURE UNIVERSITY

Ideas and Possibilities

Edited by Ronald Barnett

NEW YORK AND LONDON

First published 2012
by Routledge
711 Third Avenue, New York, NY 10017

Simultaneously published in the UK
by Routledge
2 Park Square, Milton Park, Abingdon, Oxon OX14 4RN

Routledge is an imprint of the Taylor & Francis Group, an informa business

Library of Congress Cataloging in Publication Data
The future university : ideas and possibilities / edited by Ronald Barnett.
   p. cm.—(International studies in higher education)
   Includes bibliographical references and index.
   1. Education, Higher—Aims and objectives—Cross-cultural studies.
   2. Universities and colleges—Cross-cultural studies.
   3. Education and globalization—Cross-cultural studies.
   I. Barnett, Ronald, 1947–
   LB2322.2.F88 2011
   378—dc22
   2011003860

ISBN: 978–0–415–43391–4 (hbk)
ISBN: 978–0–203–94560–5 (ebk)

Typeset in Bembo by Swales & Willis Ltd, Exeter, Devon

CONTENTS

Series Editors' Introduction   *viii*
Acknowledgements   *xi*

Introduction   1
Ronald Barnett

PART I
Emerging Futures   **13**

1 The Future isn't Waiting   15
   Sheldon Rothblatt

2 Imagining the University of the Future   26
   Louise Morley

PART II
Global Possibilities   **37**

3 Accessing Knowledge in the University of the Future:
   Lessons from Australia   39
   Leesa Wheelahan

4 The Trajectory and Future of the Idea of the University
in China   50
Shuang-Ye Chen and Leslie N.K. Lo

5 The Idea of the University in Latin America in the
Twenty-First Century   59
Mario Díaz Villa

6 The Decline of the University in South Africa:
Reconstituting the Place of Reason   71
Yusef Waghid

PART III
Ideas of the University   **85**

7 Towards a Networked University   87
Nicolas Standaert

8 The University as Fool   101
Donncha Kavanagh

9 Re-imagining the University: Developing a Capacity to Care   112
Gloria Dall'Alba

10 Creating a Better World: Towards the University of Wisdom   123
Nicholas Maxwell

PART IV
A University for Society   **139**

11 Universities and the Common Good   141
Jon Nixon

12 Teaching in the University the Day After Tomorrow   152
Paul Standish

13 The University: A Public Issue   165
Jan Masschelein and Maarten Simons

14 The Future of University Research in Africa   178
    Berte van Wyk and Philip Higgs

15 Knowledge Socialism: Intellectual Commons and Openness
    in the University   187
    Michael A. Peters, Garett Gietzen, and David J. Ondercin

    Coda   201
    Ronald Barnett

List of Contributors   *205*
Bibliography   *208*
Subject Index   *225*
Name Index   *230*

SERIES EDITORS' INTRODUCTION

International Studies in Higher Education

This series is constructed around the premise that higher education systems are experiencing common pressures for fundamental change, reinforced by differing national and regional circumstances that also impact upon established institutional structures and procedures. There are four major dynamics for change that are of international significance:

1. Mass higher education is a universal phenomenon.
2. National systems find themselves located in an increasingly global market-place that has particular significance for their more prestigious institutions.
3. Higher education institutions have acquired (or been obliged to acquire) a wider range of obligations, often under pressure from governments prepared to use state power to secure their policy goals.
4. The balance between the public and private financing of higher education has shifted—markedly in some cases—in favour of the latter.

Although higher education systems in all regions and nation states face their own particular pressures for change, these are especially severe in some cases: the collapse of the established economic and political structures of the former Soviet Union along with Central and Eastern Europe, the political revolution in South Africa, the pressures for economic development in India and China, and demographic pressure in Latin America.

Each volume in the series will examine how systems of higher education are responding to this new and demanding political and socio-economic environment. Although it is easy to overstate the uniqueness of the present situation, it is not an exaggeration to say that higher education is undergoing a fundamental shift in its character, and one that is truly international in scope. We are witnessing a major transition in the relationship of higher education to state and society. What makes the present circumstances particularly interesting is to see how different systems—a product of social, cultural, economic and political contexts that have interacted and evolved over time—respond in their own peculiar ways to the changing environment. There is no assumption that the pressures for change have set in motion the trend towards a converging model of higher education, but we do believe that in the present circumstances no understanding of "the idea of the university" remains sacrosanct.

Although this is a series with an international focus it is not expected that each individual volume should cover every national system of higher education. This would be an impossible task. Whilst aiming for a broad range of case studies, with each volume addressing a particular theme, the focus will be upon the most important and interesting examples of responses to the pressures for change. Most of the individual volumes will bring together a range of comparative quantitative and qualitative information, but the primary aim of each volume will be to present differing interpretations of critical developments in key aspects of the experience of higher education. The dominant overarching objective is to explore the conflict of ideas and the political struggles that inevitably surround any significant policy development in higher education.

It can be expected that volume editors and their authors will adopt their own interpretations to explain the emerging patterns of development. There will be conflicting theoretical positions drawn from the multi-disciplinary, and increasingly inter-disciplinary, field of higher education research. Thus we can expect in most volumes to find an inter-marriage of approaches drawn from sociology, economics, history, political science, cultural studies, and the administrative sciences. However, whilst there will be different approaches to understanding the process of change in higher education, each volume editor(s) will impose a framework upon the volume inasmuch as chapter authors will be required to address common issues and concerns.

This volume in the series, edited by Ronald Barnett, focuses upon how universities across the world are examining their "missions" and are looking to develop a renewed sense of their purposes. What then is it to *be* a university in the twenty-first century? What possibilities lie in front of it? What ideas might help to frame the University of the Future? How, in the best of all likely worlds might and should the university unfold? It is questions such as these that form the territory of this volume.

Bringing together a distinguished group of scholars from across the world, *The Future University: Ideas and Possibilities* explores these matters and offers bold and imaginative proposals. With the contributors offering differing disciplinary viewpoints and perspectives from many regions of the world, the volume is a resource both for further scholarship and also for university policy and practice, at national and international levels.

Among the issues explored are:

> The idea of the university in the twenty-first century
> The networked university
> Universities and the common good
> Universities and wisdom

Many proclaim the end of the university but this volume is a volume of hope and beneficial possibilities. The idea of the university can live on vibrantly through the twenty-first century.

David Palfreyman
Director of OxCHEPS, New College, University of Oxford

Ted Tapper
OxCHEPS, New College, University of Oxford

Scott Thomas
Professor of Educational Studies, Claremont Graduate University, California

ACKNOWLEDGEMENTS

I should like to express my warm thanks to the series editor, Professor Ted Tapper, for inviting me to plan and edit this volume and for all the encouragement, support and guidance he has given me throughout its compilation. This volume could not and would not have seen the light of day without that support from him.

Thanks are due for the following permissions:

Donncha Kavanagh's Chapter 8, "The University as Fool" draws on his (2009) paper, "Institutional Heterogeneity and Change: The University as Fool", *Organization,* 16 (4) 575–595, Sage Publications.

Nicholas Maxwell's Chapter 10, "Creating a Better World: Towards the University of Wisdom," is contiguous with some parts of Nicholas Maxwell (2008) "From Knowledge to Wisdom: the need for an academic revolution", chapter 1 in Ronald Barnett and Nicholas Maxwell (eds.) *Wisdom in the University.* Abingdon: Routledge (and previously published in the *London Review of Education* (Taylor and Francis Journals)).

Jan Masschelein and Maarten Simons' Chapter 13, "The University: A Public Issue," draws upon Masschelein, J. and Simons, M. (2010) *Jenseits der Excellenz: Eine kleine Morphologie der Welt-Universität.* Zurich: Diaphenes.

Nicolas Standaert's Chapter 7, "Towards a Networked University" draws upon his chapter "Pyramid, Pillar and Web: Questions for Academic Life Raised by the Network Society," in R. Barnett, J.-C. Guedon, J. Masschelein, M. Simons, S. Robertson and N. Standaert (2009). *Rethinking the University after Bologna,* pp 39–53.

INTRODUCTION

Ronald Barnett

Believing in the University

What is it to be a University in the Twenty-First Century? What might the university become? What limitations are pressing upon the university? And what possibilities might lie in front of the university?

These questions lie at the heart of this volume and they in turn open up a large territory. In order to tackle them seriously, we shall need to develop a sense as to the past and present conceptions of the university, in order that conceptions of the university's future possibilities might be well grounded. In turn, we shall need to identify and explore conceptions of the university from different regions of the globe, for assuredly there will be different traditions and perspectives in different countries. In many countries and even regions of the world—for example, South America—debates are being conducted over the purposes of the university and it may be that different views are emerging on the matter bearing a national or a regional imprint.

The reference to "the University" rather than to "higher education" in the proposed title of this volume is significant on three grounds. *First*, this volume focuses on the university as a social institution. This is an institution that has extraordinary longevity, being around a thousand years old since its mediaeval inception, but yet arguably is on the cusp of a new phase opening to it in the twenty-first century. This volume will attempt to explore the options that are opening to the university. *Second*, higher education is here understood to be a significant part of the functioning of the university, but only a part: the contemporary university has ever-expanding functions, not only in knowledge production and knowledge transfer but in a manifold of relationships with the state and society (in class formation and in intellectual culture). It is, therefore, the university in its totality that is in question here, rather than any particular aspect of it. *Third*, there is a long-standing literature that continues to grow on the idea of the university but rarely has an attempt been made to bring together scholars from across the world imaginatively to explore the *future* possibilities for the university.

Three ideas in that last sentence deserve, perhaps, a little emphasis—those of imagination, exploration and possibilities. Across the world, the space occupied by the university apparently seems to be increasingly defined for it as the university comes to be subject more and more to the market. The university is being incorporated, it is said, into "knowledge capitalism" (Murphy, 2009) and is being enjoined to play an ever fuller part in expanding this new form of capitalism. It may be said that this new function of the university now opens possibilities for the university that it has not enjoyed before. Now, the university is free to identify and exploit possibilities for its position in society and the global knowledge economy. There is an expanding universe of opportunities available to it. But these opportunities, such as they are, have severe constraints written into them. Now, knowledge inquiry and learning processes have to prove their worth through their economic impact. It is not enough that these activities are "applicable"; now they have to generate demonstrably an economic return in some form.

Against this background, it becomes a matter of both significance and urgency as to whether there are other possibilities for the university in the twenty-first century and as to what such possibilities might look like. "Possibilities," "imagination" and "exploration" become, therefore, key terms in addressing the current state of play; or, at least, they form key ideas for this volume. The contributors to this volume are not content simply to assess or even to critique the contemporary university but, as the title suggests, to identify and explore "ideas and possibilities" for the future university. Such a venture requires, in turn, the exercise of the imagination: only through the imagination is it possible to try to step outside the given order of things and to bring forward future possibilities for the university.

The exercise of the imagination, however, can only be a necessary condition of leaping beyond the current order of things; it cannot be a sufficient condition. Two additional conditions have to be met. Firstly, the exercise of the imagination has ultimately to be tempered by a certain realism. Hard-nosed efforts have to be made in order to assess the actual possibilities inherent in the current state of play of the university. Seriously identifying ideas and possibilities for the university is a nice example, as we might put it, of "critical realism" in action (cf. Bhaskar, 2011: ch9). Universities are real social institutions, caught amid social forces, networks of other institutions and ideologies. That complex of real factors, often hidden from immediate view, has to be teased out if the exercise of the imagination is not to have a castles-in-the-air quality. Secondly, the exercise of the imagination needs to be accompanied by a belief in the university. The university remains an extraordinary social institution, replete with possibilities. The identification and exploration of those possibilities has to be infused by a double belief, both that the university is worth struggling for and that the there are still possibilities open to the university that enable it to do some justice to its traditional value background, connected with reason, understanding and personal and social improvement. Believing in the university, therefore, is a crucial part of the inquiry represented by this volume.

In the rest of this introduction, I shall refer more explicitly to the chapters in this volume.

Emerging Futures (*Part I*)

As Sheldon Rothblatt puts it (chapter one), "the future isn't waiting." It is already with us. This, too, is a message in much of Louise Morley's chapter (chapter two). New institutional forms involving cross-institutional collaboration, a blurring of the public and the private, new learning modes (especially favouring e-learning and practice-based learning), forms of knowledge pursued for their "impact" on the knowledge economy, the rise of the "global" in higher education and the emergence of "nomadic" identities among academics: all these and more contribute to the "hyper-modernisation" of the university (cf. Lipovetsky, 2005). We can surely safely predict, with Rothblatt and Morley, that these trends will continue into the future. They will do so because they are the outturn of massive underlying forces of the incorporation of the university into the dominant structures of a post-capitalist society.

This set of considerations raises two fundamental issues. Firstly, there is a question raised by Rothblatt: under these circumstances—in which the university is being broken open, and its boundaries are not so much becoming porous as rather entirely dissolving—does the very idea of "the idea of the university" retain any substance? If, as both Rothblatt and Morley observe, a heightened competitiveness among universities is likely to develop, we can predict that universities will increasingly seek each to identify a niche for itself in the academic marketplace. In such a situation, talk of "the idea of the university" may seem to be redundant at best and pretentiousness at worst. The "idea of the university" seems to have had meaning in an age in which universities were largely undifferentiated and serving a small (actually an "elite") section of society. In an age in which the meaning of "university" simply cannot be either stable or uniform, engaging in an inquiry into the future idea of the university becomes redundant. It can have no purchase. It is also pretentious in that it pretends to a unity that is now lost from view. And it pretends that there could be ways of talking of the university that have a universal connotation, above and beyond the particularities of institutional forms and fluidities.

Rothblatt's answer to his own question is that the idea of the university can now serve as a conceptual umbrella—albeit with "untidy boundaries"—for "a collection of niches, for disciplines, for individuals." Here, in this volume, this reflection raises in turn the following question: Just what niches, conceptual and practical, are available to the university? Just what are the possibilities for the university in the twenty-first century, in ways that still retain some substance of the term "university"? Morley observes that "it is unclear whether . . . recent and current policy discourses are generating creative thinking about the future of universities, or whether they are limiting it." At least, then, we might hold out the hope that the idioms and currents of the present age are generating spaces for new kinds of thinking about and practices in and around the university.

A second issue here is this: to what extent should the recovery of any idea of the university borrow from or seek to retain remnants of earlier ideas of the university? Or are any ideas of the university from earlier ages inevitably so much conceptual baggage? Rothblatt himself notices that the "absence from discussions of globalization" of the idea of the liberal education is "particularly evident." In this weighing of the "University of the Past" with the "University of the Present" (as Morley puts it), there are two subsidiary issues. On the one hand, there is the empirical story: as governments around the world move to introduce more market elements into their higher education systems, the possibilities for the university to expand social mobility and social equity seem even to be reversing. This is, as Morley puts it, a "rapidly dessicating sector." The University of the Future seems to be becoming, in part, the University of the Past as its locus as a centre of power, prestige and inequality grows again.

But, on the other hand, there is—as we might put it—the discursive story. Can we still sensibly hold onto elements of the former ideas that characterised the University of the Past? For Morley, "the University of the Future needs to recover critical knowledge and *be* a think tank and policy driver." In other words, parts of the traditional idea of the university can still be called up, providing that they are re-interpreted in the context of the University of the Future. As Morley puts it, "We need new conceptual vocabularies and reinvigorated courage to challenge the archaism and hyperactivity that frame the sector."

Global Possibilities (*Part II*)

Each university system in each country has its own history, traditions and contemporary circumstances. Ideas of and the possibilities for the university always have their place in a context. Increasingly, too, within a university system, each university will have its own setting and positioning. This necessary *contextualisation* of the ideas and possibilities is just one of the points to be drawn from the contributors in this section. And yet, strikingly in these four contributions and across the countries and regions represented here—Australia, China, South Africa and Latin America—we see recurring themes, such as those of a shift towards "performativity" (in which efficiency and output become crucial), a driving up of knowledge that has direct applicability in society (and in which that impact can be demonstrated) and a slide away from "liberal education" towards vocationalisation *and* the increasing influence of governments and inter-governmental agencies in encouraging these shifts. These commonalities—albeit with a greater or lesser presence in each case—in the country-specific narratives point to a global context for an inquiry into the ideas and possibilities for the university in the twenty-first century.

This dual set of reflections—as to the presence of the local *and* the global contexts that surround universities—surely invites the following line of thought. The university has for a very long time—arguably even since its medieval origins—stood for universal categories. It came to have a close association with an inquiry into truth and whatever that might mean (even in its pragmatic orientations), truth was never simply my truth, or my group's truth or even my society's truth. The university's truth claims were to be subjected to validity tests for truth as such. The question "but is it true?" has always been a key question for the university. It is here, in this concern for truth, that we find the university's allegiance to reason, of which Yusef Waghid speaks. Yet the university does have to live in particular contexts many of which are closing the spaces for untrammelled reason. We surely catch glimpses of this movement in each of the chapters: Leesa Wheelahan draws attention to the promotion of vocationalism in Australia and the separation from the systematic conversations of society about itself for those who take that learning route; Shuang-Ye Chen and Leslie Lo draw attention to the struggle in China—now apparently infused with renewed vigour—to re-vivify university practices with ideas of the university fit for the twenty-first century; Mario Díaz Villa, amid the heterogeneous sets of spaces that now constitutes Latin America, points to the dominance of the economic field and of economic reason; and Yusef Waghid, borrowing from Derrida, points to the heightened production in South Africa of "technicians of learning."

And yet, despite situations that could lead to quite dismal readings, each of the four contributors is able to identify ideas and potential practices that just might lend themselves to enactment that helps to move the university forward in the twenty-first century. Wheelahan looks to "the notion of professionalism [to provide] a bridge back to . . . disciplinary knowledge (and thereby a form of liberal education)"; Chen and Lo look to a visionary institutional leadership leading, for example, radical curriculum reform; Díaz Villa boldly sets out a raft of principles framed around critical dialogue and openness through which the university might combat the "performativity" and "postmodernism" that confront it; and Waghid, by way of example, refers to the cultivation of "democratic iterations" that may be embodies in a student-supervisor relationship in which each learns from the other.

In a way, the actual weight that may be placed on each of these proposals is not, I think, to the point. The key point is that, however fast the currents in which the university finds itself may be running, the search for progressive possibilities that extend reason across society remains a worthwhile activity. It *just might* lead to the identification of realisable possibilities. Such possibilities we may term "feasible utopias" (Barnett, 2011): they may not be realised but there is sufficient available to us—both in reasoning about the character of man's place in the world and empirical evidence—to suggest that they *could* be realised. They are not fanciful suggestions.

We can draw, I think, three broad conclusions from these four case studies. Firstly, the very globalisation of the university is opening up global spaces in which the idea of the university as a space of reason *in* society may be reclaimed. Secondly, the identification of feasible ideas and practices that may carry the university forward requires hard and imaginative thinking, especially if they are successfully to contend against the main currents of the age. Thirdly, the very insertion of the university into global society—as we may term it—opens and even calls for new ideas and practices that open up possibilities for the university *for* society. There is no sliding back available: the university cannot ratchet itself back to a situation in which it is separate from society. Very well: let us see, then, if we can identify ideas and possibilities for the university both *in* and *for* society. The enactment of ideas here becomes just as important as the identification of the ideas themselves; they should yield feasible possibilities for the university, in fulfilling its new potential as a global institution able to promote learning, inquiry and even social development across the globe.

Ideas of the University (*Part III*)

Possibilities for the University, then, are already present. Spaces are opening for new practices. Those spaces present themselves differently across the world and across universities even within a single system. Yet, if full advantage is to be taken of the spaces now opening for universities in the twenty-first century, new ideas are surely needed. Certainly, the extent to which any new ideas might or should still draw upon earlier ideas of the university—of reason, truth, academic freedom and so forth—is a matter for further consideration. But the university in the twenty-first century has challenges afresh. It occupies new spaces in society. Accordingly, new ideas are needed if the university is to realise its possibilities. The four chapters in Part III seek to help precisely in this task. For each of the four contributors, there is a dominant concept and with it comes a cluster of attendant concepts.

Nicolas Standaert (chapter seven) develops the idea of the university as a set of networks within wider societal networks. Associated concepts here include those of web, places, nodes, spaces, displacement and the "in-between." For the networked university, there is no centre as such. Consequently, "in a time of fragmentation there is need of rediscovering the whole." For Standaert, a major challenge for the university understood through such concepts becomes the following: Can ways be found so that different disciplines can meet each other? "How can one create new nodes in the web of sciences?" A particular problem is that of the relationship between "the so-called measurable and hermeneutic sciences" (or, as might be said in the UK, between science and the humanities): just "how can the two meet each other?" It follows that "the space of a networked university still has to be invented." We need, therefore, a new architecture that has "in-between" spaces that in turn generate the "uncertain, vulnerable, uncontrollable or incomprehensible."

Donncha Kavanagh (chapter eight) invites us to think of the university as fool, the idea of fool taken from the mediaeval courts and elsewhere in which the fool had a crucial role to play. The role of the fool, after all, is to present ambiguity to the powerful, wittily engaging his audience but perhaps to disturb a little as well. "The fool is an irritant, a provocateur, whose modus operandi is to provoke new wisdom in others." Within the fool's foolishness, then, lies wisdom. Understood as fool, the university has had several masters or "sovereign institutions" over its near-one thousand years of history, including the crown, the nation, the state, the professions and the world of work. The idea of fool, however, implies a certain "liminality" from the main structures of power and so an issue (for Kavanagh) is the extent to which this liminal role has been or is being abandoned. If, qua fool, the university is both to institutionalise and to de-institutionalise, the university cannot become subservient to any authority. "The fool must . . . be careful not to transgress this (liminal) role." Accordingly, "there is an . . . onus on the university . . . to actively *foster* intellectuals that question and play with society's institutions."

In her chapter (chapter nine), Gloria Dall'Alba—drawing especially on Martin Heidegger—explores the concepts of care, being, responsibility and attunement. To care is to have a deep concern for something beyond oneself, both "others and things in our world." Calling on the concept of care is thus a rejoinder to a higher education that has become narrowly a matter of the intellect and of skills in the world. To have a concern with care is to take up a view as to one's being in the world. An interest in care and in being on the part of the university would carry over into all of its key practices, namely teaching, research and social engagement.

Care shows itself in being responsible, in responding appropriately, whether in pedagogical relationships or in the choice of research and in the manner of its conduct or in the possibilities that open for social engagement. Responsibility entails choice which in turn has further implications: "when possibilities are opened, we press ahead into an emergent possibility, thereby negating and foreclosing other possibilities." Part of the functioning of the space occupied by the university, therefore, is that of encouraging "the discernment of possibilities" and the wherewithal to follow through on certain possibilities: "the university can encourage thoughtful—and, at times, courageous—responses to the call to care." We discern possibilities through "attunement," through close and careful attention to matters at hand. Such an education—and such a university—for being entail commitment and risk and require courage and leadership.

In chapter ten, Nicholas Maxwell develops an argument around the idea of wisdom. Connected concepts include those of knowledge-inquiry and wisdom-inquiry, and problem-solving rationality and aim-oriented rationality. Maxwell believes that the university has long favoured "knowledge inquiry," a form of inquiry that is "grossly and damagingly irrational." This is a form of inquiry that is dissociated from a more fundamental concern with problems of living and which, as a result, violates certain rules of rational problem-solving. What is needed, therefore, is to develop universities around a form of inquiry that promotes wisdom—"wisdom being the capacity to realize what is of value in life, for oneself and others . . ." In this "wisdom inquiry," "social inquiry is intellectually more fundamental than the natural and technological sciences," helping "to develop and assess rival philosophies of life." "Whereas knowledge-inquiry demands that emotions and desires, values, human ideals and aspiration, philosophies of life be excluded from the intellectual domain of inquiry, wisdom-inquiry requires that they be included." Wisdom inquiry, therefore, would offer an interplay of sceptical rationality and emotion, an interplay of mind and heart so that we may develop "mindful hearts and heartfelt minds."

On the face of it, these four chapters constitute four quite different viewpoints, articulating and developing separate sets of concepts in helping to develop ideas and possibilities for the university in the twenty-first century. And the chapters have some substantive differences in the detail of their arguments. However, there are certain features that are to be found across them to a greater or lesser extent. Firstly, they are centrally concerned to identify and to develop imaginative concepts not currently part of the mainstream of contemporary thinking about the university. Secondly, each contains indications as to ways in which the concepts for which their authors are contending could be put into place. Thirdly, they are suggesting in their different ways that a conception of the university built around knowledge per se is inadequate. Fourthly, they are arguing—again to a greater or lesser extent—for the intellect and other aspects of human *being* to be brought into a proper and closer relationship with each other. Fifthly, we see here too a view—especially in Standaert and Maxwell—that a new understanding of the humanities needs to be developed and a new articulation of the relationship found between the physical sciences and the various forms of social and human inquiry.

There is a further issue raised by these four conceptions: if the university of the twenty-first century is to realise fully its possibilities, should it be construed as lying within the main body of society or somewhat separate from it? Kavanagh's conception of the fool is itself a point of ambiguity on the matter: the fool is both within the court but keeps his distance from it; and hence is a "liminal" character. For Maxwell, the University of Wisdom is presumably to be within society in that it is deliberately structured as a site that identifies key issues in society and rigorously brings together its total resources in addressing those issues; but it is clear that the university here too has to be permitted its own space if it is rigorously to assess all the competing viewpoints and evidence on issues. Perhaps the metaphor of the web suggested by Standaert is potent here: the university can be seen as occupying a region within a larger web of webs, with its own nodes and networks, but yet having sufficient force that it is able to exert an influence of its own on the totality of the webs that constitute the world.

A University for Society (*Part IV*)

Suppose, as part of our imagining the university in the twenty-first century, we conceived of a university not just in society but actually *for* society? What would that mean? I take it that it would mean a number of things. It would mean that the university was interested not simply in reflecting society but in helping society forward; towards a better society. It would mean, in turn, that universities would be compelled to forge some sense as to what might constitute "a good society" (to steal a phrase from the aphorism of Tony Judt with which Jon Nixon opens chapter 11). It would mean that the university had formed some sense of its own collective virtues, in helping society to realise better and more profoundly the capacities of its members to come to have a care for each other and to live more harmoniously and respectfully together. And it would mean that the university was seized of its potential in developing the public realm, especially the realm of public reason, of the giving and rendering of reasons in a public space.

This is a formidable list of conditions and yet the five chapters in this section not only, I think, imply such conditions but go even beyond them. For Nixon, the matter is essentially one of an "aspiration towards a fairer and more just society; a society shaped and motivated, that is, by a sense of the common good." For Paul Standish (chapter 12), one way of achieving such an end lies in the recovery of teaching as constitutive of the good life in itself and as, therefore, at the heart of the university. Here, the "subject matter" would come alive "in the interaction between teacher and student, . . . in dialogue or conversation . . ." Jan Masschelein and Maarten Simons (chapter 13) urge the rediscovery of the lecture as a conversation between professor and students in a public space, a space of free-thinking, unalloyed by considerations of performance, economy or informational resources or even specific interests of any kind. Berte van Wyk and Philip Higgs (chapter 14) plead for "a form of African community based research which takes cognisance of values present in the community, for purposes of fostering the communal beliefs of that community." It would be a "kind of research that is conducted by, with and for the community." Michael Peters, Garett Gietzen and David Ondercin (chapter 15) examine the possibility that new communication technologies may usher in a university that is much more open than its predecessors, structured around many-to-many interactions and knowledge creation. We may even, they suggest, be on the verge of the formation of a university that is playing its part in the birth of "knowledge socialism."

Together, these five essays provide a powerful rebuke to depictions of the university as a matter of private good, or personal interest, or as a set of marketable products (where the capacity to access those products is inevitably severely curtailed in a capitalist society). It was long part of the self-understanding of the university that, alongside teaching and research, it offered "service" to society. (This view of the university was perhaps markedly so in the US.) But these five essays suggest that a new conception of the university is both possible and necessary, a university that actually helps the remaking of civil society in a fragmented age.

Of course, there are many issues that these five chapters implicitly raise that should be tackled on another occasion. One is that of concepts. What, for example, are the meanings of, and the relationships between, the following concepts: common good, civic good, public good, public sphere, public reason, social good, communality, commons and public engagement? This is not the place to essay such conceptual analyses. I will, in closing, instead confine myself to making three points.

Firstly, as these chapters make plain, the university is well-placed to contribute *directly* to the widening of the public sphere by thinking through its own internal practices. For example, as Standish sees it, the dominant conception of teaching that "afflicts the university . . . stultifies the public realm"; so that "the threat to teaching is a threat to democracy." But if and when "the best possibilities of teaching are recovered," the university—"of the day after tomorrow"—would come to have a "public place in the democracy to come." In parallel, for Masschelein and Simons, properly conceived and practised, the lecture is precisely a collective endeavour, a gathering together (of a plurality of students and professors) giving themselves to the provocations of an issue that stands outside of themselves. "It shows something about what living and living together is about . . ." (Masschelein & Simons). The lecture is not *to* a public but itself conjures forth a "public." "Public lectures thus are associated with the emergence of a new consciousness, or an overtaking of the self that extends one's own, private affairs by making things into a public affair." As such, it "inaugurates a question about how we are going to live together." Analogously, a university for the public good would ensure that it offered spaces for learning that "might also become deliberative spaces" (Nixon) in which students might engage with "uncertainty, indeterminacy and irreducible complexity." A fundamental consideration here is that "it is precisely the capacity for living and working together in uncertainty, indeterminacy and irreducible complexity that the students of today will require [in the twenty-first century]."

Secondly, the university is well placed because of its already embeddedness in society to affect transformations in the wider society. In making its research more community based, focused on community social problems and needs, "grassroots democracy" could be strengthened while, at the same time, through "the opening of educational doors to community knowledge," the academy itself could grow in socially worthwhile ways (van Wyk & Higgs). The possibility is even emerging that the university could inaugurate a new era of collective knowledge creation and become "a locus of true inclusion and social and economic activity" (Peters, Gietzen & Ondercin).

Thirdly, there is an important distinction to be made here between the social (good) and the public (good). I take the category of the social here to refer to the capacity for human beings to take account of each other. In an individualised and economically competitive world, that natural inclination towards a care or concern for the other may be being jeopardised; and the university is well placed to help play its part in recovering the social dimension of society. The University of the twenty-first century should surely see it as a responsibility that it work towards enabling discordant voices to live together, in a world lacking sureness and certainty. In addition, the university is well placed also to develop anew the public sphere, a sphere of collective and public reasoning. This latter role in particular calls for the university itself to become much more public in its activities, not only in displaying its intellectual wares but in facilitating public reflection and understanding so that society might be more enlightened, even amid discord; and might just be better able to develop some collective and rational control over its affairs even amid differences of perspective and values.

PART I
Emerging Futures

1

THE FUTURE ISN'T WAITING

Sheldon Rothblatt

The University of the Future Is the University of Today

The historian's obligation is to the recorded past and its crooked paths to the present. Despite every temptation, I am less concerned with what a university ought to be than describing its present character and identifying the internal and external forces that have shaped its past and are shaping its future. The approach should not be taken to mean that universities while beholden to their surroundings and obedient to history, are only reactive or passive. They have never been mirror images of some other entity. Such is only true under tyrants and dictators. Otherwise the intersections with churches, the state, social classes or a particular economic system are many and complex.

The current literature on the subject is actually huge and daunting, so that what is attempted here is often a summary of arguments and observations. The principal examples are drawn from the history of Anglophone universities, but similar changes appear in other nations' universities.

The University of the Future, at least the near future, is already visible, not only in outline but in its organization, its interior values, its external relationships, its disturbing aspects but also its strengths. The university of today, whatever its origin or funding base, is a hybrid, composed of both top-down and bottom-up styles of decision-making, varying according to the type of institution or to idiosyncratic circumstances. A half century ago, Clark Kerr of the University of California coined the word "multiversity" to describe composite institutions challenged by multiple external pressures (Kerr, 1963, 2001).

The challenges most often cited today, such as the coming of the "postmodern university" relying less on social democratic government policies, to include national security and defense, and more on "networks" and diverse markets, national and global, have been a reality for decades. "Privatization" has followed closely, another vexed word that does not exactly mean "private" but relates to freer institutional initiatives operating under more flexible governmental policies. Nevertheless, governments, the principal revenue source for most universities, have by no means yielded their tendency to "guide" or "steer" or direct university activity.

Multiple external commitments have contributed to the absence of institutional clarity, which, exacerbated by funding pressures, have led to complaints about academic career prospects, working conditions and related frustrations, but the discontents are not universal. As universities vary greatly in their income and prestige, some prosper while others struggle. Universities springing up as "centers of excellence" in Asia and the Middle East (and Israel is considering them) are understandably more optimistic about the future than those preoccupied with thoughts of decline, especially those without the scientific and technological strengths most favored by politicians, civil servants and corporations.

For higher education, the last century was so revolutionary for many countries that further radical departures may well appear tame. What we can expect, however, are weightings and intensities that will affect the inner culture of specific colleges, universities or technical institutes, with undergraduate education, apart from certain places, adjusting itself to research missions, already a reality as undergraduates are increasingly exposed to research experiences. Oxbridge, the great symbol of undergraduate teaching, is now increasing its intake of graduate students. Current proposals in Britain to rationalize research missions by creating two academic classes, separating teachers from investigators, hitherto more typical of France and Germany, are likely to cause distress since status is based on research and even plays a major part in the assessment of liberal arts college professors in the United States.

The Effects of Rapid Change

A century ago, no nation met Martin Trow's criterion for mass access higher education. All were "elite," that is, admitting about 1% of the available student cohort, America a bit more at 2–4% (Trow, 2010). Secondary education was limited. Few occupations required a university education. For all western nations, America first, mass higher education was primarily a post-1945 phenomenon. For Europe, expansion of the higher education system, both the proliferation of institutions that were universities in name or would become such by the end of the century, was swift and compressed. Policies were adopted in response to political beliefs that post-compulsory education was a right and not a privilege. The intentions were admirable. However, policies were undertaken without any perspective on how rapid change might affect quality and funding. The result, carrying through to the present, has been frequent policy shifts on the part of governments. The accompanying reform of secondary education, especially in

Britain since countries such as France largely adhered to a stringent curriculum leading to the *baccalauréat*, introduced even more confusion into the articulation between secondary and tertiary education.

Once again the intentions were noble. The object was to provide alternative routes into higher education by abolishing existing barriers to upward educational and social mobility. But in all countries the results have been disappointing. Remedial instruction at universities and colleges, long a feature of American higher education, is now characteristic of many European institutions. No one appears happy with the levels of skills and proficiencies that students bring to first-year studies. At one point, Britain even had a ministry with "skills" in its name. While the emphasis may have been understandable, academics were dismayed by what appeared to be a distortion of the purposes of a university education and a drain on funding.

No matter what schools reforms have been undertaken, a familiar pattern prevails. The high achievers come mainly from homes that are relatively affluent and neighborhoods that are reasonably stable. Parents are either educated or, in the case of particular ethnic and religious groups, foster a culture of achievement. Poverty, broken homes and dangerous schools have created what is now called an "underclass" in the US. Parents with means, or children in disadvantaged circumstances who show promise, patronize private schools or "independents," the prestige sector of schooling in both Britain and America. Experiments with alternative forms of schooling—"charter" schools or "academies," voucher programmes, home schooling—have proliferated. Bypassing existing educational establishments, to include teacher unions, and accused of inflating their academic success, they are presently vastly controversial.

A Withdrawal of Trust

Although government support of an expanding higher education system naturally appealed to academics, a few wondered whether a Trojan horse had been wheeled onto the premises. This proved to be the case with the burgeoning of quality assurance, audit and assessment agencies. It is said that Asian countries favor evaluation, while Western nations lean towards audit. No one model prevails, and in some nations the participation of central government has been milder than in others. Historically, universities were accustomed to setting their own curricular and degree standards, with external examining in Britain assuring that standards across a particular segment of higher education were reasonably uniform. The system worked well when universities were few in number and polytechnics were linked to a central validating body, the Council for National Academic Awards.

However, a combination of changes produced new issues regarding quality assurance. One, already discussed, is the problem of remediation pushing up from below, or fears that grade inflation is rampant at all levels of the educational system. Another is the wide, if not universal, adoption of teaching modules in some cases replacing the single-subject honors degree that has been a mainstay of the undergraduate curriculum in the UK. Maintaining some kind of uniform academic standard across a system of modules is virtually impossible. A third is the extraordinary increase in the numbers of institutions denominated "universities" based on the model of the expensive research-led university. Whatever their initial intention, government policies ostensibly aimed at quality maintenance have become a way of rationing resources in a sector that has grown overnight.

Efforts at maintaining a common element of quality has been more European than American. The American view is consistent with what has long been a highly differentiated system of higher education composed of select institutions with high standards of entry and achievement and other institutions responding to different academic norms. One sociologist once noted that American universities and colleges could not exactly "charter" graduates, that is to say, they could not guarantee the quality of a degree, leaving the decision on subsequent employment to markets. However, the persistent problems of schooling, the current stress on institutional ranking and the prominence in public life of the graduates of elite colleges and universities, along with fears that America has lost its innovative edge, may signal a new attitude. Admission to the famous colleges and universities of the nation has never before been so demanding, competitive and nerve-wracking, further dampening the chances of entry for those without adequate schooling.

Circumstances Favor Elite Colleges and Universities

The University of the Future must cope with the contradictions (barely indicated here) carried over from the radical transformations in education that marked the second half of the twentieth century. In this task, it is evident that institutions that have the resources and national and global reputations not only will fare better than the others. They are already hugely successful, attracting the ablest undergraduates and outstanding postgraduates. They recruit from the world's pool of academic talent. They have alumni support and prestigious graduates occupying prominent positions in government, industry, think tanks and philanthropies. They have history on their side. In short, the configuration of higher education institutions in many nations is a sort of gigantic bimodal distribution of favored and less favored institutions. The favored universities in the United States are mainly private, but they include state institutions such as Virginia, Michigan, Illinois and campuses of the University of California. Michigan has long been privatized, deriving only about 7% of its operating expenses from the state; but gloom has settled in elsewhere, particularly in once-wealthy California, where talk of a "crisis of the publics" is continuous.

The universal adoption of some kind of research mission, basic or applied science, and the phenomenon of incubator policies, start-ups, spin-offs and science parks have positioned higher education more firmly within national and world economies than in the industrial age, although we cannot forget that two world wars enlisted academic-based science and technology in the fight against militarism and totalitarianism. Within single universities, the resources flowing to particular fields and subjects have also created wider income disparities between knowledge domains and between professional and liberal education. No study that we have absolutely indicates the extent to which such disparities affect institutional morale. Americans are fairly well accustomed to the existing reward structure, but satisfaction depends upon overall working conditions as well as income. Recently concerns have emerged over retirement and health benefits as universities find themselves unable to meet accustomed obligations. Grumbling is widespread, but the elite sector has the means of mitigating discontent to a greater degree than other kinds of institutions, especially those dependent upon low-paid part-time instruction, unhappily more and more the rule.

Futurologists might speculate that the elite university already born will be even more loosely designed, with more professorial movement in and out to industry, government, philanthropies and even private life than presently exists. Multi-campus systems in the US, justified on the grounds of cost-effectiveness, may in future actually prove less attractive, too bureaucratic and more difficult for states to support. At any rate, the case has so been argued. However, alternative schemes envisage branch colleges, possibly two-year community colleges, associated more closely with the research universities in order to improve the opportunities for receiving first degrees. The looser organization of a "postmodern" university enhances the options for individual academics, depending upon field. In other words, contrary to the managerial model of institutional governance currently a topic of irritable discussion, the disaggregated type of university is neither purely managerial nor collegiate. Another way to summarize the situation is to say that adjustments between top, bottom and outside will be continuous and unstable. Education has historically relied upon a certain element of predictability regarding governance, the appointments process, curricula, examining and scheduling. But like other institutions within contemporary society, uncertainty has become a norm.

Towards a Global University

To what extent can we also expect student transfer *a là* Bologna to contribute to the looser organization of the university? Is it possible to expect a return of the *Wandervogel* phenomenon of the nineteenth-century German university, with students seeking professors rather than specific universities? This would be a major readjustment for many institutions. A bedrock aspect of vertical mobility in the American university, transfer is less pronounced in the select private sector where alumni support is vital. Undergraduates are particularly loyal to their institutions since attendance is so closely associated with coming of age, making friends and finding spouses. Because transfer students spend only half their time at flagship state universities, postgraduate instruction became particularly important. Today institutions in search of enhanced revenue streams are conspicuously recruiting students from abroad, and particular American universities are increasing places for out-of-state undergraduates for similar reasons (Douglas & Edelstein, 2009).

As the national university moves offshore, so to speak, concerns are expressed that the connection between universities and national cultures established in the later nineteenth century will be disrupted. That connection featured models of undergraduate liberal education based on assumptions about citizenship and nation-state identity. There are many reasons why liberal education scarcely exists in any recognizable form, but its absence from discussions of globalization is particularly evident.

We can surmise that as linkages between universities, especially research-led universities, become more global, the relations between specific institutes, departments, programs, laboratories and area studies within single campuses and their counterparts elsewhere become stronger. One can reflect upon a kind of University of France composed of disciplines informally organized on a regional, national or even global pattern, more possible within the European Union than elsewhere. Degrees can be awarded conjointly (I recently had experience of a doctorate shared between Bergen and Sciences Po). "The College Invisible," today's network, then becomes more visible. Embryonic colleges, if limited in scope, are presently formed around great international laboratories for example, the research facilities at Cern and Fermi and around the linear accelerator at Stanford.

Another if related scenario is more direct cooperation between separate institutions. The notion still persists that a genuine university is one that is complete and can offer every subject whatever student demand. That has never been absolutely true. It may well be less true than ever. We can expect mergers in an effort to improve economies of scale, or, short of mergers, cooperative efforts between neighboring institutions to encourage library sharing or improve purchasing like those being utilized by the colleges of Oxford. We can also envision more schemes like the Five Colleges of the Amherst, Northampton, South Hadley area in Massachusetts composed of four liberal arts colleges and the flagship campus of the University of Massachusetts, or the three Quaker colleges of Main Line Philadelphia. Shuttle buses take students from one campus to another. Carleton College south of Minneapolis offers no instruction in Italian, but Carleton students can take classes at cross town rival St. Olaf's. Given the unfortunate propensity for hard-pressed institutions to close down humanities subjects, especially languages in response to bottom-line targets, the sharing of courses across campus boundaries is one way of recalling that universities are conservers as well as generators of knowledge.

Drivers of Internal Change

The driver of all strategies and departures is multifaceted. Knowledge generation in particular has been primary in the evolution of systems and structures.

Knowledge acquisition and dissemination are imperial, continuous and move sideways to embrace adjacent disciplines. This is most often an "autonomous" process, subtle and even imperceptible, a step-by-step accumulation of ideas and methods. Organizational reforms may strengthen the advance of disciplines (Clark, 2004), but they can also be trendy, designed for publicity, suggesting profound changes where none exist. Whether structural reforms are generally more "efficient" in some measurable way, or enhance institutional prestige or improve teaching and research is debatable. Today's high-ranking universities are for the most part conventionally organized, incorporating familiar disciplines and professional studies. Yet campus administrations can support and abet networking initiatives, which then find linkages to regions, communities, cities and industries. The city planner, Sir Peter Hall, has explained how "creative milieu" arise when this happens, citing Silicon Valley as one example (Hall, 1997).

Knowledge expansion will unquestionably continue to drive all essential aspects of the university, but financial drivers are at present not far behind. Research, research dependent upon the latest technologies, and fixed costs are vastly expensive. More of the costs of attendance are being offloaded onto students; and although many institutions attempt to increase tuition discounting and provide various forms of financial aid through their own and government sources, debt levels have risen and create genuine hardships. The present White House has attacked irregularities in the private administration of loans, but it is hard to see how the general situation can be altered.

The Broadband Revolution

The search for cheaper forms of higher education is by necessity on the rise, a by-product of the movement from mass to universal higher education. Advocates of on-line instruction, a relative of predecessors such as distance learning and open universities (some with drop-in centers), speak prophetically of the demise of the "broadcast" or "industrial model" of instruction. For-profit institutions are well into the game, reaching hundreds of thousands of users. However, financial improprieties have increased existing suspicions about the commodification of knowledge. Completion rates are low, and the costs to students mount up. Yet controlling costs will continue to drive providers towards less expensive ways of delivering education, even though, in the US, students enrolling in for-profit institutions have access to government-derived financial aid.

Some academics deplore efforts to bypass or denigrate the inherited classroom, regarding them as yet another dumbing down of education and another contribution to a denatured university environment. Proponents can, if they wish, counter by pointing to the huge impersonal lecture halls in France and Italy or the large classes in many American universities and the widespread use of graduate teaching assistants. They welcome on-line instruction as in keeping with today's student computer-based, any-time cultures. A further argument is that insofar as today's undergraduates are easily bored and attendance at lectures has fallen, on-line instruction makes perfect sense. Freed from the need to cover a routine sylla-bus, lecturers can use the time for a more creative approach to learning, including personal attention in a few instances. This is a large claim where some angels may well fear to tread (Guri-Rosenblit, 2009; Harley, 2009).

The decline in state funding has made it impossible for the University of California system to meet its demographic obligations framed in the famous State of California Master Plan for Higher Education of 1960 (Geiser, 2010). Con-sequently a debate has just started—certain to be acrimonious—over whether courses offered in the freshman and sophomore years ought to depend upon on-line instruction. Trials have begun. How much of an education will be forgone if digital teaching is the main instrument of education will doubtless occupy endless hours of discussion and renew interest in the educational benefits of peer-group interaction. Controversies over the use of internet teaching will unquestionably carry on well into the present century. Although select institutions use and will continue to make use of newer digital tools, sometimes systematically, more often piecemeal, according to classroom styles, the degree to which this occurs will sharply separate elite from other types of institutions, with implications, as yet unclear, for employment and career prospects. This is a vexed subject in any case. Most studies fail to distinguish between initial employment following the award of a degree and lifelong career chances. Elite institutions appear to continue to have an advantage in the first, and they may also possess an advantage in the sec-ond, but at that point many other variables enter relating to occupation, leader-ship qualities, personality, emotional stability and actual job performance.

Securing an Advantage

Competitive pressures, global rankings, the pursuit of status, student anxieties over being left behind in a race for the top are fueling an academic propensity to cheat. Cheating is not in itself a consequence of the digital revolution. As long as there have been written examinations, cheating has prevailed. Attempts to game examinations even existed at eighteenth-century Cambridge when examinations were oral, although the evidence is largely anecdotal. One reason why intelli-gence testing was so widely adopted in America in the first decades of the twen-tieth century is that its supporters could claim that cheating was impossible on a correctly-designed "objective" IQ test that measured natural aptitude.

Still, the advance of on-line education, accompanied by the revolution in gadgets that defines the world of young people, has exacerbated what is almost a natural tendency to gain an advantage wherever the stakes are high. In the rich democracies, cheating appears to be strongly correlated with lower achievers, those who are desperate to succeed. Student cheating has become so prevalent that the University of Central Florida, the nation's third largest campus as measured by enrolment, has created a testing center stocked with technology designed to catch reprobates. In a battle of wits, gum chewing is forbidden during examinations because it can mask use of a hands-free cell phone linked to a collaborator. Computer screens are recessed so that they cannot be photographed and information transmitted outside. Scratch paper is dated and turned in. Proctors use overhead cameras to spy on potentially suspicious activity. One student tattooed possible answers onto his body. Elsewhere professors design software intended to catch students who are plagiarizing or somehow copying papers and answers. Or they can employ the services of industries with huge data bases designed to catch plagiarists (*New York Times*, 2010; *Boston Globe* online, 2010).

An Orwellian educational environment of surveillance is frighteningly distant from the kind of idealism about learning that is presumably every teacher's wish. Academics are understandably uncomfortable. Where is the trust that ought to exist between teacher and taught? But the most disturbing casualty of wide-scale cheating is moral; a refusal to admit that a cut and paste style of composition stolen from the internet is wrong.

For researchers, the desire for recognition has produced scandals from Korea to the United States that are even more disturbing than student fiddles to obtain degrees. A world of celebrity cultures has brought increased attention to numerous violations of professional ethics such as the falsification of evidence or fake degrees. Concerns about whether the actual, hidden or subtle pressures exerted by huge pharmaceutical or bioengineering conglomerates will compromise objective research standards have long been expressed. Since outside support will continue to be sought, the matter demands extreme vigilance. For the humanities and social sciences, objectivity has already been compromised by the intrusion of political partisanship into teaching and publication. The degree to which this has occurred is difficult to measure. Numbers do not always a controversy make.

But there are also new neighbors on the block, and their influence is yet to be felt. Academics still rely on peer review to catch malpractices and correct bias, but just as the internet has provided a major challenge to honesty, so is it beginning to affect broadband assessments of research results. The division between specialists and non-specialists is breaking down. On the internet, anyone can have an opinion, and anyone can express it. What are the implications of this pastime for academic autonomy, peer review and individual reputations? How is it possible to separate mere opinion, rumor and innuendo from genuine critical expression when hundreds or thousands of internet users come out of cyberspace? How is it even possible to summarize this mountain of commentary as if deciding upon the purchase of an automobile?

Finally, it is necessary to make a point about institutional leadership in contributing to the national and global race for an advantage. So prevalent is the search for standing, and the rewards associated with rank, that campus leaders market their institutions as products superior to others in some specified way, often in a way that has little do with core missions. Modesty is not a present-day attribute. The worry is that noise is required in order to attract attention.

Conclusion: Does a University Require an "Idea"?

The value of an "idea," its function, is to gather the disparate disciplines around a core, to unify the academic professions and to provide a university with a clear commitment that can be defended in plural environments. These objectives are unobtainable. Two traditions of the nineteenth century created the idealist litera-ture that has substantially grown since Cardinal Newman in England and philoso-phers in Germany posited the view that a university either embodied a specific mission or that knowledge had a specific purpose. Not all of many commentators find the arguments compelling (Maskell & Robinson, 2001). Newman and the Germans are not always clear and precise. Nor did they agree.

Newman did not find research an appropriate function for a university. His model was the Oxford of his youth, with colleges devoted to undergraduate teaching and character formation. The German view of knowledge was rather more ethereal, less applied, although the "high culture" of self-cultivation—*Bil-dung* and its Scandinavian variants such as *bildning* and *danelse*—was expected to result in a desirable personality change. Historians have written about the intel-lectual difficulty of penetrating such conceptions. However noble, they were sometimes exclusive, easily distorted and encouraged unpleasant prejudices. Yet the hope of some intellectuals was that the high culture once associated with class privilege would in time become democratized, the possession of all. The univer-sity, it was supposed, would lead the way towards a more elevated conception of moral conduct: less crass, less vulgar, less absorbed by the bottom-line (Rothblatt & Wittrock, 1993; Rothblatt, 2008).

Individuals may meet this obligation, and doubtless some do. We can-not know the numbers. But the multiversity of the twenty-first century, by definition, is a house of many mansions. No single idea prevails, but many exist. The extent to which they are actually operable, so to speak, is impossible to determine apart from their rhetorical use. Some see the essence of a university in Newman's terms, or better yet, the essence of knowledge, as excellence; others as discovery, others as the life of the mind. Still others speak of the university as an agency for problem-solving. Politicians want a commitment to economic development. Political activists seek the transformation of society on partisan grounds. Conservatives prefer to speak of tradition. Ronald Barnett states the ideal as open discussion, the free exchange of views and respect for them. The effect of this is emancipatory, he says, a necessary stage for self-understanding and self-improvement, values that support proud and free democracies I would add (Barnett, 1990). Can all of these exist simultaneously as a single and uni-fied commitment? No, because they lead in different directions depending upon circumstances. Can they exist if knowledge domains are disaggregated and free to establish their own priorities and connections within untidy boundaries? Yes. *A fortiori*, the multiversity is a collection of niches, for disciplines, for individuals.

While the university has not altogether lost some of its historical characteristics, it is nevertheless a far different kind of place from what was known even a half century ago. Positive elements exist. The university's fluid boundaries and networking possibilities are suited to problem-solving. Arguably, it is a more generous-minded place than its predecessors, particularly those whose history is sadly marked by ready acquiescence to the bigotries and injustices of states and society. But this is a reminder that universities are only as tolerant as their societies and governments allow. Academic freedom and institutional autonomy can only thrive when generally respected.

The university of today is part of a national system of "higher education" composed of many types of institutions subject to contradictory tendencies. One promotes greater cooperation between colleges and universities, a fuller sharing of resources and commitments in the interests of the greater good. The other encourages competition, rankings, hyperbola and the exploitation of multifarious markets.

Yet taken as a whole and with all of its perceived drawbacks, this world holds great possibilities for intellectual discovery, for social betterment and—to return to Newman—for teaching. Students still want to learn, and adult education is thriving. Weaving and bobbing through the "terribly tangled skein of modern life" (homage to Tolstoy), and within porous borders, the university is more important and more vulnerable than it has ever been in a breathtakingly long and continuous history.

2

IMAGINING THE UNIVERSITY OF THE FUTURE

Louise Morley

Desire, Desiccation and Distributive Justice

This chapter will raise questions about the morphology of the University of the Future and whether creative visioning has been eclipsed by pressing concerns and tensions in the present. It will also consider whether the University of the Future might also be seen as the University of the Past. The global economic recession means that higher education could move from expansion to contraction, with a reinforcement of social hierarchies and privilege. Opportunities for participation could become spaces of closure in the emerging austerity economy and creeping privatisation.

We live in times of policy turbulence, and change has been rapid and extreme. Transformation has largely been driven by the perceived needs of the economy rather than by academic imaginaries or social movements. The academic imaginary has tended to be harnessed to critique, protection and defence rather than an engagement in futurology. Counter hegemonic advocates did not necessarily predict the scale of neo-liberal driven change. Traditionalists did not foresee the industrialisation and massification. Higher education currently abounds with a sense of crisis. Movements and political demonstrations in many countries have been mobilised to attempt to protect what we had in the past, and interrupt the rapidly desiccating sector. The shock therapy of disaster capitalism means that the future of higher education is under threat in a range of national locations. For example, in the UK Comprehensive Spending Review of the public services, higher education funding is being cut—ostensibly in relation to the global fiscal crisis. However, these cuts are also ideologically driven and the financial crisis is embedded in and re-producing political and democratic crises. Economic crises "soften the ground" for radical political changes (Klein, 2008). Austerity measures can also be seen as ideology posing as technology, with higher education re-positioned as a private positional good and luxury product. It is important to question what is worth protecting, and what type of higher education would be of value in the future. Desire, that is, for what the different stakeholders and constituencies actually want for the future of higher education that goes beyond immediate concerns with economics, as well as loss, needs to be considered.

Higher education is caught between hypermodernism (Lipovetsky, 2005) and archaism. It is characterised by the development of global, entrepreneurial and corporate universities and speeded up nomadic public intellectuals. There are new student constituencies, literacies and modalities of communication. Borders are dissolving and academic (hyper)mobility is promoted (Kenway, Bullen & Rob, 2004). However, the hyper-modernisation of liquified globalisation (Bauman, 2000), and edgeless universities (Bradwell, 2009) are often underpinned by the stasis, archaism and desiccation of poor quality employment and learning environments, unequal employment regimes, elitist participation practices and globalised gender inequalities (Morley et al., 2008; Morley & Lugg, 2009). These factors are set to deteriorate further in times of economic crisis. The recent UK Browne Review of higher education funding suggests that increased tuition fees will raise quality and standards as students will demand value for money for their investment (Browne, 2010). This is an interesting logic—cutting the government teaching grant by up to 80% implies loss of permanent staff, closure of many specialist departments and an instability caused by the fluctuations in demand of a market economy. It is questionable how the reconstruction of students as customers in this impoverished climate will drive up quality.

The University of the Past was associated with elitism, exclusion and inequalities (Morley, 2010a). The University of Today is diversified, expanded, globalised, borderless/edgeless, marketised, technologised, neo-liberalised and potentially privatised. Dominant discourses and imagined policy futures focus on excellence, innovation, digitisation, globalisation, teaching and learning, employability and economic impact (BIS, 2009). It is unclear whether these recent and current policy discourses are generating creative thinking about the future of universities, or whether they are limiting it. Policy priorities are not always commensurate with aspirations and desires of students and staff, and there have been fears over the past decade that universities are being reduced to delivery agencies for government-decreed outcomes (Young, 2004). The delivery has demanded a degree of compliance and performativity that can stifle creative thinking. This has been particularly the case with audit cultures that have devoured and diverted vast temporal, material and intellectual resources (Morley, 2003).

The emphasis now is on the economics of higher education. In a recessionary market economy, the questions of the value of higher education, and the rate of return and who should pay become even more relevant. Higher education is positioned as a private, rather than a public good (Singh, 2001). Current UK policy debates on fees, graduate tax and the graduate premium focus on what the capital is worth in terms of the exchange rate of qualifications (Curtis, 2009). There are also discussions about how universities are valued. In the austerity economy, higher education has been recast as profligate and extravagant. However, higher education itself has been a profitable product. For every one million pounds the treasury invests in universities, the return is £1.3 million in other parts of the UK economy (UUK, 2010). Underpinning all these debates on the economics of higher education is the question of whether universities should exist to create knowledge for wealth, for social and public good, or for its own sake. Knowledge is now coded for its optimisation and exchange value in the labour market, rather than for its pleasure, power, democratic or critical possibilities.

The commodification of knowledge is apparent in the growth of the private sector. Private universities have expanded massively in some geopolitical regions e.g. sub-Saharan Africa, Eastern Europe, South East Asia and Latin America (Altbach & Levy, 2005: Bjarnason et al., 2009). Now there is the suggestion that the UK should follow suit (Shepherd & Vasagar, 2010). As demand is now exceeding supply in the UK, the state is looking to the private sector to fill the gap. This strategy has been a feature of low-income countries, for example in sub-Saharan Africa (Varghese, 2004). Many high-income countries are now examining the role of the state in the provision of higher education. Boundaries between the public and private are blurring. The private sector has been infiltrating state provision for some time (Ball & Youdell, 2008), and looks set to benefit further from the state's policy to raise aspirations. Privatisation is often posed in the vocabulary of modernisation and disguises the potential major changes in the ethos, curriculum and values of higher education.

Widening Participation: Opportunity or Coercion?

Archaism is observable in patterns of participation, and more recently in relation to policies on participation in higher education. Social variables raised their head in some of the recent debates on widening participation (BIS, 2009), but largely in relation to poor students. Their inclusion into higher education could be classified as a form of democratisation. It could also be interpreted as an act of incorporation and an attempt to make the working classes more like the middle classes (Archer et al., 2003). In the UK, there has been a movement from expansion and widening participation under the former Labour Government to policies of retrenchment and contraction under the current Conservative/Liberal Democrat coalition. Whereas previously the policy momentum was to widen participation for social justice (and human capital), now the emphasis is on cost-cutting, privatisation and how to finance higher education. Difference is contradictorily conceptualised both in terms of disparagement and desire. For example, widening participation policies and social movements suggest that universities should want to be more socially inclusive. Yet, new constituencies of students are still regarded as a high risk by many elite organisations.

I do not wish to set up a binary between the golden ageism of the recent past and the economies of the austerity culture. There have been some notable global successes in increasing participation under diverse governments in the past half century, but some uneven distribution across regions, suggesting that there are still powerful geographies of knowledge. There are now almost 153 million tertiary students in the world, a 53% increase since the year 2000 and a fivefold increase in less than 40 years. It is predicted that the demand for higher education worldwide will expand from 97 million students in 2000 to over 262 million students by 2025 (UNESCO, 2009). Much of this growth has been in East Asia—in China, enrolment is now 20%. In South Asia, India has the world's third largest system and plans to raise enrolment from 11% to 15% by 2012, while in Bangladesh, enrolment rates are just 6%. Sub-Saharan Africa has experienced the highest average regional growth rate. For more than three decades, enrolments have expanded by 8.7% annually, compared to 5.1% for the world as a whole, and have tripled since 1990, to almost four million students. However, in sub-Saharan Africa, regional enrolment rates are 5%, the lowest in the world. Nigeria and South Africa enrol 10% and 15% respectively but Uganda and Ethiopia just 3% and Tanzania 1% (DFID, 2008). At the other end of the axis, Iceland and Austria lead the world with the highest graduation ratios of 65.6% and 60.7% respectively (UNESCO, 2009).

It is important to ask who these new constituencies are, and whether quantitative change has challenged middle class capture of higher education. Recent research and reports in the UK suggest that it has not. There is still a toxic correlation between poverty and access. Only 4% of the UK's poorer young people enter higher education (David et al., 2009; Hills Report, 2009), and only 5% of this group enter the top seven universities in UK league tables (HESA, 2010). Morley et al. (2010) also found that poor students in Ghana and Tanzania were absent from almost all the programmes included in the research sample in two public and two private universities—in spite of quota systems for disadvantaged students and affirmative action programmes for women in science. It is relevant to ask why it matters that elitist participation patterns prevail under diverse governments, and in different locations. The university is a major site of cultural practice, identity formation, knowledge formation, capital and dissemination and symbolic control. Graduates from elite universities in the UK dominate the media, politics, the civil service, the judiciary, the arts, the City, law, medicine, big business, the armed forces and think tanks (Monbiot, 2010). In short, participation is about power, and higher education continues to play a dominant role in reproducing social privilege.

Widening participation targets of 50% in 2010 in the UK are in the process of being repealed. It was always a highly contentious policy intervention, even though the target has almost been met with a current 45% participation rate (BIS, 2010). Widening participation policies unproblematically construct higher education as a social good, and become a formulaic or techno-rational prescription for economic and social development, and for adding capital to members of marginalised groups. Participation gets constructed as much as a duty as a right (Biesta, 2006). Widening participation can be a force for democratisation. It can also map onto elite practices and contribute to further differentiation of social groups. Research has demonstrated that those with social capital are able to decode and access new educational opportunities (Crozier et al., 2008; Heath et al., 2008; Morley et al., 2010; Reay et al., 2005). Those without it remain largely untouched by initiatives to facilitate their entry into the privileges that higher education can offer. There can be an affinity between capital and the capacity to aspire to higher education (Appadurai, 2004; David, 2009). What is interesting, however, is that recessionary driven graduate un/under employment has not satisfied the hunger for higher education. Aspirations have been raised and applications in the UK rose by 23% in 2009 (HESA, 2010). This could be a recession-proofing strategy, the return of the scarcity-value of higher education or perverse resistance that is desiring access after the state has stopped trying to coerce you into raised aspirations.

Closing the Gender Gap

Gender inequalities are another example of archaic practices. The Global Gender Parity Index of 1.08, means that there are now slightly more women undergraduates than men (UNESCO, 2009). It could be argued that relays of power are being disrupted by the changing gender profile of undergraduate higher education. The number of male students globally quadrupled from 17.7 to 75.1 million between 1970–2007. However, the number of female students rose sixfold from 10.8 to 77.4 million (UNESCO, 2009). Instead of celebrating the gains for gender equality, some constituencies have created a feminisation crisis discourse, with fears that women are taking over the academy to the detriment and exclusion of men (HEPI, 2009). This suggests that women's successes have come about by damaging men. It also implies that a woman's place is in the minority, and reconstructs the dominant group as victims. There are fears of imbalance, contamination and domination by socially disadvantaged groups, suggesting that there should be a ceiling on their participation, and that their place is in the minority. When the symbolic order appears destabilised, policy debates utilise normative vocabularies and commonsense, binaried understandings of gender to justify repositioning dominant groups as victims (HEPI, 2009). Fortunately, this crisis discourse has been eloquently deconstructed by feminist scholars who have unmasked the misogyny that lurks beneath the engulfment fears (Leathwood & Read, 2008).

A further feature of the feminisation discourse is that it ignores gender in wider civil society. While women's participation in higher education might be increasing, gender equality is falling in wider UK civil society. The UK was ranked 13 in the 2008 Global Gender Gap Index and 15 in 2009 (World Economic Forum, 2009). The index benchmarks national gender gaps on economic, political, education and health-based criteria, and provides country rankings that allow comparisons across regions and income groups, and over time. Each year, the UK has been sliding down this scale. While Nordic countries tend to dominate the top three positions (Iceland was top in 2009), population size and wealth do not always influence the scores. Ghana is higher (ranked 80) than Japan (ranked 101), and Lesotho is now in the top 10. Women might be entering higher education, but are they accessing wider benefits?

Women are still under-represented as knowledge producers and leaders in higher education, with their academic capital seeming to have a lower value in the labour market. Only 19% of European Union professors are women (She Figures, 2009). 13% of UK Vice Chancellors are women (Deem, 2010). In 70% of Commonwealth countries, *all* universities are led by men (Singh, 2008). In 2007/08, the median gender pay gap in universities in the UK higher education sector was 18.2% (ECU, 2010). Current policy concerns about impact seem to evaporate in relation to research evidence about gender inequalities. Gender tends to get ignored when women suffer discrimination or under-representation, but amplified in crisis form when women start to be "over-represented." Gender inequalities appear to be resistant to hypermodernisation forces, in spite of legislation in different locations.

The UK now has the Gender Equality Duty (2007), which moves gender out of individual grievance modalities and into recognition of the need for a radical new approach to equality—one which places more responsibility with service providers to think strategically about gender equality, rather than leaving it to individuals to challenge discriminatory practices. This framework suggests that gender should be taken out of crisis mode and into proactive, resourced, strategic interventions e.g. gender mainstreaming (Morley, 2010b). Gender mainstreaming involves the creation or strengthening of national machineries and other governmental bodies for the advancement of women; the integration of gender perspectives into legislation, public policies, programmes and projects; and the generation and dissemination of gender-disaggregated data and information for planning and evaluation (United Nations, 1995). Instead of simply noting gender inequalities, institutions should develop strategic plans and procedures for monitoring and evaluation. The University of the Future needs to be accountable for gender in quantitative and qualitative terms, with its leaders making clear where they stand on gender, and what strategic re-distributive action they propose to take.

Multiple Knowledges

Higher education typically involves accredited learning, which assumes that complex processes, activities and knowledges can be measured objectively (Pryor & Crossouard, 2010). However, assessment is bound up with normative judgements and power relations that can involve misrecognition. New ecologies of knowledge are developing in technologically driven societies. The University's DNA is still largely literary in structure—especially in relation to modes of assessment, whilst new generations of students have been attributed with and inducted in technological literacy. One tension that appears to be developing is between the diverse social identities of knowers and orthodoxies about what counts as knowledge and what counts as appropriate assessment of knowledge. If new constituencies are bringing new literacies and modalities of communication into higher education, this might be accompanied by new sites of conflict.

While this might sound like technological determinism (Clegg, 2010), research is informing us that younger undergraduate students can often spend longer interacting with social networking sites than with their university set texts (Morris, 2010; Robson, 2009). Morris (2010) points out that these social practices and digitisation are producing new identifiers including: *Millennials, Digital Natives, Digital Generation, Google Generation, Generation Y, MySpace Generation, Nintendo Generation, Net Generation* and *YouTube Generation*. The sacred/profane binary of knowledge could be challenged by new "just-in-time," "wiki" knowledge producers. Brabazon's (2007) study examines how this can sometimes result in cut and paste practices for many students. Students too have been speeded up, so why read a whole book, when summaries of grand theories are available on Wikipedia?

New research is suggesting that many of us no longer have the concentration or time to read texts to their conclusion (Carr, 2010). Carr believes that hyperactive online habits mean that we are in perpetual locomotion, and losing our ability to process and understand lengthy textual information. A new movement has been created to introduce slow reading, just as it was for slow food (Miedema, 2009). New generational power relationships could be producing a tectonic relationship between ideal/imagined students and actual new constituencies in terms of knowledge codes, assessment and learning practices. In other words, the University of Today could be constructing students using the reference points and values of the University of the Past. The University of the Future needs to strike a delicate balance by speaking to diverse generational and geographical power geometries while simultaneously safeguarding academic values and standards.

Nomadic Subjects

A site of hypermodernisation is the globalised knowledge worker. Just as digitisation has speeded up knowledge work, so too has the generative power of the global. Academic success is evaluated for its location in the international community. Parochialism equals cognitive dispossession. An indicator of success is academic hyper-mobility and animation—being always on the move (Kenway, 2004). The life of the mind assumes a robust, normative and able body. It is also requires a diffusion of bodily and textual selves into multiple locations. Cosmopolitanism, nomadism and spaces of transition are features of academic production. Yet the

construction of the nomadic academic assumes, as Lynch (2009) argues, a *doxa*—
a common belief or popular opinion—of "carelessness" that is, that academics
are "carefree"—without care responsibilities—for themselves or for others. She
maintains that this nomadism is underpinned by a highly individualised entrepreneurialism that is at the heart of the academy. This has allowed a particular "careless" form of competitive individualism to flourish, and this careless character of
higher education culture is entirely driven by new managerial values and norms.
We might surmise that the austerity economy, with its emphasis on over-work,
and progressive austerity (Reeves, 2009)—doing more (creatively) with less—is
exacerbating these unhealthy work practices.

Re-location without dislocation is a professional imperative. Expectations
of performativity involve an unsustainable neglect of one's health, well-being
and relationships. Having worked on five continents for the past fifteen years,
I am aware of the pressures that the global imperative places on bodies, con-
nectivities and the environment itself. I have a global network, but lack time to
see friends who live a few miles away from me. Whereas universities are often
leading scientific research on climate change, it could be argued that they are
also making major contributions to global warming via international mobility
of students and staff. The University of the Future needs to balance de-
pariochialisation and global velocities with environmental and personal sustainability.

Futurology

There are competing and multiple visions of the University of the Future. Expansion to multiversities is predicted by some that is mega, multi-campus institutions (Fallis, 2007). Others have more nakedly dystopic visions. Bousquet (2008)
predicts a callousness of prestige—a type of Darwinism that means that well-
endowed, elitist research intensive universities will happily see the closure, rather
than the incorporation of teaching-led universities. This prediction has recently
come true, with the Vice Chancellor of University College London, advising
that the UK Government should slash student places at "pile it high, sell it cheap"
universities—even if it means some being forced to close—to protect Britain's
"world class" research institutions (Vasagar, 2010). Instead of university heads
joining forces to oppose economic cuts, some are competing and identifying
other candidates for closure. Bousquet (2008) foresaw this when he suggested
that countercultures and opposition would be crushed. His other predictions
are, unhappily, materialising; he prophesised a decline in academic freedom and
increased political, cultural and economic assault.

One way in which the decline in academic freedom is being enacted is via
policy interventions such as the research impact agenda. In the austerity economy,
the use of public money is under even more rigorous scrutiny. Research has value
if it contributes to the economy. Funders need more evidence of certainty about

what counts as a positive, sustainable change, or a sound return on research investments. The Higher Education Funding Council for England (HEFCE) in the UK has published its criteria for assessing research quality (2009), which includes 25% for impact. McKibbin (2009) believes that this implies a colonisation of universities by business and the private sector. This echoes Bousquet's (2008) fears about creeping corporatisation and academic-capitalist values. Saunders (2010) highlights the problem of attribution or the difficulty in identifying the extent to which a particular intervention, or set of research findings, have created a specific outcome. Complex social research findings now have to be presented in techno-rational packages of certainty of outcomes and impact.

The certainties of the impact agenda are set beside uncertainties of funding for higher education. Insecurity is the dominant ontological position in many parts of the sector. The state rescuing of the banks in the UK has resulted in severe cuts in the public sector. Disinvestment and the transfer of debt and risk from the private to the public sector means that employees are permanently temporary—another of Bousquet's (2008) Cassandraesque visions. This is the landscape of closure, decline and domination.

Ball and Exley (2009) question who is influencing policy futures. They suggest that unelected, non-academic think tanks might be having more "impact" than academic research findings. Furthermore, these think-tanks are strongly networked and staffed by the elite. Bradwell (2009) embodies a think-tank approach to policy. Taking the metaphor of the edgeless university, he discusses ideas that have been in circulation in academic domains for some time. In contrast to Bousquet (2008), he uses metaphors of openness—somehow implying that the University of the Past was closed to external influences. He predicts open access publishing, flexible learning outside the university, the increased use of social media for teaching and learning, strategic technological investment, new providers, collaborative research and open research communities, universities as partners, and not sole providers of learning and research, engaging stakeholders in course design and new forms of accreditation.

Conclusion

Globally, the higher education sector has become associated with the hypermodernisation of the knowledge economy. Yet there are some archaic practices that continue to prevail, such as gender inequalities, feminisation fears and the exclusion of poorer communities. Modernisation has been via a form of unsustainable hypermobility that poses threats to bodies and the environment. The narrative of the austerity economy has now been layered on to these frenzied cultural practices. We need new conceptual vocabularies and reinvigorated courage to challenge the archaism and hyperactivity that frame the sector. I believe that the University of the Future needs to recover critical knowledge and *be* a think-tank and policy driver. We need to discover new conceptual grammars to include equalities, identities, environmental and affective domains. Knowledge should not be reduced to its optimisation value. We need to find a way to speak to diverse generational and geographical power geometries, while preserving some enduring values e.g. democratisation. There is a lot of talk about how higher education can contribute to wealth creation. The University of the Future should also consider opportunity and wealth distribution.

PART II

Global Possibilities

3

ACCESSING KNOWLEDGE IN THE UNIVERSITY OF THE FUTURE

Lessons from Australia

Leesa Wheelahan

Introduction

Durkheim argued that theoretical knowledge is society's "sacred" knowledge—
the knowledge that it uses to think about itself. Universities have, since medieval
times, been a key site for mediating access to the sacred, but do they continue to
do so in mass and near universal, stratified systems of higher education? This is a
key question for the university of the twenty-first century. At stake is the question
of democratic access to "society's conversations."

This chapter argues that social justice requires access for all to the sacred, yet
the stratification of higher education systems means that the access mediated by
universities to this knowledge is not equal. Many (mainly wealthy) countries
are approaching universal systems of higher education. "Universal access for all"
brings with it the promise of realising the meritocracy in which all have the
opportunity to achieve according to their ability rather than their social class.
However, unless such access is accompanied by a theory of knowledge, universal
higher education becomes a key mechanism for reproducing social disadvantage,
albeit in a less visible form. With the advent of universal systems, the formation of
"consciousness, identity and desire" (Bernstein, 2000) is no longer mediated by
mechanisms of inclusion and exclusion from higher education, but by the *type* of
higher education that students have access to. The chapter relates these arguments
to an examination of higher education in Australia.

The first section of this chapter is a Durkheimian argument about the nature of
knowledge, its sacredness, and its role in society and in constructing autonomous
individuals. The next section critically appraises Trow's extraordinary, prescient,
and enduring analysis in which he distinguishes between elite, mass and universal
higher education systems to explore the way they mediate access to different

types of knowledge, while later rejecting his conclusion that such structuring is necessary and good. This is followed by a discussion of vocationalism in Australian universities and then an exploration of the way in which the stratification of higher education distributes different forms of access to consciousness, identity and desire. The following section discusses the reasons why there has been a retreat from knowledge in higher education curriculum, and this is followed by an argument about why it is necessary to have a theory of knowledge to underpin curriculum. The final section considers the way in which a theory of knowledge can be used to support more democratic access to knowledge in the university of the twenty-first century, and thus to society's conversations, even in more vocationalised higher education programs.

A Durkheimian Analysis of Knowledge

Durkheim (2001) argued that all societies distinguish between two forms of knowledge—the sacred and profane. Esoteric or abstract theoretical knowledge is sacred knowledge because it has its origins in religion, whereas profane knowledge is knowledge of the profane, everyday world. The distinction between sacred and profane knowledge, or theoretical and everyday knowledge, is universal and each is necessary for the existence of society. Knowledge of, and life in, the profane, everyday world is necessary for society to materially reproduce itself.

Esoteric knowledge performs two functions. First, it consists of "collective representations" of a society that allow it to understand and develop knowledge about the nature of the (natural and social) world beyond that which is accessible through individual experience. Collective representations are society's "work-in-progress," which are "the product of a vast cooperative effort that extends not only through space but over time" (Durkheim, 2001: 18).

Durkheim (2001: 10) argues that religions constitute "a cosmology as well as a speculation on the divine" and that societies historically have used religion to make sense of the world. Religions are in essence the collective representations of societies and reflect societies back to themselves. They express the general social relations of particular societies, and this is why religions differ between societies and epochs. Consequently, ". . . there are no false religions. All are true in their fashion: all respond, if in different ways, to the given conditions of human existence" (Durkheim, 2001: 4).

Religion was paradigmatic for theoretical, abstract knowledge because both are specialised forms of knowledge that societies use to see beyond the individual to make connections between the material and immaterial worlds. They do so because ". . . both involve connecting things to one another, establishing internal relations between them, classifying them, and systematizing them" (Durkheim, 2001: 324). They allow societies to connect the here and the not here, and the past, present and future and to consider alternative futures. There is thus continuity between religious and academic knowledge in the way society uses sacred or esoteric knowledge and its purpose.

Moreover, the medieval universities have their origins in the church and this provided the basis for the emergence of the academic disciplines. In providing frameworks for the interrogation of faith and knowledge, the medieval universities provided the discursive space for the unthinkable (Durkheim, 2006). Durkheim (2001: 324) argued that there is continuity in the concerns of religion, philosophy and science: "they are nature, man, society." The academic disciplines have developed, proliferated and changed since the medieval universities. They tend to be concerned with different aspects of the natural and social worlds, reflecting the growing complexity of society and its increasingly differentiated division of labour (Bernstein, 2000); however, all are ultimately connected with the traditional concerns as expressed by Durkheim.

The second function that esoteric knowledge plays is a normative function; collective representations are the means through which society conducts its conversation about itself, considers alternative futures and debates what it *should* be like. It is the way society establishes its values, norms and mores. Bernstein (2000: 30) argued that theoretical knowledge constitutes the site of the unthinkable and alternative possibilities and that it "is the meeting point of order and disorder, of coherence and incoherence." The reason it plays this role is because it is not tied to the contextual and everyday—it is general, principled knowledge and not particularised knowledge. This is why abstract, theoretical knowledge is socially powerful, and why access to it is socially mediated and distributed. Those who are successful will have access to such knowledge, and "will become aware that the mystery of discourse is not order, but disorder, incoherence, the possibility of the unthinkable" (Bernstein, 2000: 11).

Collective Solidarity and the Individual

Durkheim's argument has mostly been interpreted as an over-socialised one in which the social determines the individual thus denying agency (Archer, 2000), but it can also be interpreted as one that expands the space for agency (Moore, 2004). It is through engaging in the social that the individual emerges, and more importantly, provides the individual with scope for subjectivity. Collective representations are the basis of social solidarity because they are shared, but they are also the basis of individual freedom because they are the structuring principles of consciousness, although consciousness cannot be reduced to them because it is always mediated by subjectivity (Moore, 2004). Just as possession of a language provides the parameters for, but does not determine what people actually say, so too society's collective representations provide parameters for, but do not determine, what people will think and do. They are the tools that society and individuals use to mediate their lives, but these tools can be used in creative ways because they can be used to think the unthinkable.

To have access to theoretical knowledge is still to participate in the sacred even though it has been secularised in the academic disciplines because it comprises "powerful symbols . . . that make and remake society's collective existence" (Cladis, 2001: xxiii). These symbols allow individuals to transcend individual experience thus extending their horizons and participate in something bigger than themselves. Access to theoretical knowledge is thus an issue of social and distributive justice because society uses collective representations to conduct its conversations about itself and what it should be like. It provides the basis for collective solidarity in society and for the development of the autonomous individual. I will return to this last point later in this chapter.

Elite, Mass and Universal Higher Education Systems

Martin Trow (1974) famously distinguished between elite, mass and universal higher education systems. Trow described a higher education system in which half the population or more of the relevant age group participates as a universal system, while a mass system has between 16–50% participation, and an elite system has up to 15% participation. Most industrialised countries have been progressively moving from elite towards universal systems over the last 30–40 years in response to changes in society, the economy and technology (Trow, 2005).

Trow argues that the nature of higher education institutions, curriculum and pedagogy change as the system moves from being elite to mass and then universal. The purpose of elite systems is to prepare the social elite, and this is reflected in a curriculum that is based on "shaping the mind and character" of students through the academic disciplines and professional knowledge. Institutions are relatively small and homogeneous with clear boundaries that distinguish the academic community from the rest of society. In contrast, the purpose of mass systems is to transmit knowledge and to prepare this segment of the population for a broader range of technical and economic leadership roles. The curriculum is modular, more flexible, and consists of semi-structured sequences within institutions that are comprehensive with standards that are more diverse and boundaries that are more fuzzy and permeable. Mass systems started to develop after the Second World War, and this is the beginning of the ascendency of the vocational over more liberal purposes of education. The purpose of universal systems is to prepare the whole population for rapid social and technological change. The boundaries between formally structured knowledge and the everyday in the curriculum begin to break down, as do the distinctions between the educational institution and other aspects of life, including the workplace (Trow, 2005: 64).

Trow initially presented a linear model of development from elite, to mass and then universal higher education and this has been criticised because there were many aspects that he did not get right. However, many have argued that Trow's model is helpful in providing a framework for analysing the stratification of higher education and different types of institutions within universal systems (see, for example Teichler, 2008). Trow (2005: 36) later revisited his model, and argued that the elite and mass systems (and institutions) were not supplanted by the universal system, but were subsumed so that their role and function continued within the universal system. This analysis lays the basis for understanding the current expansion of higher education.

Vocationalism in Australia's Universities

Australia is preparing to undergo its third period of major expansion of higher education since the Second World War, and this is reflected in ambitious targets set by the government for participation in higher education (Commonwealth of Australia, 2009). The first period was after the war when new universities were created along with colleges of advanced education and teachers colleges. The second was in the late 1980s, when Australia's teachers colleges and colleges of advanced education merged to form new universities or merged with existing universities. While Australian universities traditionally have had a strong utilitarian emphasis (Marginson & Considine, 2000: 205), each period of expansion has been accompanied by a growing emphasis on the vocational purposes of education. Marginson (1997: 12) explains that following the Second World War, private individuality and social need were (somewhat uneasily) reconciled through policy that sought to develop human capital. Individual aspirations were linked to broad social concerns through the mechanism of upward mobility based on occupational progression, and achieved through higher levels of education.

However, education was more explicitly tied to economic purposes as a consequence of neo-liberal reforms of the late 1980s, which resulted in a more thorough going vocationalisation of education and the creation of markets in education. The latter was to ensure competitive and entrepreneurial behaviour by educational institutions, including universities. Education was reshaped to produce the economic citizen and systems of education, including curriculum, were shaped to meet this goal so that "the way of thinking about education, and the new systems and behaviours emerging from reform, were neoclassical and market liberal" (Marginson, 1997: 152). Vocationalism emphasises preparing students with the skills they need for work, particularly generic or employability skills. It is based on a notion of the human actor as one who instrumentally invests in education that will develop their human capital and position them in employment markets. The purpose of education is to enable the "project of the self" expressed as the self-maximising, instrumental market individual. Vocationalism emphasises the profane world and ties knowledge and skills directly to that.

However, vocationalism and marketisation have been mediated in different ways in different groups of universities. For example, in discussing Australia's elite universities which they have labelled as sandstone universities, Marginson and Considine (2000: 194) argue that the:

> Sandstone commitment to Newmanesque notions of higher-education-for-its-own-sake is selective. The rhetoric is in one moment sincerely felt, in another it constitutes a form of marketing in itself, albeit one based on non-utilitarian and anti-commercial values. Anti-marketing, marketed with care . . . Other worldly rhetoric survives, but the Sandstones are as utilitarian as other institutions.

In other words, the Australian sandstone universities are able to position themselves in the education market through emphasising the more liberal purposes of education.

Mediating Access to Consciousness, Identity and Desire

As I have argued, different levels and forms of access to knowledge mediate different forms of consciousness, identity and desire; it produces different subjects and subjectivities. This is exemplified by two universities in Australia; one is an old university established in the 1850s in the early days of Australia's development as a British colony, and the other is a new university formed in the early 1990s through merging institutes of technology.

The new university says that its students will develop "the knowledge and skills required for the development of the knowledge economy" and that its curriculum will "strengthen the work values employers look for in new employees." It "will ensure that . . . [its] graduates are job ready with both job specific and generic employment skills and values." In contrast, the old university says that its students will be "academically excellent; knowledgeable across disciplines; leaders in communities; attuned to cultural diversity; [and] active global citizens" (Wheelahan, 2010: 179).

Each is providing students with a different form of access to knowledge. The new university's emphasis is on preparing students for the workplace (and moreover, to the workplace as it currently is), and it is looking to employers and the workplace to shape the kind of knowledge and skills it should include in its programs. The underlying notion is an idealised worker who has the subjectivity needed to be a desirable employee from the perspective of the employer. The old university is preparing its students for leadership, and it is linking knowledge with social leadership. It is inviting students to participate in a different form of preparation for the future. The curriculum matters.

The Retreat from Knowledge

As knowledge producers, universities play a key role in producing knowledge for the knowledge economy, and they also prepare students for the knowledge economy. Students are expected to know more than ever before, but there is less demand that they systematically engage with disciplinary structures of knowledge. The rapid pace of change accompanying globalisation has led to an emphasis on the contingent nature of knowledge and "authentic" knowledge which is cross-disciplinary, problem-oriented, applied and less hierarchical (see for example, Nowotny, Scott & Gibbons, 2001). However, this is to mistake disciplinary knowledge and the specific contents of that knowledge. Disciplinary knowledge consists of structured systems of meaning, while the specific content may change as the discipline produces further insights and changes and evolves through engagement in the world and with other disciplines. Interdisciplinary work will often lead to changes in disciplinary knowledge, but this is on the basis of engaging with the methods and concepts in each.

The importance of knowledge in curriculum has also been undermined because disciplinary knowledge is associated with elitism, and this is because socially powerful knowledge is mobilised and monopolised by social elites (Young, 2008). Paradoxically, the response of many progressives has been to say that because knowledge is associated with social power then we should deny its importance and the need for those outside social elites to have access to it. The alternative is to proclaim "other ways of knowing" as of equal value. Arguably, proponents of this argument confuse "powerful knowledge" with "knowledge of the powerful" (Young, 2008). Powerful knowledge is powerful because it provides epistemic access to the social and natural worlds, even if this is imperfect and always subject to revision as our practice in the world and attempts to extend knowledge provides us with better understandings (Bhaskar, 1998). On the other hand, knowledge of the powerful is shaped and distinguished by unequal social access to knowledge production, acquisition and use, and this is exemplified by the over-representation of social elites in elite schools, universities and professions.

It is true that knowledge always bears the marks of its producers and this is because it is *socially* produced. However, knowledge cannot be reduced to the conditions of its production, so while it bears the mark of social elites, it also provides at least some epistemic access to the world because it is our best effort to date in understanding the world. This is an argument for *democratising* knowledge by including those from less privileged backgrounds in its acquisition and, as members of the academy, in its production in the longer term. Moreover, arguing for access to powerful knowledge is not the same as arguing against valuing other ways of knowing. These are not mutually exclusive propositions, even though they are often represented as such by a deep-seated anti-intellectualism by some progressives. It is possible to argue that the less powerful should have access to powerful knowledge *and* that we should value other ways of knowing at the same time. Indeed, providing the less powerful with access to the academy has resulted in the emergence of new disciplines such as cultural studies and women's studies as the voices of the hitherto excluded were included in changing and extending the boundaries of the traditional disciplines.

As discussed in the previous section, knowledge has been marginalised in curriculum through the triumph of vocationalism in curriculum and through the instrumental alignment of education with the requirements of work. This includes the subsumption of liberal education as a component of generic skills. For example, the previous Australian Department of Education Science and Training (2002: 3) explained that:

> A liberal, general education and a professionally focused education are not necessarily mutually exclusive. The broad conceptions of a liberal education as espoused by Cardinal Newman in 1852 may be unsustainable, but the development of generic skills and knowledge should remain an essential part of all undergraduate education.

The emphasis on generic skills, graduate attributes and employability skills at the heart of curriculum in higher education reflects the purpose of curriculum, which is to ensure students have appropriate dispositions and attributes for the labour market. Rather than participating in collective representations that make and remake society, neoliberal visions of education privatise and commodify knowledge so that it is bought and sold in the credentials market as individuals make decisions to invest in their human capital, and employers to purchase their human capital. The focus is on the pursuit of private gain because the public good consists of aggregating the private good.

Rather than an inner dedication to bodies of knowledge, students are expected to have a commitment to lifelong learning and retraining. This is not a bad thing, but the discourse around lifelong learning has been used to diminish the centrality of knowledge in the curriculum so that learning takes place less through engaging with disciplinary knowledge, and more in response to the externalities of markets and the pursuit of "useful" knowledge. The argument used to justify the retreat of knowledge is that it is subject to flux and change in the context of globalisation.

In the case of newer professions that have emerged in the last 30–40 years (for example, hospitality or tourism or business studies), these externalities are driven more by the exigencies of the market, and less by an inner dedication to a professional identity of the traditional (and generally elite) professions (such as medicine or law), and the specialised knowledge base they have developed over time. Bernstein (2000: 85–86) argues that the basis of knowledge creation over the last 1000 years was a humanising principle based on inner commitments to knowledge, first expressed as religious knowledge and later as disciplinary knowledge in the case of the academic disciplines or applied disciplinary knowledge that provides the basis of practice in the professions. He argues that this has been replaced by a dehumanising principle, which is not inner commitments to knowledge or practice, but to the market. In this way, knowledge is divorced from knowers, a process which in the long run must have profound effects on the formation of identity.

Why a Theory of Knowledge Is Needed

If theoretical knowledge is crucial in providing students with access to society's conversations and in shaping identity, consciousness and desire, then we must have a theory of knowledge to guide the construction of curriculum so that the different modalities within society are available to all on the basis of choice, and less on social background. Providing access to knowledge should be the *raison d'être* of higher education regardless of the institutional context in which it is offered (Young, 2008). We must reclaim the importance of knowledge as the organising principle of curriculum in higher education. Young (2008: 10) argues that those who emphasise increased choices available to students may have a theory of *access* but not a theory of *knowledge*. Policies that seek to widen access to higher education that emphasise student choice in the absence of a theory of knowledge acquisition fail to recognise the unequal cultural resources that students have available to them in making choices. Such a failure is the basis for new, even if less visible, inequalities. Including students from disadvantaged backgrounds in higher education requires considering the *type* of access that students have. It is not enough that students have access to higher education; they must also have equitable access to elite universities or access to the knowledge that the elite universities offer.

Placing knowledge at the centre of curriculum provides students with access to ways of understanding that they would not otherwise have. However, there is more to it than that, because as Barnett (2009) explains, it is through access to disciplinary knowledge that students become knowers and thus engage in a process of becoming. They do this because to enter a discipline is to enter systems of meaning that have key "threshold" concepts, and rules for producing knowledge, reasoning and argument. In particular, they provide criteria for judging truth claims. It is not being claimed here that the disciplines provide unmediated access to the world or to truth—they don't—but they represent our best efforts and work-in-progress towards doing so.

Barnett (2009: 436) argues that the academic disciplines "call for discipline on the part of those who are trying to work within them." We may call the discipline that is developed the structuring principles of consciousness. Acquiring this discipline is the basis of autonomy because it provides students with the critical understanding they need and capacity to navigate boundaries, particularly the boundary between theoretical and everyday knowledge. Students need access to systems of meaning and not just contextual knowledge if knowledge is to be under their control. They need to be able to *choose* appropriate contextually specific applications of knowledge in new and different contexts, and they need to understand theoretical concepts and the relationships between them if they are to do so. This is the basis of moral autonomy and for constructing one's life because it provides the basis for the individual to make her or his own decisions and to participate in society "in such ways that social guidance shall be a matter of his own mental attitude, and not a mere authoritative dictation of his acts" (Dewey, 1966 (1916): 301).

Reclaiming Knowledge

Arguably vocationalism in Australia is so deeply embedded in higher education that it cannot be wished away. In discussing the United States, Grubb (2005: 2) argues that the only possible strategy that can be used to overcome the narrow instrumentalism of the new vocationalism is to seek to "integrate vocational purposes with broader civic, intellectual and moral goals." He argues that the notion of professionalism provides a bridge back to liberal education because each profession has an ethical dimension, is situated within a broader social, civic and political context, has a history, and a relationship to knowledge, theories and concepts (Grubb, 2005: 16).

This provides a useful way for thinking about different ways of responding to vocationalism and for structuring the relationship between vocationally specific programs and the disciplines or applied disciplines that underpin their field of practice. In the case of the new occupations and professions, this means structuring the curriculum around disciplinary knowledge as it is in the elite professions. Higher education should not be that which is designed to foster in students those work values desired by employers. Rather, it should engage students in the sacred, by providing them with access to the knowledge they need to participate in debates and controversies in their field of practice and in society.

The logic of this argument is that the occupations that the new higher education is preparing students for must also be imbued with a notion of the sacred. Just as the elite professions developed their own knowledge base when they moved into the academy towards the end of the nineteenth century (Grubb, 2005: 5), so must also the professions and occupations for which students are being prepared in the vocationally oriented new universities. These institutions must of course continue their mission of widening access for students who have not previously had access to higher education, and to provide the supportive pedagogy they need to *become* higher education students. However, this needs to be on the basis of providing students with access to systems of meaning and not just contextual applications of knowledge. In this way, new universities that do not have the resources of the elite universities can help to realise the democratic project of the university.

Conclusion

Trow argued that the stratification of higher education into elite, mass and universal systems is the only affordable way for a democracy to provide universal higher education while at the same time ensuring that the traditional role of preparing social elites was maintained. He argues that while ideals of egalitarianism are laudable, that they are unaffordable and would lead to a decline in quality. Consequently, stratified and differentiated systems provide the only means of meeting the range of society's needs. Such systems provide the basis of a meritocracy because at least some students are successful in moving from less prestigious to more prestigious institutions (even if it is not too many), while at the same time protecting the quality of elite provision.

However, Trow is surely wrong in this argument, particularly if the implications are that only the elite get access to the site of the unthinkable and alternative possibilities. Apart from intrinsic concerns with social justice and democracy, the scale of the social problems that we face today, particularly issues such as global warming, means that the only way forward is to involve more people in the conversation, based on *understanding* the issues at stake. We all have a stake in this conversation, but we do not all share the same means to participate in it. While I cannot see equitable resourcing of higher education institutions in the near future, nonetheless it is possible for all higher education to take seriously its obligation to provide students with access to the sacred.

4

THE TRAJECTORY AND FUTURE OF THE IDEA OF THE UNIVERSITY IN CHINA

Shuang-Ye Chen and Leslie N.K. Lo

Introduction

The first modern Chinese university was established in 1895, during the last imperial dynasty. Organizationally deriving from the medieval European university, the early Chinese universities lacked two salient institutional elements, namely institutional autonomy and academic freedom, in the borrowing process from the West via Japan (Hayhoe, 1999; Altbach, 1998). In the Republic Era (1911–1949), Chinese higher education flourished with distinctive dynamics from Christian private universities, private universities funded by local entrepreneurs and national public universities. After 1949, Chinese universities in the New China were restructured by the Chinese Communist Party after the former Soviet Union model and required to be ideologically conforming and educationally specialized. Since the Open-up and Reform policy (gaige kaifang) was implemented in 1978, Chinese universities have changed continously and grown into the largest higher education system in the world.

In the globalized context of universities, the idea of the university is challenged by the postmodern conditions of knowledge, massification, and diversification. Over the past century, the *idea* of the university in China has been shaped by the joint forces of state, market and academia. In recent years, the Chinese higher education system has been expanding dramatically and the tension between quantity and quality poses a challenge to the traditional idea of the university. Furthermore, the practice of building world-class universities and the higher education quality assurance movement have left little room for the idea of the university. This chapter maps out the trajectory of the changing idea of the university in China, and analyzes its contents and enactment in the Chinese context. A narrative approach is used to illuminate the future of the idea of the university in China, and the exploration of university identity is proposed.

Changing Ideas and Changing Universities

With the advent of a new century, two major underminings of higher education, the epistemological and the sociological, are now more visible than when Ronald Barnett (1990) put forward this thesis two decades ago. Universities all over the world have been and are being transformed by the global forces of the knowlege society and the dramatic massification of higher education. Discourses of public accountability and audit (Barnett, 1990; Delanty, 1998) are prevailing in and among universities. Their allegedly falling quality and failing role in the knowledge society have brought universities to a crisis of legitimacy.

The ideas of the university across Plato, Newman, Kant, von Humboldt, Weber, Jaspers, Parsons and Habermas to Minogue, Kerr, Barnett and Delanty have been fading from the present discussion about higher education. The intrinsic values of the university, which are usually carried by the ideological statements concerning "the idea" are drawing to an end (Barnett, 1990; Readings, 1996; Delanty, 1998). Universities and higher education are appreciated for their extrinsic values, and their functional and instrumental contributions to students, governments and the public.

Now that higher education has become an institution "of" society as distinct from its being an institution merely "in" society (Barnett, 1994), universities are seen to generate economic objects either to be invested in or to be consumed. The idea of the university that helped to sustain the university as an "ivory tower" in the time of higher education "in" society (Barnett, 1994) cannot withstand the powerful impact of society on universities. Moreover, in the postmodern condition of knowledge (Lyotard, 1984), the idea of the university is losing its own power and standing and, at the same time, is incorporating numerical calculations of efficiency and performativity.

Given such a pessimistic trend, it becomes a necessary but also a formidable project to raise again a discussion of the idea of the university in looking into the future. This set of considerations is worked out here in the narrative of Chinese universities.

The Idea of the University in China

The idea of the university is ideological and qualitative in nature. It is a phenomenological idea constructed by people with sets of normative values and justifications. How could the future of the idea of the university be predicted or foretold? The narrative method offers a feasible way to connect the past and the present with the future. It comprises a series of materials in a sequential way, a selection or appropriation of those materials, plots and logics to line them up, and a coherence and a meaningful wholeness (White, 1987; Ricoeur, 1991). The narratives of the idea of the university are public and conceptual at the same time. They are attached to cultural and institutional formations beyond individuals, and constructed as concepts and frameworks for social action (Somers, 1994). In such a way, dimensions, ownership and enactment of the ideas of the university in China may be analyzed across different periods.

The Maturing of the Idea of the University in China (1895–1949)

In Chinese, "the idea of the university" is translated as "Daxue de linian." Another term in Chinese, "Daxue de jingshen" (the spirit of the univerisity) is used frequently to refer to the idea of the university in English. Since the founding of the first university in China, there are two major narratives concerning the idea of the university. One is following the storyline of the western model of universities (Yang, 2000; Xiao, 2001; Chen, 2006), but the other is captured by the Chinese traditional understanding of higher learning (Hayhoe, 1999; Chu, 2006; Chen, 2009).

In the early stage of establishing a modern university after the Japanese model, the idea of the university in China was embodied in Zhang Zhi-Dong's slogan, "Chinese learning as its essence, Western learning for its usefulness" (cited from Hayhoe, 1999: 38). In traditional Chinese learning, there was no division of subjects, nor practical programmes to assist students in applying learning and practice to the real world. The last Qing Imperial Court agreed to import the Western institution of university as a powerful learning strategy to defeat the Westerners. As a result, institutional autonomy and academic freedom, which feature strongly in the European university, were neglected in the process of borrowing the form of the university.

In the process of introducing the university model into China, a group of selected young people were sent out from 1872 onwards by the Qing government to Japan, America, Britain and Europe to receive higher education (Bevis & Lucas, 2007; Qian & Hu, 2009). Ten to twenty years later, these people returned to China as educated elites and they sought to instil their understanding of the idea of the university back into Chinese universities.

The Republic Era (1911–1949) was a time of wars and social turmoil, but the achievement of universities and the development of the idea of the university were significant and were highly recognized (Yang, 2000; Yang, Vidovich & Currie, 2007). The two major widely-quoted ideas of the university were put forward by Cai Yuan-Pei and Mei Yi-Qi, then presidents of Peking University and Tsinghua University respectively. Cai Yuan-Pei was appointed as president of Peking University from 1917 to 1927. He committed himself to transforming Peking University into a university of higher learning with academic freedom after the Humboltian German University model (Chen, 2009). Mei Yi-Qi phrased the idea of the university from a quote of an old Chinese book, *The Great Learning*, as "Daxue zhidao, zai mingmingde, zai qinmin, zai zhiyu zhishan" (the way of the great learning involves manifesting virtue, loving the people, and abiding by the highest good) (cited from Yang, 2000: 80). Another aphorism from Mr. Mei about the idea of the university is "Daxue zhida, fei dalou zhida, nai dashi zhida" (the greatness of a university is defined by the great masters it has, rather than its magnificent buildings) (cited from Yang, 2000: 353).

In his anthology of "Daxue jingshen" (spirit of the university), Yang (2000) classifies the selected texts into six categories: the idea of the university, academic freedom, general education, student autonomy, words to young students, and master leaders. In the first part of the idea of the university, most texts were selected from the then-presidents of the few top comprehensive universities. They covered the topics of the purposes of university education, the configuration of a modern university, the idea of a free and independent spirit, and general education.

The Chinese idea of the university shared many of the elements that have come to characterize the Western idea of the university (Barnett, 1990), but was weak in two aspects, namely knowledge creation and rationality. While European universities emerged and developed in a spontaneous manner, their Chinese counterparts were established by active intellectuals and political elites who were seeking for a solution of the national crisis and the project of saving the nation. Therefore, the legitimacy of the Chinese universities was justified more by its social and political function, rather than by its epistemological values.

In narrating the idea of the university in China, scholars, public intellectuals and presidents of universities were three dominant groups. They were cultural elites in the public sphere where the weak state at that time didn't intervene much. The higher education system was elite in nature, enrolling just a few rich and capable students (Wang, 2007). Therefore, it was a small elite higher education system that was influential in promoting the idea of the university.

The idea of the university was a set of normative statements and values proposed by the cultural elites. The university was seen as an end in itself but this conception could not be held separate from the realities of university practice. How much in reality did the idea of the university matter or make a difference to Chinese universities in that period? There is no empirical work giving any clue in answering this question but there are some indications of an influence taking place. The South-Western United University (Xinan lianda) was an example of the idea of the university being realized in the war time. University presidents, academic scholars, students and intellectuals were agents in bringing alive the idea in the lifeworld of the university.

The Disappearing Idea of the University in the New China (1949–)

After 1949, the Chinese Communist Party replaced the former Nationalist Party in ruling China. The new regime eradicted Christian private universities and re-engineered the existing universities into the Soviet Union model of higher education (Pepper, 1996). Comprehensive universities were dismantled and reorganized into specialized colleges; general education was replaced by a common curriculum of political-ideological courses. Researchers in the universities were regrouped into specialized research institutions separate from the university. And last, but not least, scholars and intellectuals were disciplined out of their free minds and independent critical thinking through a series of ideological remolding movements. President Mei Yi-Qi—as an icon of the idea of the university—chose to escape from the Chinese Mainland and rebuild Tsinghua University in Taiwan. Peking University and Tsinghua University as the flagship institutions in Chinese higher education were restructured into the proletarian people's university (Luo, 2010; Pan, 2009). The idea of the univerisity was muted and forbidden under the state revolutionary discourse.

It was not until 1978, when the Reform and Opening-up policy initiated societal change from the ideopolitical revolution to economic development, that universities were released gradually from the tight control of the state. Institutional autonomy and academic freedom were desired by Chinese universities. The state did delegate tasks and decision-making authority to universities but it did not necessarily turn Chinese universities into autonomous institutions with academic freedom. State patronage (Lo, 1991) penetrated and prevailed in the operation of universities.

In the societal transition from the planned economy towards a market economy, Chinese universities suffered from a shortage of public money and were forced to generate revenue with market-like activities (Yin & White, 1994; Wang, 2007). The idea of the university was jeopardized by a strong state and unregulated market at the same time (Chen & Lo, 2004).

The year of 1999 marked another stage in the development of higher education in China. The number of university enrolments increased significantly in 1999. The gross enrolment ratio rose from 10% in 1998 (Levin & Xu, 2006) to 22% in 2008 (MOE, 2009). The number of bachelor degree granting universities was doubled in ten years to 1079 in 2008 (MOE, 2009).

The former elite higher education system could not accomodate such a significant but rapid expansion with the same level of "quality." In order to ensure both the pace of expansion and the maintenance of quality, the Ministry of Education started a compulsory quality assurance project of "Benke jiaoxue shuiping pinggu" (an evaluation of University Baccalaureate programmes) from 2002 to 2008. Every university with Baccalaureate programmes was evaluated by a delegate team with reference to a set of "observable" indicators in eight areas of teaching, learning, research and management.

Another project named "Jianshe shijie yiliu daxue" (Building world-class universities) was initiated in 1998 to improve higher education quality and to gain an edge in the global competition across states (Cerny, 2000). Peking University, Tsinghua University and other selected top universities in China have been funded by the state with more than 30 billion Renminbi Yuan. The category of "world-class" was created in the local context of China but with its symbolic power, it has accelerated a fierce status competition across the world, among both universities and nation-states (Huisman, 2008).

The quality assurance movement and the world-class university project are two salient technologies to orient Chinese universities towards performativity. Performativity in Lyotard's work (1984) was seen as a way of optimizing performance by maximizing output and minimizing inputs. Stephen Ball (2006) further developed the concept in the following way:

> Performativity is a technology, a culture and a mode of regulation, or even a system of 'terror' in Lyotard's words, that employs judgments, comparisons and displays as means of control, attrition and change. The performances – of individual subjects or organizations – serve as measures of productivity or output, or displays of 'quality', or 'moments' of promotion or inspection. They stand for, encapusulate or represent the worth, quality of value of an individual or organization within a field of judgment.
>
> *(Ball, 2006: 692)*

The idea of the university in China has been neglected and marginalized in a series of performativity exercises and the audit culture (Delanty, 1998). Instead, another kind of fabricated phenomenal existence (Ball, 2003) prevails over the idea of the university, now seen in terms of productivity and empirically observable items of academic life for fulfilling accountability requirements and ranking competitions. In contrast with the fabrications connected to the university in an era of performativity, an idea of the university still worth defending is that essentially the university is unquantifiable, unproductive, useless and unobservable in any obvious way (such as any accountability exercise). This latter—and longstanding—idea of the university doubtless needs to be developed in the modern world but it has actually been impaired by the overwhelming climate of performativity.

Reviving the Idea of the University in China: Possibilities and Challenges

In sixty years, Chinese universities have been confronted with political control and domination, financial shortages, market developments, a dramatic expansion and a rapid process of massification, and new technologies of performativity for quality assurance and competition (Zha, 2009; Chen & Lo, 2004). The idea of the university has little room to grow and gain wider recognition among the public. Marginalized as the narrative of the idea of the university has been, it has survived among some public intellectuals in and out of the university. Here are two exciting examples of the weak but noteworthy development of the idea of the university in China.

In the mid 1990s, Chinese universities were merging on a large scale. This was a trend to reverse the 1950s restructuring of universities into specialized colleges. Universities were encouraged to merge small specialized colleges into comprehensive institutions of various academic disciplines. The process was not without problems or criticism. But one major change in the process within universities was to bring general education back into common core curriculum of the university. Peking University, Fudan University, Zhongshan University and others have been experimenting with their versions of general education like Harvard or Chicago. However varied in practice they were, the idea of general education and liberal education were referred to, relied on and revived in an indigenous way.

Another encouraging case is related to academic freedom and the idea of the university. In 2003, a heated public discussion was stirred up by a human resources reform policy being implemented in Peking University. It resulted in an edited book (Gan & Li, 2003) of which editors were active and leading public intellectuals speaking out in public. Academic freedom as the essence of the idea of the university was used in the book to justify the editors' criticism of the personnel reform policy in Peking University. Ariticles included in the book ranged from traditional pieces on the idea of the university by famous scholars in the Republic Era such as Cai Yuan-Pei and Mei Yi-Qi, to contemporary criticism and argument by active scholars and public intellectuals.

However, this long-standing idea of the university is fragile in the present era; it has become faint and is threatening to disappear. Its rapid growth and expansion carried the Chinese higher education system away from an elite to a mass but highly stratified system. Now, the legitimacy of the university lies in its responsiveness to external expectations and demands, rather than in its instrinsic values connected with the worthwhileness of knowledge in itself and enlightenment.

Marginalized as it is, the idea of the university continues among public intellectuals and some people in the universities. General and liberal education, and academic freedom, are revived and practiced, even if in a compromised way. However, in general, the university presidents who are appointed by the state and the Chinese Communist Party do not have an ear for the idea of the university. They play no part in enacting the idea of the university.

From Idea to Identity and Enactment: For the Future of the University

The future is a temporal concept, which is beyond our experience to observe or to capture. How can the future university be imagined, proposed and discussed? How can the idea and possibilities of the university be narrated into the future?

In an age of "supercomplexity" (Barnett, 2000) and "liquidity" (Bauman, 2000), "all that is solid melts into air'" (Berman, 1983). In such an age, ideas of the university and the institution of university are configured by all kinds of ideologies. There seems to be no longer an institutional solidity that could serve as a space to hold and appreciate the internal goods of the university: they are now jeopardized as performativity and accountability are imposed from the outside. It is not easy to recover from this crisis of legitimacy.

Drawn from the above analysis of the development of the idea of the university in China over the past century, two possibilities for the idea of the university and future university suggest themselves.

Responsible Enactment by University Leaders

The idea of the university is a set of normative values and judgments put forward by different people across time and place. It could not be a holistic and coherent consensus. It is varying, invisible and ambiguous. But it functions to support and distinguish this institution (of "university") from others. How could Church and University be the two oldest surviving public institutions in history? Only through the power of the ideas, values and beliefs that sustain them.

Ideas are weak without being enacted. How is such enactment possible? In the history of Chinese universities, public intellectuals and scholars in the university read, discussed, and spoke out in the public sphere. Their voice and texts have been fixed as part of the narrative and influenced others. Therefore, university leaders should be aware of their leadership role and their potential influence in developing, articulating and enacting the idea of the university. Accountability and performativity have exerted considerable influence and even constraints on univerities, but institutional leaders can be brave in developing a public discourse as to what university should be responsible for. To engage openly with the public is a preliminary form of the enactment of the idea of the university.

From Idea to Identity

The idea of the university is value-laden and normative. It defines what a university is and what university should do. In the past narrative of the idea of the university in China or other places, it was an idea narrated for a small number of elite universities with a history and reputation through an association with public elites.

In the age of higher education massification and diversification, it offers a good opportunity for us to reflect again on the idea of the university itself. With a massified and stratified university system both in China and in other places, the old storyline of the idea of the university should be studied and reflected critically. In seeking to develop that storyline into the present and future ages, could a switch be possible, such that an idea originated from an elitist imagination form an idea of and even an identity within the university that can be applied in the modern era to different universities having varied concerns and interests? Perhaps a new university identity can work as an analytic concept to allow both universality and distinctiveness in a new narrative of universities as a continuing meaningful unity (Somers, 1994).

Conclusion

The trajectory and future of the idea of the university in China can be seen through a narrative approach from the establishment of the first modern Chinese university to the present. Dimensions, ownership and enactment of the idea of the university can be observed across the stages of its development, namely the stages of maturing, disappearing and reviving. Currently the idea of the university in China is challenged by the massification process, and further impaired by a rising performativity in the higher education system.

For the future development of the idea of the university in China and other places, the traditional way of narrating and studying the idea needs a change. The enactment of the idea should be emphasized over the specific content or dimensions included in the idea of the university. The elitist idea of the university developed in old times needs to accomodate the massification and diversification of higher education.

5

THE IDEA OF THE UNIVERSITY IN LATIN AMERICA IN THE TWENTY-FIRST CENTURY

Mario Díaz Villa

> To ask whether the university has a reason for being is to wonder "why the university" but the question "why" verges on "with a view to what?" the university with a view to what? What is the university's view? What are its views?
>
> *Derrida (2004: 130)*

Introduction

The aim of this chapter is to examine the current meaning of the university in Latin America, especially to establish its goals and dimensions in the present century, characterized by substantial changes in the production of knowledge, in its own nature, and by a profound transformation in the collective bases of society (Bernstein, 1998), all of which prompts a refocus on education, subject, identity, work, and their intrinsic relations. In turn, the idea of the university in the twenty-first century becomes unstable, due to the fact that its meaning is determined by historic conditions and transformations in the contexts in which the positions, relations, and functions of knowledge produced within society changes. It is from this point of view that I will sketch several problems that cannot be avoided when referring to the idea of the university in Latin America.

The chapter does not provide answers. It only opens a field of critical possibilities about the idea of the university in Latin America. This idea is controversial if one considers that to this day there is neither an absolute concept of university nor a general notion of what Latin America means. The university has always been an object of semantic—not to mention epistemological or sociocultural—transformation. Its grammatical organization has been multiple and diverse. Each time that society recodifies its organizational models and generates new forms of production and reproduction in its institutions, subjects, discourses and contexts, a reconfiguration of the university's being and doing takes place. In adopting this reflection to illustrate the university in modern and postmodern societies, I can agree with Barnett (1994) that university is "both in and of society." This idea refocuses the historical interests of the university by means of recontextualizing its emancipatory principles and values. As Barnett states, the university has lost its way in an "unknowable world" (2003: 151). This statement embeds the questions: Is the university possible? Can we, indeed, any longer speak of "the university"? (Barnett, 2005: 1) What is its nature within higher education? (Barnett, 2007).

For this reason, with all the problems brought by the restrictions of space, the following analysis will attempt to present the ideas of university around Latin America in the current century, a century full of social upheavals; commotions which broke the institutional forms of the nineteenth and twentieth centuries (Lipovetsky, 2002) but which failed to transcend the principles of the classic university. In the first place, some historic principles will be explored which identify the idea of the university related with Latin America; secondly, I will sketch the basic changes occurring during the second part of the twentieth century; thirdly, I will examine the current condition of the Latin American university; and finally, I will consider what, from my point of view, should be the twenty-first-century university in Latin America.

The Idea of the University in the Twenty-First Century

It is not easy to construct an idea of the university in the contemporary context. There are many perspectives that have evoked the possible conditions of its existence: historical, economical, sociocultural, institutional, associated both with international and national macro-justifications, and expressed in policies, objectives, purposes, missions and even visions. The idea of the university, its *raison d'être* (Derrida, 2004: 129), has oscillated between the assumption of an institution dedicated to open reason, in the Kantian sense, and an institution founded on a rationality based on policies, principles, objectives, purposes and forms, as well as organizational and reorganizational criteria.

Reason and rationality have historically coexisted in the idea of the university. Reason remains fundamental in comprehending the ideal of *universitas*[1] as an expressive voice, faculty and core of the convergent ontological unit of knowledge and truth (Barnett, 2005; Borrero, 2008). Rationality allows us to comprehend the modern roles of the university in responding or reacting to socioeconomic interests, in de-centering its historical tasks of critical discourse, and in becoming an organization of and for performative knowledge (Barnett, 2000). What we could denominate as the "university's rationality" has been carried out in the last centuries in terms of delimitations, assimilations, and demarcations, which regulate the dimensions of its fields, domains, subjects and objects. In the same way, "different paradigms have determined both the inner configuration and the outer delimitation of their domains differently" (Welsch, 1998: 17). It is through this means that the university has historically legitimated the production and reproduction of discourses, practices and identities within specific fields and contexts of knowledge/practice.

However,

> As a result of changes in the field of rationality, rationality itself is distinguished by a peculiar disorderliness . . . Rationality is certainly intended to establish and guarantee order. But disorder is an inevitable consequence of the modern development of rationality, characterized by pluralization and entanglements.
>
> *(Welsch, 1998: 18)*

This seems to be what has happened to the twenty-first-century university, an institution embedded in the plural basis of an allegedly flexible society. Given this situation, how can one now reflect on the university? How can one understand the fields of the university's rationality under the new conditions of flexibility in knowledge, technology and society? Is it possible to assume disorderliness in the modern and postmodern university? Or is this new rationality in conflict with its historical foundation, namely the principle of reason (Derrida, 2004)? What is the university's identity in the present millennium? These are difficult questions that challenge the dominant social thought of the modern university.

The main assumption here is that the twenty-first-century university has an abstract identity. University has become a kind of common name without a specific ontology. It represents different things. It has neither a specific space nor a specific discourse. Today, university means the beyond, the beyond of boundaries, a constellation of meanings and realizations, a plurality of "standpoints," "interests" (Moore & Muller, 1999) and contexts. In contrast with the classical ideas of the university as the foundation of the world, humanity and truth, signifier of sciences, basis of scientific knowledge, and synthesis of faith, reason and culture (Newman, Humboldt, Jasper, Ortega y Gasset), the university in the twenty-first century has become itself a site of dissolution of unity and the end of a singularity of discourses, identity and knowledge. It is the means and end of the blurring of boundaries.

If the classic university represented the adequate order of world and knowledge—the universal in the university in Barnett's terms (2005: 1), the twenty-first-century university is a particularist organization ready to solve the imperatives of policies, open to vocationalism and to the logics of performativity, entrepreneurialism and virtuality (Barnett, 2005; Robins & Webster, 2002). Its principles have subscribed those of the global market. Academic knowledge has become a commodity ready to consume; learning has become the foundation of neo-individualism, a new economy for the production of pedagogic identities; and, even its organization has adopted the most sophisticated division of labor (Slaughter and Rhoades, 2009). It witnesses, as Virno (2004) states, the theoretical-commercial triumph surrounding the university. This has configured a tremendous change in the university identity and in its internal values.

The classical university's task of cultural transmission inherited from the middle age, and that of social mobility and socialization proper of modernity, has been replaced in the twenty-first century by the scientific and technological market, determined by the multidimensional pluralizing of knowledge and by multiple changes in the mode of its production. In the same way postmodern society has changed the historical course of its objectives and modalities of production and reproduction (Lipovetsky, 2002), so the university in the twenty-first century has de-centered its historical reason. The postmodern university celebrates the instrumental condition of hegemonic discourses, the erosion of academic life, the weakening of epistemic spaces and the plurality of structures, rationalities, standpoints, histories, and identities. The pure essence of its morality and autonomous ideas, the autopoietic sense which made the spirit of the classic immune university has been transformed. The external boundaries of university have become more flexible and adaptable to the language of the new capitalist spirit: "autonomy, spontaneity, mobility, looping capacity, coexistence, opening of other innovations, availability, creativity, visionary institution, differences sensibility, multiple experiences, aptitude for learning and adapting" (Boltansky & Chiapello, 2002: 148).

The university has ceased to be a place of public debate—*agora* or *forum*. In the process of change, the place of critique and wisdom has been converted into a market place, subordinated to being a business scene of knowledge, ready to offer to its clients the services and certificates which they require for the labor market. This has weakened the credibility of the historic meaning of the university in its creation and promotion of values.

The Idea of Latin America

In general, the idea of Latin America is founded in a system of representations which bring into play a division of temporalities, political subordinations, territorial divisions, cultural and linguistic similarities and differences, and unequal development. The historic and political retrospective of the construction of a "new world," its increased colonization and modernization and the precipitate entrance into modernity, have a great weight in these representations. This means that regardless of the opening of Latin America to modernity, the colonial image (Mignolo, 2007; Lastra, 2008) is a repressed ghost in the Latin American subconscious. We can add to this point Mignolo's reflection for which "the colonial image in the present keeps the contradictions which were not resolved in the past." It is, therefore, a commonplace to say that Latin American way of thinking has been constructed, in a large part, through the modern modulations of an historical euro-centric colonial logic, and in the twenty-first century, dominated by the widening power of the United States.

On this basis, it is not easy to claim autonomy within Latin American epistemic fields, whose historical structuring have been dominated by European or Anglo-Saxon epistemologies. It is probably fair to say that the colonial logic dissolved the idea of Latin America into hybrid and ideal views under the mantle of European humanism (Ardao, 1993; Henriquez Ureña, 1978), but also under the rhetoric of development addressed by international agencies (CEPAL, BID, BM, IESALC-UNESCO), which continually tune their sociocultural and economic horizon to that of the globalization politics. In the former case, the dominant discourse displays ontological and epistemological inferiority (Mignolo, 2007). In the latter case, the economic voices define decontextualized principles for Latin America, no matter the disastrous effect of global market economy for this part of the so-called "third world."

As can be observed, the idea of Latin America has a semantics that make it difficult to depict and understand the complexity of its present and prospective scenarios. How, then, might one delineate a new image of Latin America in the context of the avalanche of the global economic and sociocultural processes?

In economic matters, it must be recognized that the uneven development of Latin America has been produced by the historical dependence on the dominant expansion of capitalism in the international and the global economy. This issue, underlined by the systematic development of dependency theories (Cardoso & Faletto, 1979; Sunkel, 1969, 1973) and their later developments (Wallerstein, 2005), seems to be relevant for the explanation of the weaknesses of Latin American countries in their insertion into the unequal exchange of the present global economy. Despite the deep commercial reforms determined by the global competition, Latin America is characterized by the existence of incomplete and precarious internal and external markets (Ffrench-Davis, 2001). On one hand, the economy of most of the countries in the sub-continent depends on the export of natural resources, despite the efforts of international agencies for designing and improving competitive economic policies, and for opening the countries to international trading and foreign investments (CEPAL, 2008; 2008a). On the other hand, the accelerated commercial development and the deregulation and flexibility of the organizational patterns of production in Latin America have weakened the productive and technological capacity of the economy. In addition to this, the lack of technologies and the low capacity for research and innovation must be considered. For example, the Latin American expenditure on university research and development between 2000 and 2003 shows the mediocre growth of 2.3%.

The mixture of neoliberalism and developmentalism, more than being the trigger of socioeconomic transformations, has been the means not only of stagnation, but also of increasing rates of poverty and unemployment. This has given rise to the production of a broad grammar of political and social conflicts. As an example, the poverty rate rose in 2008 to 32% (184 millions of poor people, including 68 millions of indigents). For 2010, the OECD foresees an increasing level of poverty of almost seven points as a consequence of the fall in the gross domestic product (GPD) and of an increase in the economy of a mere 1.3% (CEPAL, 2008a: 23).

As can be seen, despite the alleged benefits ascribed to globalization, the growth of economic rates in Latin America neither reflects an improvement in the socio-economic situation of its population, nor a strengthening of the wellbeing of the unprotected population in access to education and health. The same has happened with the Latin American integration processes (Altman, 2009; Rueda, 2001).

The rhetoric that international agencies and Latin American governments have developed represent dominant voices in economic matters that have made very few contributions to advanced changes and transformations in Latin America. The market situation has gone always in the opposite way to the labor situation and social welfare. The figures above (180 millions of poor people and 68 millions of indigents) show the very slow progress in raising the wellbeing of poor Latin American people. What is most striking is the pessimistic picture of social change over time.

In relation to socio-cultural processes, the retrospective idea of Latin America was proclaimed by the mystifying euro-centric voices of colonial and post-colonial culture. However, today new voices tend to oppose the metropolitan approaches to the subcontinent and propose new explorations about the Latin American identity (Lienhard, 1996). Among the current debates is the one related to "cultural hybridity." This perspective, developed by García Canclini (1990) has become most influential for the comprehension of modern cultural grounds in the subcontinent. García Canclini understands Latin America "as a complex articulation of unequal and diverse traditions and modernities, an heterogeneous continent composed of countries where, in each one, coexists multiple development logics" (García Canclini, 1990: 23). This viewpoint, that is more phenomenological than structural, presents a socio-cultural explanation of modernization produced in Latin America.

In fact, the idea of hybridity which is associated with a "multi-temporal heterogeneity" can be useful for describing the apparent coexistence between high and low culture, tradition and modernity, and the depictions of the globalization of the local and of the localization of the global. Hybridity dissolves the class struggle dilemmas and neutralizes the structural conflicts embedded in the historical dynamics of what can be called modalities of capitalism in Latin America.

It is likely, therefore, that the sociocultural idea of Latin America needs a review of the relations of economic production and of their interactions with the dominant modalities of cultural production. In this sense, it would be possible to understand why, in hybridity, the idiosyncratic particularisms coexist in a subordinate way to class hegemonies that allow control over the rules of political, economic, moral, educational and cultural logics, and the differentiated production of fluid, non standardized, dynamic, and internationalized identities for the dominant groups, and the consumption of standardized identities for the dominated groups. This hybridity, no matter its fluidity, flexibility and liquidity, reproduces the class "*habitus.*" The hybridity perspective has allowed a recontextualization of Latin American particularisms and localisms, generating through this way consensus which legitimate social stratification and differentiation processes. Some authors have pointed out the limitations of the hybridity theory (Kokotovic, 2000) and have developed other concepts—heterogeneity, transculturation, deterritorialization (Cornejo, 1994, 1997; Quijano, 1990; Rama, 1987) to locate socio-cultural identity, and the idea of Latin America in a different way, and reflect a subcontinent that even today appears divided and marked by unequal development.

The Latin American University During Recent Decades: Modernization and Technocratization

For the Latin American university, the situation has been crucial since 1960, when the idea that the university should adapt to the demands of social and economic development gave ideological support to this process, and led to prepare, at the same time, the managers, politicians and technicians for such a duty (Atcon, 1961; Herrera, 1965, 1966). Today's modern and postmodern university seems to be an institution of the techno-science market, although in Latin America techno-science does not seem to be a supporting principle of the university. Latin American diversification of higher education has become more a principle for the generation of hybrid educational markets than a principle for the development of new epistemic and sociocultural spaces open to alternative principles, values, knowledge and interest, against the legacy of inequalities underpinning the global society.

In Latin America, the second half of the twentieth century can be understood as an open totality of transformations in different dimensions. This constitutes a wide field of events and problems, and represents the spirit of a period in which the process of modernization has been proceeding along with substantial changes in the economic and sociocultural structures in Latin American nations. In what follows, I will focus on the *substratum* of the university.

The entrance of Latin American countries into the so-called "modernity" can be understood as a complex web of induced economic, sociopolitical and cultural processes. A political and ideological theory of development has been constructed to generate accelerated structural changes in these fields (García, 1985). According to Melo (1990: 26), this theory led education from the 1950s to the 1960s and was based on the rationalization of political administration in the Latin American states, and on the transfer of metropolitan economic, political, and cultural models, abstracted from the historical particularities of each country. Thus, the entrance of the Latin American countries into "modernity" introduces the idea of "modernization."

For Marshall Berman, modernity is a "form of vital experience, the experience of time and space, of ourselves and of others, of the possibilities and dangers of life" (Berman, 1988: xi). From the Weberian perspective, it is a process of progressive rationalization of society in its economic, political and cultural institutions, it is "the institutionalization of economic and administrative action with final arrangements" (Habermas, 1989: 12). It is also considered a "general movement toward the opening, rationalization and secularization" of society (Touraine, 1988). This can also be defined as a step from traditional order to modern order (Lechner, 1989: 36).

However, modernity in Latin America does not mean a substitution of the traditional forms of life, nor a rupture with the economic and sociocultural colonial foundations. Hence, its modernization has been considered unfinished and as a project that can never be finished. It has been named as half way modernization or as a cartoon of modernity (Corredor, 1990), forced modernity (Melo, 1990), or pseudo modernity (Brunner, 1992).

We can also add that modernity in Latin America has been associated with powerful mechanisms of exclusion and marginalization. Even though these concepts are dated to the sixties of the last century, they currently have a close relation to the poverty and the precarious nature of these forms associated with work, nutrition, health, education, security and social integration (Costa, 2001; Cortés, 2006). From García Cancilini´s perspective (1990), modernity in Latin America should be understood as a form of hybridity, a cultural heterogeneity, produced under the parameters of colonialism. This has given rise to diverse forms of political space and of societal expressions in a continent distributed in different regions with different cultural logics, chronologies, prospectives and utopias. These can be understood as the mixture of democratic institutions with authoritarian governments and new social movements with messianic regimes.

As diverse and different as its geography, geopolitics and culture, the university in Latin America, a precarious system constructed at the beginning of the fourteenth century, has retained traces of the Spanish culture and the French Enlightenment, despite its democratic development at the beginning of the twentieth century. References to its organization agree that, in Latin American universities, a plurality of organizational logics is proliferating that, in turn, have given rise to a structural heterogeneity. With some exceptions, the Latin American university is still premodern (Ferrari & Contreras, 2008). The "knowledge society" and "flexibility" dominate the rhetorics of most institutional discourses but old disciplinary knowledge is the main organizational principle. This fact raises doubts about the capacity of the Latin American university to meet in a critical way the challenges posed by the global interests.

My hypothesis is that the Latin American university has blurred its social space in the light of its crises. If during the middle of the twentieth century, the university was assumed to be the leading carrier of modernization, it is surprising that today it has ceased to be a social agent of solutions and has become a setting for contemporary knowledge markets in which flexible trainability is the generating principle of a new economy of professional identity. Currently we are seeing a semantic modification of the university. Global processes and social realities challenge its traditional academic meaning. Its growing rhetoric of diversity is embedded within the uniformity generated by a series of globalized policies: self-regulation, programme accreditation, self-financing and privatization and the university as a set of cultural businesses in the making.

This has meant that the Latin American university at the end of the twentieth and during the present century has been converted into an artificial place whose substantive work has been blurred due to the laws of the market. As a result of global politics, in the current Latin American university there can be found many varieties of offers and demands: an education that is dissolved by a generalized flexibility of all types of competencies; a diversity of model programmes in accordance with flexible mechanisms for clients' choices; a reorganization of learning, with autonomous working programmes supported by the most diverse interactive technologies; many types of outreach projects that mobilize its "academic resources"; the decentralization of financial management and auto-management; and a variety of curricular offers, research and services that support the productive model due to the need for economic expansion in the institutions of higher education.

As we can see, the twenty-first-century university in Latin America has undergone significant transformations, most of them influenced by the weakening of the boundaries between the higher educational system and the economic field. The response of the university to such transformations has been influenced by the technocratic discourses of international agencies, which have increasingly generated the optimistic and democratizing global version of economy and culture, and recontextualized through this means the national and regional purposes and policies of Latin American universities. What this suggests is that the discourses of international agencies are, in essence, "hegemonic discursive formations" (Laclau, 2006), that in Latin America have been characterized by the extension of neoliberal policies which, in education, emphasize efficiency and more instrumental forms of professional training. This has brought conflicts within higher education as university responses have been matched by structural differences which oppose the pretended unity of this institutional system in Latin America. However, the recontextualizing logic of international agencies acts as a re-centering force due to the hegemonic unity of their discursive dynamics.

The Democratic Idea of the University: A Latin American Possibility

The construction of a democratic idea of university, and a democratic university in the twenty-first century requires a review of higher educational systems in the context of numerous problems present in the region: backwardness in education, violence, inequality, poverty, corruption, discrimination, lack of scientific and technological development, and fundamentally, a lack of democracy and social sensibility. The efforts of the international and national education agencies have been characterized, on one hand, by the production and reproduction of a rhetorical discourse focused on the development of the expansion process, democratization of the educational services, and strengthening of equality and, on the other hand, have consolidated the neoliberal political project, which cut the support of the State to higher education and obliges it to change the nature of its cultural and multidimensional institution to that of a market organization.

Within this context, how can one think about the Latin American university? In trying to answer this question I will present some suggestions about an alternative idea of the university in the present century. They represent a challenging voice against the mystifying discourses of the postmodern views of this historical institution:

1. In front of the rapid changes brought about by globalization, the Latin American university must recover its capacity for promoting the participation of all social actors in reflecting on and analyzing the external economic interests and purposes that have assaulted its historical principles, values and identity.
2. The Latin American university must reconsider its present foundations and go beyond the narrow interests of the dominant economic values defined by the paradigm of economic globalization.
3. Without forgetting the significance of higher education in promoting social and economic development, the Latin American university must work on the inclusion of the present and future generations in their individual, social and political growth, opening knowledge to all, and integrating the fragmented postmodern world which has reduced mind and identity to the consumption principle of performative positions in life, education and work.
4. The acceptance of the metamorphosis of the Latin American university, in correspondence with the new demands of postmodern rationality, does not imply an uncritical assumption of plurality, flexibility, autonomy and cultural integration values or reducing them to economic principles. The Latin American university must challenge the performative criteria through which knowledge has been reduced to experience and "know how" competences.
5. Against the new functional and multidimensional view of knowledge sustained by the educational international agencies, the Latin American university must be able to debate new frames of knowledge for socializing its actors (academics, students, administrators) in terms of competence, responsibility and compromise, and in the debating and thinking of alternatives necessary to deal with the crucial social problems that affect most of the population in the continent.
6. Latin American university academics must be aware that postmodern epistemologies are embedded in the economic reason that regulate most of the

dominating narratives of the so-called "knowledge society." From this perspective, it is crucial to debate the extent to which "knowledge society" is a legitimate principle to describe the fundamentals of the twenty-first-century Latin American university that has built its historical consciousness within the uncertainties, vagueness, and misunderstandings of the euro-centric discourses. In consequence:

7. The Latin American university must critically assume the postmodern challenges, and redirect its task by reorganizing its goals and ends, in the light of the consideration of the crucial social gaps increased by the power of the economic global forces that in their own interests have invaded with a plurality of narratives all the sociocultural spaces of the Latin American way of life.

These axioms are, in some way, guidelines to what must be the Latin American university in the twenty-first century, that is:

a. A democratic and pluralistic university that promotes respect for cultural differences within and between groups, and works for weakening its aberrant educational stratifications.

b. An institution able to promote dialogue, tolerance and respect for the axiological, ideological and political discrepancies between individuals and groups.

c. An institution open to all, which promotes access and inclusion, through the offering of diverse modalities of education and the development of knowledge and values necessary for making professionals, committed and responsible to and critical of the society in which they live and work.

d. A university that privileges dialogue, criticism and self-criticism; open to the scrutiny or revision of its tasks, and able to solve its internal dilemmas and conflicts, but also to contribute in the solution of those of the continent.

e. An institution able to deal critically with flexibility and to articulate professional trends and needs with social ones, on the basis of the equity, priority, and social principles. From this perspective, the Latin American university must reconceptualize the "knowledge society," or better, the "skilled society" (Sennett, 2009) which has eroded its capacity for dealing with the macrodimensions of theory and practice, and has been obliged to produce curricula centered on generic and specific competences.

f. An institution open to the understanding of the impact of technological developments, and of their uncertainties and ambiguities of their limits. This means being aware of the unpredictable consequences, conflicts and disasters of the technological development intrinsic to scientific dynamics of research.

g. An institution able to reconsider its eroding plurifunctional tasks. This means reviewing the new functions and performances that celebrate its postmodern rationality. The spread of tasks such as services; the acceptance of multiple joint ventures; the entrepreneurial criteria that must be adopted and adapted in training, research and extension; the competitiveness linked to the need to collect proper financial resources: all these have endangered the historical reason, goals and ends founded on objectivity and truth with respect to knowledge, thought, consciousness, and identity.

h.   A university that assumes critically the entrepreneurial principles, but promotes innovation and development on the basis of socially useful and relevant knowledge. Whatever may be the type of knowledge, its production and innovation must not be regulated solely by economic laws. Knowledge must be socially useful, democratically distributed and relevant to solve the growing damaging conditions of the world.

i.   A university that is self-regulating, self-evaluating, and without restrictions to its critical spirit and culture.

In brief, the features assigned the twenty-first-century university in Latin America must be an expression of the cultural and social richness of the continent and not the result of the determination of economic forces which have eroded and distorted its historical condition. The university in Latin America must fight for its autonomy, sovereignty and social compromise. Appealing to Derrida, I conclude by saying that university in Latin America—and possibly all over the world—must be a "university without condition" (Derrida, 2002).

Acknowledgement: I should like to acknowledge the helpful comments of the Editor, Ronald Barnett, in the preparation of this chapter.

Note

1   From **unus,** the unit and **verto** which entails the idea of returning.

6

THE DECLINE OF THE UNIVERSITY IN SOUTH AFRICA

Reconstituting the Place of Reason

Yusef Waghid

Introduction

Universities face many challenges on the African continent. Assie-Lumumba (2006: 71) poignantly claims that from the 1990s higher education, especially universities in Africa, was characterised by great instability as indicated by numerous confrontations between students, faculties, administrations and governments. This instability is further compounded by economic failures, stagnation and regression, which adversely affect the advancement of higher education on the continent (Assie-Lumumba, 2006: 75). Some of the main reasons for the ill-preparedness of African universities to meet societal needs are their alienation from the broader society and business community, as well as the inefficiency of university administration, organisation and management (Assie-Lumumba, 2006: 78). Likewise, Teferra and Altbach (2003: 4) argue that the influence of colonialism on African higher education contributed towards restricting student access, undermining the teaching of students in indigenous languages, limiting academic freedom and constraining the Africanisation of the curriculum.

In view of the challenges faced by several African universities, for more than two decades the South African public universities have been changing fundamentally: from exclusive apartheid knowledge producers to institutions of higher education focusing on research, teaching and learning, and community engagement. In response to the government's National Plan for Higher Education (2001) all universities in South Africa have stressed the strong interrelation between research, teaching, learning and community engagement. From this perspective the function of universities seems to be to produce advanced, high quality scientific knowledge and technology, to train highly skilled professionals and researchers as a necessary workforce and to cultivate a democratic citizenry through social engagement. Yet, like universities in Africa, South African universities also have limited impact on the citizenry. For instance, firstly, universities do not adequately address inequities in terms of race, gender and disability, and do not contribute towards the eradication of global problems such as poverty, environmental degradation and conflict; secondly, universities seemingly do not commit themselves first and foremost to the education of enlightened, informed and critical citizens and can be said to be elitist because such an education would not engender in people (students) a capacity for judgement and for informed participation in democratic life. Such universities do not succeed to develop in students a questioning, critical and democratic attitude. The implications are threefold: they (universities) remain sites of exclusive expertise (only the academics know best); students (like many during the apartheid years and perhaps today too) do not have the critical minds to initiate social change; and third, universities remain representative of a small percentage of the population (as if scientific research of a high quality is the preserved ownership of only a few privileged intellectuals). The knowledge monopoly would remain confined to those who speak with authority and whose arguments are given priority because they speak with superior knowledge and rationality. Such universities would remain elitist and would not necessarily make a contribution to the democratisation of knowledge and society—the latter involving the production of academics from the marginalised sector who eagerly await being taken up in the knowledge monopoly of such universities.

With the aforementioned background in mind, drawing on Jacques Derrida's (2004: 148) compelling work on what constitutes the university, specifically his idea that the university is "the responsibility of a community of thinking," I shall attempt to show that this institution in South Africa is limping. Since the first democratic elections of 1994, I have witnessed the university's decline. Simply put, the university has abandoned its responsibility of being a place of reason and instead has chosen the path of producing only "technicians of learning." If the university in South Africa was to break with its current objective of attending to mostly utilitarian demands (in service of the democratic government) and reconstitute the place of reason, then it has a real chance of walking on two feet as a responsible university without external controls and concerns for utility in the twenty-first century.

The Controlled and Utilitarian South African University

From the outset I want to acknowledge my personal complicity in the academic position the South African university has assumed since the first democratic elections in April 1994. When I joined the university sector two years after the establishment of the new government, I witnessed without the freedom to speak out how the newly elected African National Congress (ANC) government legislated one higher education policy text after the other: from the 1996 White Paper on the Transformation of Higher Education and the Higher Education Act of 1998

to the National Plan for Higher Education in 2001. At the core of these education policy initiatives has been the government's most serious ambition to break
(some would argue symbolically) with the apartheid past, while simultaneously
advocating for a university (the now 23 universities and universities of technology
are mergers of the previous 15 universities and 21 technikons) that can achieve
utilitarian demands in the service of the government and public. Thus, one finds
that the National Plan proposes the achievement of 16 outcomes that range from
increasing student access, particularly of black communities into the university
sector, to enhancing their (the students') cognitive abilities *vis-à-vis* technical and
professional competences that would not only ensure greater competitiveness
in an ever-evolving labour market economy but also increased participation as
democratic citizens in service of the "public good."

Moreover, the performative role of the university is enhanced through the
government's funding formula, which favours subsidising the university according to student enrolments, throughputs and research publications in what has
become known in South Africa as "accredited journals." This means that a faculty's funding is secured through its student input and output, and publication
output. Often rigorous scholarship seems to be exchanged for increased student
throughput and publications and, subsequently, impending state subsidy. It seems
as if more emphasis is placed on producing a large quantity of academic papers
which often appear in local journals rather than the production of fewer papers in
perhaps more reputable journals. From my conversations with colleagues, it does
seem that academic rigour and caring supervision are waning and that research in
the university has been "pledged in advance to some utilitarian purpose" (Derrida,
2004: 111). Too often I hear the country requires so many doctorates to be economically competitive. The cliché "publish or perish" has assumed a monetary
priority with universities being compared and assigned rankings in terms of their
high productivity in research.

How oddly we are continuously reminded that the university cannot survive
if throughputs are not sustained. Such instrumental utilitarianism implicates the
university in South Africa as an institution without autonomy. Less autonomous
universities are in fact those institutions that place more emphasis on their ranking
on the basis of high quantity and not necessarily high quality research outputs.
Autonomy is linked to the credible research outputs universities produce and not
just to increase the number of articles as expected by the government. And, a university without autonomy cannot be a university. For Derrida (2004: 104–105), a
university which is autonomous "must be able, according to Kant, to teach freely
whatever it wishes without conferring with anyone, letting itself be guided by
its sole interest in truth." Contrary to such an idea of the university, the South
African university has abandoned its internal quest for truth to being a technical
agent of state bureaucracy. Annually, the financial income through state subsidy
of the university is determined by the quantity of research outputs; student enrolments and throughputs as part of the government's control of the imperatives of

technological production. Recently, the Vice-Chancellor of a prominent university in the country was reminded by the government's spokesperson that his institution should transform, considering the state subsidy the institution receives. Such a not so unusual response from the government confirms its concern in guiding the university towards the interests of government.

Of course, I am not suggesting that the university in South Africa should not have ends, that is, should not strive to become financially sound on the basis of increased research outputs. But if such ends are the only outputs of the university system then the university has lost its soul. This implies that the university in the first place:

> Is there *to tell the truth*, to judge, to criticise in the most rigorous sense of the term, namely to discern and decide between the true and the false; and if it is also entitled to decide between the just and the unjust, the moral and the immoral, this is so insofar as reason and freedom of judgement are implicated in it as well.
>
> *(Derrida, 2004: 97)*

For instance, the South African university's apparent reticence to "speak out" against social ills on the African continent confirms the university's erosion of its power and free judgement to take a stand on truth and falsity.

At the level of research, the university is in even more trouble. Increasingly the university can be seen as dancing to the tune of large business corporations that invest enormous sums of money in research that can be applied for some or other utilitarian purpose. In South Africa several universities are beginning to augment their budgets on the basis of contractual agreements with large corporations. As Derrida (2004: 143) confirms, "the end-orientation of research [I would add in South Africa as well] is limitless." For instance, my institution has decided to approach large corporations to invest in research on the basis that the university's strategic initiatives will be aligned with corporate investment goals. If the university endeavours to pledge in advance the use of research for some techno-scientific purpose then the possibility that fundamental or basic research might be neglected is a stark reality.

Does agricultural research in poor farming communities contribute to eradicating poverty when the produce is still under the control of the rich farmers who now become more entrepreneurial? Does research in violent communities secure peace if some people are challenged to deal with choices of engaging in drug trafficking often in the face of unemployment? Does research about democracy necessarily ensure that societies behave according to the ideals of democratic action? What I am wondering about is whether this kind of envisaged "end-oriented" research actually achieves its desired or intended consequences. The fact of the matter is that the university in my country has been pursuing this kind of instrumentalist research for some while and very little if any substantive societal changes have ensued. By far the majority of people remain poor, and joblessness escalates. But maybe this is not what the university is supposed to be doing? It is for this reason that I now focus my attention on what the university ought to be doing.

Reconstituting the Place of Reason in the University

I now wish to elucidate a distinction between "technicians of learning" and scholars of knowledge (the latter constituting the university), before moving on to a discussion of reconstituting the place of reason. Following Derrida's neo-Kantian analysis, "technicians of learning" are in fact former students of the university who have been educated to perform functions to the ends determined by the state and not to the ends of science—the latter being the work of scholars at the university.

"Technicians of learning" wield enormous power not only as a result of displaying "technical mastery" within their professions, whether as doctors, journalists, lawyers, magistrates, accountants, geneticists, biochemists, engineers, teachers or theologians, but also through their influence on and shaping of the public. For Derrida (2004: 96) "they are all representatives of the public or private administration of the university, all decision makers in matters of budgets and the allocation and distribution of resources . . . all administrators of publications and archivisations, publishers, journalists, and so forth." In a way they are technical consumers of knowledge(s) who professionally serve their own interests.

University prospectuses clearly confirm the interest of all current South African institutions to produce "technicians of learning" that can vocationally practise their careers to the benefit of the public. But of course, herein also lies a potential danger to the university. "Technicians of learning," like most state bureaucrats involved in the technical administration of knowledge(s), often present themselves as judges and decision makers in the public practice of their careers. Mostly they usurp the right to judge and decide in the performance of their professions without being subjected to the authority and censorship of the university and its faculties (Derrida, 2004: 97). How common is it for some doctors today to prescribe inappropriate medications, or for some teachers to use archaic learning strategies without conferring with the university, or for some judges to wrongly convict an innocent person? The point is that "technicians of learning" often use their university-acquired qualifications to project themselves as paragons of knowledge(s) who at any time usurp the power of scholars of knowledge to decide and judge. Yet, this is not what they have been educated to do. But maybe the university has stripped itself of its responsibility to judge and decide on truth and falsity, with the result that "technicians of learning" now masquerade as arbitrators of knowledge(s).

Some critics might take issue with me for arguing that the university in South Africa produces mostly "technicians of learning." Let me illustrate my point further with an example from another salient development in the restructuring of higher education in the country. The recent upgrade of several technikons (polytechnics) to universities of technology means that these former technikons with their overwhelming emphasis on experiential learning are now expected to perform at the level of research. In other words, these institutions should now produce master's and doctoral candidates and research publications, and their academics should at least be in possession of a master's qualification. Despite the existence of pockets of outstanding research, most staff members at the universities of technology cannot cope with the demands of research outputs and some even publicly express their dissatisfaction at what they perceive to be their new academic roles that are incommensurate with their task of preparing students for the world of work—that is, producing technicians of learning. Many staff members who are now expected to supervise advanced postgraduate students themselves do not possess an advanced qualification or are currently enrolled for such a qualification. Now how does one expect these academics to provide research leadership and to produce outputs at their respective institutions if they are themselves not adequately trained to do so? I am not suggesting that possessing a PhD is a prerequisite for research leadership and productivity but considering the lack of research in this sector in South Africa, these academics will perpetuate and exacerbate the university's crisis which axiomatically seems to be connected to the production of technicians of learning.

Although some of the older universities (at least four to five) are highly productive in terms of research outputs and student throughputs, it would not be unfair to claim that one reason for the university's under-performance is a lack of credible scholarship at most South African universities. If one wants to go the performative route, not a single university features in the top hundred institutions listed on any world ranking index. Of course I am not denying individual pockets of excellence at some universities, but overall, the university in this country is in serious trouble. Furthermore, by far the majority of South African universities have appointed many staff members who do not hold a doctoral qualification. These staff members are therefore not as research-productive early in their careers as they should be, because they spend much of their time finishing their doctoral qualification. Without being too disingenuous towards the university which has struggled since the demise of apartheid to increase its levels of research and to offer more support to staff for their professional development as academics considering that many have been denied access to higher education before, I now turn to a discussion of what the university should be doing to enhance its credibility as it endeavours to establish itself as a research intensive institution.

Implications of a "Community of Thinking" for the University

There is not a single university in South Africa that does not want to be recognised for its research or quality of thought. And, for this to happen, universities ought to take seriously the idea of what it means to be an academic community of thinking. Firstly, characteristic of a community of thinking is the idea that "reason must be rendered" (Derrida, 2004: 136). Literally, thinking means to explain or account for something, that is, to ground, justify, motivate, authorise. Only then, a reason is said to be rendered. So, if a university's academic staff can justify their association with a particular action it does the work of a community of thinking because of rendering and evaluating a reason for action. For instance, if a university can justify why it aligns itself with a "pedagogy of hope" (Freire, 2004) such a university can be associated with a community of thinking because it renders a reason (by which others might be persuaded or not) in defence of the project it embarks upon. Following such an account of thinking, a university does not pledge in advance its association with a pedagogy of hope for some utilitarian purpose. Instead, it renders a reason or reasons for its epistemological journey. In doing so, it functions within the parameters of a community of thinking—that is, it leaves open the possibility of grounding an institution's non-instrumentalist course of action.

Often universities in South Africa too readily reveal their strategic plans for action to indicate their public responsibility. Yet, they seldom render reasons as to why they prefer to embark on a particular form of action. Put differently, such a university too often displays its intended utilitarian ends. What the university seemingly does not do is to render a justifiable reason for its actions. If the Vice-Chancellor of Stellenbosch University could motivate the institution's commitment to a pedagogy of hope on the grounds that such a pedagogy would establish opportunities for deliberative engagement, unhindered academic freedom, and equitable change, then such a university can be associated with a community of thinking. However, if the aims for such a strategy of hope are geared towards fundraising for the institution's future plans and to ensure the achievement of corporate investment goals, then such an institution cannot be said to align itself with the work of a community of thinking. This is so for the reason that the university would programme its actions through considerations of utility.

In the words of Derrida (2004: 148, 150), "this [community of] thinking must . . . prepare students to take new [non-instrumental] analyses" and "to transform the modes of writing, the pedagogic scene, the procedures of academic exchange, the relation to languages, to other disciplines, to the institution in general, to its inside and its outside." Certainly, for South African universities this makes a lot of sense, considering that many of the theses produced at postgraduate level are often claimed to be lacking theory (Balfour, 2010). Generally these theses have been soft on theoretical knowledge—they have not always "rendered a reason."

Secondly, a "community of thinking" would go beyond the "profound and the radical" (Derrida, 2004: 153). The enactment of such thinking is "always risky; it always risks the worst" (Derrida, 2004: 153). A community of thinking that goes "beyond" with the intention of taking more risks would become more attentive to unimagined possibilities, unexpected encounters, and perhaps the lucky find. Nothing is impossible because it opens the university not only "to the outside and the bottomless, but also . . . to any sort of [non-instrumental] interest" (Derrida, 2004: 153). And, if students and staff are prepared to take more risks, what seems to be unattainable could well easily be achieved. Certainly in South Africa where the moral fabric of post-apartheid society is withering away, universities require thoughtful, highly inspired and risky research contributions that can address issues of racism, gender inequality, patriarchy, domestic violence and the HIV and AIDS pandemic—that is, research for non-instrumental purposes. Risky efforts would enhance the possibility of highly contemplative and theoretical contributions that go beyond practical usefulness and provide us with more to know than any other instrumentalist form of action (Derrida, 2004: 130). I am particularly thinking of the need for risky intellectual contributions in cosmopolitanism, which might address the sporadic xenophobic outbursts in South Africa.

Thirdly, I agree with Derrida that the university was "supposed to *represent* society. And in a certain way it has done so: it has reproduced society's scenography, its views, conflicts, contradictions, its play and its differences, and also its desire for organic union in a total body" (Derrida, 2004: 154). In Derridian fashion, the "organic language" which used to be associated with the institution where I work happened to *reflect* apartheid society—hegemonic white academics, a majority white student population and the use of the Afrikaans language to shape academic conversations. In fact, the university produced apartheid politicians who advocated racial segregation and the oppression of a disenfranchised black majority. That is, its discourses were seemingly in opposition to pluralism and democracy. But when a university *represents* society then reflection is also given to another form of thinking—one which is provocative and which guides the university to act accountably and responsibly (Derrida, 2004: 154).

Derrida (2004: 155) refers to this form of thinking as an "etymological wink" or "twinkling of thinking" which calls on the university to act with "renewal" during a period of decadence. This implies that the university has an instantaneous "desire for memory and exposure to the future." Put differently, the university uses its knowledge discourses to pursue truth(s), yet at the same time uses its truthful knowledges to contribute towards a non-instrumentalist "renewal" of society's decadent situations—albeit physical, moral, cultural, political and/or economic. This form of thinking opens up a university to "chance" in a non-instrumentalist way—that is, what a society does not have and what is not yet. Fifteen years after the first democratic elections in South Africa, the university where I work has embarked upon a "hope project" in order to create opportunities for previously disadvantaged communities in particular to share in and gain from the academic successes of the institution. For this university, a pedagogy of hope implies, increasing access to previously disadvantaged students, improving the pass rates of students, and doing research in the interest of community development. This implies that the university has initiated a thinking that could contribute towards "what is not yet"; for instance, by using its knowledge truths to the benefit of the socio-economic development of the broader South African society.

In essence, such a form of thinking that demands that reasons are rendered, encourages risk taking, and contributes towards renewal is a kind of "critique" (Derrida, 2004: 162). This critique is a form of dissonance and questioning which is not dominated and intimidated by the power of performativity. "This thinking must also unmask—an infinite task—all the ruses of end-orienting reason, the paths by which apparently disinterested research can find itself indirectly reappropriated, reinvested by programs of all sorts" (Derrida, 2004: 148). This is basically always asking: "What is at stake (in technology, the sciences, production and productivity)?" (Derrida, 2004: 149). It is a kind of critique which allows us to take more risks, to deal openly with the radical incommensurability of the language games that constitute our society, and invites new possibilities to emerge.

Critique is a matter of enhancing the possibility of dissent and diversity of interpretations (Burik, 2009: 301); of complicating what is taken for granted, pointing to what has been overlooked in establishing identities (Burik, 2009: 302); an active opening up of one's own thought structures that is necessary for other ways to find an entrance (Burik, 2009: 304). In a different way, it is performing a kind of thinking innately concerned with creating possibilities for dissent, diversity of interpretations, complicating the taken-for-granted and opening up to the other.

Living Critique Through Scepticism

In order to show how critique can be enacted, I offer a narrative account of postgraduate student supervision focusing on a doctoral student, Masasa, over the past five years. Drawing on the seminal thoughts of Harvard philosopher Stanley Cavell (1979), particularly on his ideas on "living with scepticism," postgraduate student supervision ought to be an encounter framed by scepticism. Supervising students sceptically might engender moments of acknowledging humanity within the Other, attachment to the Other's points of view with a readiness for departure, and showing responsibility to the Other—a matter of exercising critique.

Masasa became a doctoral student on the basis of having impressed me academically with a presentation made at the Annual Kenton Education Association (KEA) Conference held in Didima (in the Drakensberg Mountains, South Africa) in 2005. He came to me after his presentation and told me he would like to work with me on his doctoral research. Hailing from Malawi, he had completed his master's in Education at another South African university and subsequently applied to Stellenbosch University to pursue doctoral studies under my supervision on the grounds that my area of educational research connected with his own interests in democracy and citizenship education. His application reached me with a request for financial assistance as well. Having recognised in him the capacity to work well with students, and considering that he was a lecturer in Philosophy at the University of Malawi, the university offered him a tutorship for three years which he gladly accepted on the condition that his studies would be sustained. On his arrival in the Faculty of Education he was offered an office, a computer with internet connectivity, and access to our library—the same support as for permanent academic staff.

Since Masasa is an intelligent, proud and hard-working person, we soon connected and developed a mutually respectful, trustworthy and impeccably professional relationship. This relationship still exists today, although Masasa now holds an academic position at a different South African university—a position to which he was appointed just after having completed his PhD. The fact that our friendship developed so remarkably over the past five years is testimony to how both of us recognised our humanity within ourselves and in association with one another. I wanted to know more about him and subsequently visited his institution and family in Malawi—a visit that made me understand Masasa's humble beginnings and his desire to serve African higher education. Subsequently, our friendship began to flourish even more. I knew how important it was for Masasa to obtain a PhD in Education and how he wanted to become an academic achiever, particularly considering the poor economic conditions in his country, which I had the opportunity to witness for myself. Although I thought he would return to Malawi to serve his fellow citizens after completing his PhD, I came to terms with his decision (like those of so many African academics) to live and work in South Africa, as part of the African diaspora.

My friendship with Masasa was further enhanced when I asked him to represent the Faculty of Education's students at the Regional Education Students' Forum that was responsible for the organisation of the Annual Western Cape Regional Education Students' Conference involving students from all four universities in the province. Masasa became joint chair of this forum. He would inform me regularly about developments and a kind of trust developed which was spawned by an interest on my part to make him realise that he should become more involved in regional student activities beyond the confined "walls" of Stellenbosch, where on occasions he encountered racial taunts such as not being served by white students in a local restaurant or being scorned by white students while walking in town. He saw in me—I think—someone with whom he could communicate his exposure to bigotry. Thus our friendship was further consolidated primarily because he felt that I had acknowledged him as a fellow human being.

In acknowledging others as human beings worthy of respect, one should simultaneously acknowledge oneself as a person who should exercise respect. Student supervision became a form of life whereby I recognised Masasa's humanity, and as he struggled along with his writing I acknowledged his cultural connections and personhood as major contributing factors to the arguments he articulated in his writings.

Responsibility Towards Others and Critique

If one were to perform one's duty to others as human beings, should one engage in social practices with something, say, morally just in mind—that is, a just society, justice for all, values of democracy, cosmopolitanism, and so on? Of course, as supervisors we are responsible to effect changes in the lives of our students, so we teach them to be civil. And this I have done through exposing Masasa to academic writings that aim at cultivating democratic iterations (learning to talk back, that is, disagreeing with others and offering reasons in return), citizenship rights and cosmopolitan justice, particularly in relation to the production of theses that aim to contribute towards justice in and about education in Africa. But this does not mean that we ought to censure students' actions so that we determine in advance what students ought to research in order to connect their work with achieving civility (a way of achieving democratic justice in African communities, commonly known as *ubuntu*), or what consequences they may be faced with if they do not write theses that connect with issues of civility (for example, having their work rejected by me). Teaching our students to connect with issues of civility, following Cavell (1979: 325), makes us "open to complete surprise at what we have done."

In other words, supervisors and students can be initiated into practices about what is morally good for society, but with the possibility that what is perceived as good for society is always in the making, continuously subjected to modifications and adaptations. For instance, it may be morally good for society for its students to produce work (theses) about advancing provocative dialogical educational encounters at some stage in its history—and we may decide this in advance. But when hostility emanates among people and makes distressful confrontations that may result in excluding the Other, we may want to suggest that peoples' distressful encounters be constrained. That is, our students' writings should be about what is desirable for society (in especially humanities and social sciences) with the possibility or readiness of departing from such practices if the situation arises—that is, advocating belligerence (provocative) in deliberations might not always be desirable for the public good.

Furthermore, students' theses can depart from making arguments for their (theses) defence, that is, what seems to be desirable for the public good. So, I have learned from Masasa that some (if not most) African communities consider belligerently challenging traditional leaders to be a disrespectful practice. Consequently I have had to depart from my earlier view of advocating provocation in most conversations. The point I am making is that my thoughts alone did not influence students' theses. Masasa's independence of mind and critical insights determined the thoughts that have gone into his formulation of arguments—a matter of engendering critique.

Cavell's remark, "we are alone, and we are never alone," is a clear indication that one does belong to a particular group (being alone with others, that is, "we") and that by virtue of being human one bears an internal relation to all other human beings—especially those who might not belong to the same group as one. In demonstrating one's responsibility towards others one immediately acknowledges one's capacity for intimacy with others—thus limiting one's idiosyncratic privacy.

It is for this reason that Cavell (1979: 463) claims that "human beings do not necessarily desire isolation and incomprehension, but union or reunion, call it community." Our private actions may lead to a betterment of our communal actions. I might privately contemplate doing something about improving human relations between foreign nationals (say from African countries) and South African citizens in my neighbourhood, but doing so autonomously without also penetrating the thoughts of other community members may not necessarily contribute towards a desired action. If my privacy remains restricted to me with the intention of not exercising my responsibility to others, my practices would remain unshared and separated from the people with whom I happen to live. So, my privacy opens a door through which someone else can tap into my thoughts—which might be of benefit to society. But if my privacy is prompted by narcissism, the possibility that others might gain something valuable for the good of society might be stunted. If I were to think about social practices in a balanced way, I should acknowledge the private efforts of individuals yet at the same time I should not avoid the possibility that their private actions can be of good public use. And so it happened that Masasa and I were concerned about the xenophobic conflicts which had erupted in several township communities and we contemplated how we could privately attend to the situation.

In a Cavellian fashion I have learnt that supervisors ought to be responsible human beings with regard to their students. Responsibility towards one's students implies that one has to create opportunities for them to think, argue and write their texts. Writing is a truly laborious yet imaginative exercise. I have taught students to continue writing even though the comments they receive would at times not be as encouraging as they might have expected—a matter of exercising critique.

In sum, what the aforementioned narrative foregrounds is that postgraduate student supervision ought to be an instance in which critique should be lived out. This implies that students at university ought to be engaged in relationships with supervisors whereby reasons can justifiably be offered. In turn, such reasons should be of a non-instrumentalist kind whereby students take responsibility for their research and supervisors as scholars of the university create opportunities for them (students) to nurture reasons. Only then can the university be considered as a space which engenders the possibility of reasons being offered—that is, reconstituting the place of reason.

Conclusion

In this chapter, I have argued that universities on the African continent, specifically those in South Africa, are challenged by performativity and some of the utilitarian technical demands of the state. In most instances, universities have been intent on complying mostly to the technocratic demands of the state. Consequently, I have posited that this institution in general is limping and, if it intends to move beyond its current malaise ought to consider reconstituting the place of reason—that is, it ought to reconsider its sense of judgement, discernment and risk taking. I then showed how scepticism as an instance of critique can be used to reconstitute post-graduate student supervision. In this way, the possibility exists for the university to enact a critical responsibility.

PART III
Ideas of the University

7

TOWARDS A NETWORKED UNIVERSITY[1]

Nicolas Standaert

Introduction

The birth of a "network society" appears to be a fundamental paradigm shift in the present world. It greatly affects the way society and also education will be organised in the future. As such a whole new world enters into universities: web-thinking, accessibility, internet, linking, nodes, hubs, clusters, hotspots, open source, open access, virtual, free, space, distant learning, are key words of this shift.

A central question emerging from this shift is: What are the new or alternative ways of organising, practising and conceptualising university life in a network society? This question forms the background of the present contribution, which takes the "networked university" as its main focus. Yet, the concept of "network" is taken here as a challenge for universities, rather than an ideal.

In the following pages, I will first trace a short history of the university on the basis of the images of "pyramid," "pillar" and "web." Next, I will argue that by paying attention to "displacements between spaces" one can start to frame the University of the Future. As such, a networked university may come into being.

I will raise questions rather than provide answers. This is due to the fact that in a period of transition there are no immediate or ready-made answers. I will mainly use visual images or metaphors. In an article entitled *'Metaphoric Imaginings': Re-/Visions on the Idea of a University*, Susan Robertson insisted on the importance of metaphors and showed how new metaphors are driving a set of alternatives to education which offer a refreshing change to what was before. As has been proven in practice, images also help more profound reflection on certain essential aspects. I hope in this way to stimulate reflection on the possibilities in front of the university in the twenty-first century, which is the objective of this book.

First Metaphor: Pyramid, Pillar and Web—Three Forms of Academic Practice

In the history of the university and of the sciences, there has so far been one major paradigm shift: from renaissance to modernity. This transition occurred gradually and took about two hundred years before resulting in the university structure with which we are acquainted today. One could represent these two structures with the images of "pyramid" and "pillar." The question that is raised today is whether we face a new paradigm shift which could quite radically influence the structure of the university and of scientific practice. The image of the new structure is that of a "web." In order to understand the present situation, it is helpful to look back at the characteristics of the medieval-renaissance and of the modern university.

Pyramid

As an image of the medieval-renaissance university, one can adopt the form of a "pyramid." Universities emerged at a time when both secular and religious society in Europe was organised like a pyramid: a hierarchical society of stratified social classes going from lower levels to the top (king or pope), the ultimate reference points in an all-embracing organisation.

Education was organised in a similar way and one can find this reflected in the classification of sciences. At the bottom were the *artes serviles* (agriculture, surgery, military sciences) which were usually not taught at universities; next came the *artes liberales* consisting of the *trivium* (grammar, rhetoric, dialectics) and the *quadrivium* (geometry, arithmetic, astronomy and music, all different disciplines belonging to mathematics), which were the foundation for the *artes superiores:* (Aristotelian) physics, ethics, metaphysics and theology respectively. Theology, as a speculative science concerning the coherence of things, was considered the "Queen" of the sciences, while the other sciences were her ladies-in-waiting.

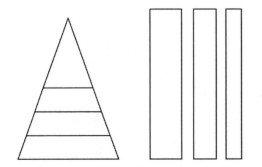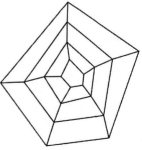

Figure 7.1   Three forms of academic practice

Noteworthy is that the acquisition of knowledge was consecutive: one first had to study the *artes liberales* (at least partially) before proceeding to the higher sciences. One also has to underscore the place of mathematics in Aristotelian philosophy: it was an essential preparation to theology.

The social structure of the medieval university was not as unequivocal as the image of a pyramid suggests. The organisation of a university consisted in the fact that it was a *universitas magistrorum et scholarium*, a community of study, a *studium*, a guild of teachers and students, which formed the core of the relationship between teachers and students and which was spatially expressed in the colleges where the students and teachers lived. The *studium* was characterised by principles of autonomy and free research. As it was believed that there was one all-compassing and ultimate truth, any particular truth could be put into question. Pedagogy consisted of a culture of debate (*disputatio*) in which students entered at least once a week in a public debate with each other. Finally one can point out that the *ius ubique docendi* (the right to teach everywhere) broke through the territorial demarcation of a particular university.

Pillar

As a result of developments during the Renaissance and the Enlightenment, a new structure came into place. During this transition, which took circa two hundred years, secular society moved away from the pyramid model towards a pillar (or silo) model, in which different entities no longer belong to one all-embracing structure but manifest themselves separately and independently from each other. This happened in society as a whole: Church and state were separated; independent nation-states were created; and different political parties, trade unions and Christian denominations were established. In academic life, the Enlightenment and the birth of "modern" science radically changed the former pyramidal structure. We are the heirs of this shift and the existing system can still be described in terms of pillars.

One important evolution was the autonomous place that mathematics acquired. This resulted in a conflict with theology which ended with the lady-in-waiting knocking the "Queen" from her throne and becoming queen herself, or even better, all former sciences becoming queens. From that time onwards, they were to a large extent separated from each other, working in a parallel way. Characteristic of these "new" sciences is a specialised way of knowledge acquisition. In the structure of a modern university, theology, philosophy, language and literature, mathematics, physics are all separated from each other in distinct faculties and departments with their own study programme adapted to their own discipline.

The relationship between teachers and students also underwent a significant change: a vertical transmission of knowledge (increasingly specialised) replaced the previous layered acquisition of knowledge: now omniscient teachers could proclaim all wisdom and knowledge in their field. Truth no longer belongs to theology alone: each science has its own (ultimate) truth. The pedagogical consequence was the replacement of the medieval debate by a one-way instruction in many European (mainly Catholic) countries. In terms of territorial demarcation the creation of the nation-state consolidated this pillar system since the international character of the *universitas magistrorum et scholarium* (with its *ius ubique docendi*) was abandoned. Universities were increasingly distinguished on the basis of their national character: empirical in Great Britain, rational in France, idealistic in Germany. Professors only taught in their own national language at their own university.

Web

The thesis of this contribution is that a new transition is taking place, one that is at least as revolutionary, if not more, than the one that led us into modernity. We are quickly moving towards the realisation of the "network society," which will tremendously influence the way both secular society and education as a whole will be organised in the future (Castells, 1996; Grewal, 2009). This new reality, which mirrors the "internet," is driven by networks, interdisciplinary connections, real and virtual meeting points and collaborations, both at a local as well as at an international (global) level. This so-called web-model also entails fundamental structural changes from a vertical towards a more horizontal approach and away from the current linear structures towards multidimensional ones.

In the new structure of classification, the sciences still have their own discipline but become organically linked to each other within one space (cf. an ecosystem). This shift already appears in new names: e.g. "life sciences" for medicine, agriculture, health, ecology, pharmacy and biology. Sciences themselves become dynamic spaces ("tissues"). Medicine, for example, had a hierarchical structure of body and head during the Renaissance; in modernity it differentiated various limbs with their own specialisation and students had to get acquainted with them separately. The new programs in medicine now use dynamic terms: "anatomy" becomes "blood and blood cell producing organs"; "histology" becomes "reproduction and development." Moreover, new forms of acquisition of knowledge consist of not remaining enclosed within one's own discipline but to search for multidisciplinary, interdisciplinary and even trans-disciplinary links with other sciences. Methodologically speaking, the mode of "analogy" plays an important role: how changes in other sciences can be analogically applied to one's own discipline. In the structure of a university, the classrooms and separate spaces interconnect and form open networks.

In the relationship between teachers and students, exchange and communication become central and both parties are encouraged to treat each other as equals. In the acquisition of knowledge and its evaluation, the principle of authority is transferred to the peer group. The principle of a single absolute truth is put into question (cf. postmodernism). In the search for truth, one uses converging principles. In terms of pedagogy, one uses interactive methods and education itself becomes a process (project education, life-long learning). All kinds of internet programs allow new forms of teaching. Territorially speaking, strict demarcations are no longer respected. In Europe, Erasmus-Socrates programs allow students and teachers to establish border crossing networks with colleagues.

If the rough sketch is correct, if indeed we are in a transitional period, then the question is how to deal with this new situation. Yet, this short historical overview has shown that a new system builds on a previous system and that the answers always preserve the essential characteristics of a university.

Second Metaphor: Displacements Between Spaces

In the subsequent section I will review some of the previous questions related to the shift to a network society on the basis of a new set of images. The underlying metaphors are those of "place" and "space." At first, it can be observed that the notions of "place" and "space" are constitutive of the present-day discourse on universities and education, since in such a context one often uses a topographic vocabulary: e.g. expressions such as teaching *environments*, knowledge *spaces*, the European Higher Education or Research *Area*, a global higher education *landscape*, etc. (Weymans, 2009). At the same time there is also a "crisis of place," since the importance of place, as an integrative and stabilising force in human experience, is waning. Indeed, our experiences of time, space, work, communication and social relations are increasingly becoming mediated by a series of devices and systems (especially communication and information networks) that diminish the impact and meaning of place (Verschaffel, 2009: 133). This also has its impact on an institution such as a university. When investigating networks from the perspective of place and space, I also want to look at their dynamic aspect by extending these metaphors to the one of "displacement."

Place, Space and In-between

Terms such as "place" and "space" are not only used by geographers, but also by observers of culture. Michel de Certeau, for instance, made the following distinction between place (*lieu*) and space (*espace*).

> A place is an instantaneous configuration of positions. It implies an indication of stability. By contrast, a space exists when one takes into consideration vectors of direction, velocities, and time variables. Thus space is composed of intersections of mobile elements. . . . In short, space is a practised place.
>
> *(de Certeau, 1988: 117)*

These concepts gain a new significance in a network society, in which, according to Manuel Castells, another important observer of contemporary culture, "spaces of flows" form part of the network society, i.e. the material organisation of time-sharing social practices that work through flows (exchanges and interaction between social actors) (Castells, 1996: chapter 6, especially 441 and 453). Castells registers the motion, and retains its stable, but static, trace, which he calls "space of places." Yet, the relationships between the "space of flows" and "space of places," between simultaneous globalisation and localisation, are not predetermined in their outcome.

These concepts gain a new significance for universities in this network society. In the story of universities in such a network society, the opposition between "place" and "space" will thus rather refer to two sorts of determinations (following de Certeau): the first, a determination through objects that are ultimately reducible to the being-there; such as the concrete university buildings, labs, teaching halls, offices; the second, a determination through operations by the actions of the subjects involved, the students, the professors, the administrative and technical personnel. Subsequently their stories result in an interplay between places and spaces, which constantly transform places into spaces and spaces into places. This, of course, has always been the case, but in the present-day internet society we often tend to communicate without "place," even within one particular institution. This is because, as pointed out by Bart Verschaffel, communication networks entail that the act of speaking is disconnected from a specific place:

> The place occupied by the speaker in reality (that is, where his or her body is) has no bearing on the speaking or listening, and does not determine the distance over which the voice carries. Virtual contact and virtual ubiquity result in the body being left behind on the edge of the network, as well as in new types of relations, unconnected to bodily presence, substituting for place-bound relations.
>
> *(Verschaffel, 2009: 133–134)*

Thus the challenge for the university is how and to what extent to "connect" the place of speaking with the place of listening and understanding, even at a local level. But following Castells, there is also the opposition between on the one hand the global and the local: the former is dominated by the space of flows, constituted by circuits of electronic exchanges of e.g. scientific material, databanks, and by nodes and hubs of important academic centres, international conference halls, etc.; the latter is dominated by the space of places, with the concrete local dynamics, such as academic power relations or the teaching or scientific experience in a given local university. Here the challenge for the university is how and to what extent to "link" the local to the global. But in both cases concrete encounters "between" the actors involved are the result of "travelling or walking": they transform places into spaces.

Here I want to introduce the concept of "in-between," because it is at the centre of the "encounter" that takes "place" in "spaces," as is well reflected in the earlier image of the web. "In-betweenness" or "the between" draws the attention to one particular aspect of space: instead of focussing on oppositions, on either/or, on Self or Other, the focus moves to the "between," to the search for the "inter-action" in space "between" the opposites, to various forms of encounter and conversation ("*entre-tien*" in French). This notion of in-betweenness shows that many human activities come into being due to the existence and creation of space "between" the Self and the Other, or between the transmitter and the receiver, between the teacher and the student, etc. This space acts both as that which allows an encounter to take place (leading to interaction and communication) and as that which is produced by the encounter as such. Encounters "between" persons result in stories that take the form of a text, image, research project, social network, community. The interaction is considered a permanent tension: between the possibility of understanding (and being understood) and the impossibility of such an understanding, between the local and the global. The interaction therefore causes the partners to readjust, rethink and reformulate ideas of themselves and of others. Thus in-betweenness is the space in which an encounter can take place.

All these concepts may appear rather abstract, but they become concrete when applied to universities, especially since universities in the future will not only be places of knowledge "production" or of "virtual communication" but also spaces of encounters. One challenge for networked universities is to become in new ways such privileged spaces of encounters. This supposes an ethos of a renewed attention to "in-betweenness," to concrete places where the actors (teachers, students, researchers) encounter each other by treating each other as subjects. Many universities are already searching for such alternatives. For sure, many of these alternatives are often rather local and still waiting for a language and opportunity to manifest themselves, but they indicate how universities actively search a place in the network society.

The Networked University as a Space

In an essay in a recent book entitled *Rethinking the University after Bologna*, Ronald Barnett takes the networked university fully into account. Universities have their being in networks, he says, both intentionally and unwittingly. It was always so, but today, networks are a vital part of what it is to be a university in the twenty-first century. "The networked university" has emerged. Thus the question is not whether universities have the choice of becoming networked universities or not, but rather what kind of networked universities they will become. Barnett raises several questions in this regard: What is the ethical basis of these networks? To what ends is the university involved in these networks? Is it engaging thus for its own ends? Or is it reaching out to others—other institutions and organisations—to help to bring about a better world?

In the next series of questions Barnett raises, the metaphor of "space" is central: What spaces, what new networks, might universities open out and be part of? . . . What spaces . . . are now available to the university? Are there other kinds of spaces that will encourage forward an alternative set of knowledge interests? In response to such questions, "the ecological university," as he terms it, prompts itself.

> The ecological is none other than a university that takes its networks and its networking seriously. That is to say, it understands that it lives amid networks and that, therefore, the responsibility arises as to which networks are to claim its primary allegiance. [. . .] The networked university becomes the ecological university when it intends deliberately not merely to safeguard the public realm but actively to enhance it. [. . .] This, then, is a university that has a care for the wider society, for the unequal life chances of its people, and for the severe challenges that society faces. [. . .] The ecological university, accordingly, may also be termed . . . "the public university."
>
> *(Barnett, 2009a: 114–115)*

The concepts of "place," "space" and "public" occupy an important position in the article by Jan Masschelein and Maarten Simons in the same book (Barnett et al., 2009). They first observe that present-day universities are places that permanently and relentlessly *mobilise* researchers, lecturers, and students. Through the well-developed systems of quality control, excellence financing, rankings, etc. they are all asked to mobilise their intellectual (human) capital. Next, they plead for a "world-university": by the space called "the world" they mean the place and time where things are made public. Paradoxically the proposal for a world-university is a proposal to slow down the construction of a common world, to create a space (one amongst others) for hesitation. Their proposal aims precisely to disrupt this mobilisation and thus requires a different *ethos*. And they continue:

> One could think, then, of the world-university as the place where we are not mobilised, but slowed down and provoked to think, and where this provocation finds (its) place (and the university as this place), the place where research is put on the table (made present) and its protection (by methods and theories) undone.
>
> *(Masschelein & Simons, 2009b)*

In their eyes, the world-university is, too, the place where teaching is stripped of its protections (by teaching methods, didactic devices) and is no longer instruction but becomes what they like to call lecturing, i.e.

> precisely not teaching a lesson but making things public, reading them before an audience, exposing them (and being in the presence of), making them speak as it were, giving them a presence that calls a thinking public into existence. Making things public, then, is not only making them

known, but making them present and inviting us to explore new ways of relating to them (i.e. to the matter and to ourselves).

(Masschelein & Simons, 2009b: 95–97)

Despite the differences between the approaches of these authors, they share the conviction that networked universities will be public spaces with attention to the world, to hesitation, to fragility, to the uncertain and unknown.

In this context one may draw further attention to the metaphor of "displacement." While the images of pyramid and pillars are linked to "stability" or minimal mobility within the pyramid or pillar, the images of web, space and place are associated with mobility: circulating from one hub to another, or better "between" the nodes. "Displacement" means that one moves from one (physical) place to another, thus creating new spaces for encounter. Yet, displacement not only takes place through one's own *self* initiative; it also happens when one is moved by initiatives by *others*. That is why we are often reactively "displaced," for instance by metaphors, rather than that we actively displace ourselves. The search for new forms of university life supposes this kind of displacement. These deregulate, but next allow reconfiguration. In this context, one can discern different types of displacements: mental and physical, though they most often operate together.

Mental Displacements

The landscape of classification of sciences (Standaert, 2009: 46–48) presents a challenge that a knowledge culture addresses to the university and to broader society: the acknowledgment of, and respect for, different approaches to knowledge, its development and its type of evaluation. Therefore the variety of sciences and disciplines contains an invitation to a first—mental—"displacement" within the landscape of knowledge. Can we, in our own research and our evaluation of it, move to the places occupied by other sciences? Even more important is whether we can allow ourselves to be displaced. Such a displacement may lead to new discoveries. The confrontation with other sciences may also lead to the discovery of the space where we lose control over what we think we master. Such an in-between space is present in any science. Indeed, the drive for knowledge has its roots precisely in what we do *not* know (Vest, 2005: 99). The more we know, the more we want to know, but a displacement within the field of knowledge confronts us with vulnerability and lack of control.

At present there is a tendency towards strengthening the pillars, even within the classification of sciences, instead of moving towards nodes between them, illustrated by the image of the web where the sciences are interlinked with each other. I am of the opinion that the major challenge is to search for new ways as to how different disciplines can meet each other: in other words, how can one create new nodes in the web of sciences? This call of displacement is not a return to the pre-modern system, in which one could cover several sciences, but a challenge of a different kind. The main reason is that, in contrast with the Renaissance period, modern sciences have reached such a high degree of specialisation that it is no longer possible to cover all sciences. Thus the question becomes, given that specialisation is inevitable for research, how to prevent specialisation in one field from enclosing itself into itself, which is entrenching the pillar system. Is the simple accumulation of various specialisations the only alternative? Or is the challenge to search for ways of combining in-depth knowledge of one field with a more comprehensive view that takes in sciences beyond one's own? This problem still needs to be explored, but it may require a kind of "horizon" perspective: this means the more in-depth mastering of one's field should not lead to a further confinement to one's field, but rather to a greater perspective on other fields. In a time of fragmentation there is need of rediscovering the whole. Thus, academic research and teaching will be more networked, if one's own specialised research is "linked" to a wider context, a new type of *universitas*.

This is also true for the polarisation between the so-called measurable and hermeneutic sciences. In the transition between renaissance and modernity, "measurable" sciences, which express and process their data arithmetically and statistically, came to be opposed to sciences that try to understand (hermeneutically), that search for meaning, or that at times express a judgment of value about what is true, good or beautiful, though the latter are at the foundation of what the university is (Illich, 2010). The measurable sciences are cumulative, since any invention or discovery forms the basis for the next scientific development. They tend to univocality: one language (English) and one exclusive method (mathematics/statistics). The hermeneutic sciences are cyclical because they re-read and reinterpret previous knowledge over and over. They are multivocal: they avail themselves of and publish in different languages and employ a variety of methods. The former seek to "explain" (*erklären*) phenomena in terms of cause and effect; in contrast, the latter seek to "understand" (*verstehen*) in terms of the relations of the part to the whole (as pointed out by Wilhelm Dilthey). Yet today, at least in the dominant discourse, a break is established between the two, with the measurable sciences (based on "counting" or "reckoning") almost excluding the other (based on "recounting" or "narrating"). I am of the opinion that the major challenge today is to search for new ways how the two can meet each other: in other words, how can one create new nodes at the centre of the axis of knowledge? Here the issue is also whether language should not perform a new role, which is how "counting and recounting" could meet each other and forge a new narrative? In fact the whole operation of "counting" not only requires a "recounting" but also finds its origin in a broader narrative; it is only when this link is established that the results can be accounted for and estimated. As such they will become more universal and public.

In the meeting of "reckoning" and "narrating," of "measurable" and "hermeneutic" sciences at this level of language, analogy and metaphor will play an important part as nodes or contact points. In scientific discoveries, metaphors make us travel and be displaced from one scientific discipline to another. In this respect Alan Lightman (2005), who is both physicist and novelist, points out that one distinction that can be made between physicists and novelists, and between the scientific and artistic communities in general, is what he calls "naming." Roughly speaking, the scientist tries to name things and the artist tries to avoid naming things. And he goes on to show (with examples from Isaac Newton, James Clerk Maxwell, and Georges Lemaître), that analogies and metaphors are aids to scientific discovery.

> In doing science, even though words and equations are used with the intention of having precise meanings, it is almost impossible not to reason by physical analogy, not to form mental pictures, not to imagine balls bouncing and pendulums swinging. Metaphor is part of the process of science.
>
> *(Lightman, 2005: 50)*

Likewise analogies with biomedical or exact sciences help processes of understanding in hermeneutical sciences. By such metaphorical displacements encounters "between" sciences are established. The use of imagination also leads to a greater universality, thus *universitas*. Very often academics see their problems or solutions as absolute, but by confronting them with problems and solutions in other places, they are put in a universal perspective.

Physical Displacements

At present the web-like structuring of universities still needs to be invented, since most universities are still organised into faculties and disciplinary departments that reflect the pillar system; and the financing, recruitment (of staff and students) is organised likewise. It is not yet clear what a more network-like structuring of universities should look like. In the transition period there is probably need for "nomadic" practices within a university.

One can observe that the most creative search is situated in these nomadic practices. Stef Langmans, a student in pedagogy at the K.U. Leuven, for instance, made a survey of such alternative practices which he found on the web and brought them together under the title "publiversity." They are oriented towards the university space and its "public" role. His blog devoted to this topic brings together 175 examples of academic initiatives intended to create public practices (http://publiversity.wordpress.com/). These examples were brought together on the basis of keywords such as "free, open, public, mobile, nomad, informal, invisible, interdisciplinary," which indicate the movement between places, and arranged under the headings "art & social, educational, knowledge system, publishing & archiving, research, student, organisational." These examples reveal that at least the following aspects enter into play in the reconfiguration of academic practice in a network society: *space* (Is it concrete, virtual, mobile?), *access* (Is the public gaining access to the organisation or is the organisation stepping towards the public? Is it focused on an elite or a broad public?), *values* (Are activities oriented towards excellence and submitted to quality-control? Is any university rank required for teaching? Is research fundamental or society oriented?), *outcome* (Do the institutions provide a diploma or is knowledge spread for its own sake? Are there any (public) knowledge repositories?), *interrelation* (What is the level of cooperation, interactivity in workshops, internet-forums, community service?).

Langmans' survey shows a large variety of displacements and nomadic practices by which institutions and individuals look for new ways of organising, practising and conceptualising university life. They search for alternatives in different directions: new practices inside the university as well as practices outside the institution and at its edges, which might inspire university institutions. They point at examples that created new links, that made students work together in a transdisciplinary way, that have made research publicly accessible, that opened spaces in which creativity could bloom or where researchers could meet each other not only to count but also to recount. There are also many institutional examples in which displacement is at the forefront: *Barefoot University* works with the marginalised, impoverished and poor in South Africa (http://www.barefoot-university.org.za/); *Communiversity* is an adult education program taught by volunteer teachers of the University of Missouri, Kansas City (http://www.umkc.edu/commu/); *Campus for Peace* of the Universitat Oberta de Catalunya is at the service of NGOs (http://www.campusforpeace.org/). This search is open-ended, many initiatives are experimental and their outcome is unpredictable.

One concrete example of education through physical displacements, is the course on "world-forming education" organised by Jan Masschelein at K.U. Leuven. During the last several years, he travelled with students to post-conflict cities (Sarajevo, Belgrade, Tirana, Bucharest, Kinshasa) and non-tourist megacities in China (Shenzhen, Chongqing) for 10 to 14 days. Students were asked to walk day and night along arbitrary lines drawn on city maps: lines starting and leading nowhere particularly, lines without plan, crossing at random neighbourhoods, buildings, or areas. Everyday, during long talks, he asked each of them very simple questions: What have you seen? What have you heard? What do you think about it? What do you make of it? At the end of the travel they had to present in the streets somewhere in the city their "look at the city." He calls these travels experiments in "e-ducating the gaze": it is not getting at a liberated or critical view, but about liberating or displacing our view. Walking, in his eyes, is the physical activity of displacing one's gaze (i.e. leaving one's position, one's ex-position) along an arbitrary line, a trajectory that at the same time exists (and is recaptured) and is paved anew, a way for new perspectives, and so not leading to somewhere given before, but somewhere without a destination or familiar kind of orientation. This opening our eyes, is the opening of an existential space, a space for practical freedom. (Masschelein, 2009; 2010)

This walking through cities raises the question of the territorial demarcation of a university, which is directly related to its place, in the physical and stable sense. The changes of the network society are obvious, since many places are transformed into virtual spaces (through internet), that connect subjects without having to change places. They enhance virtual displacements. But, as Jean-Claude Guédon points out, networks also grow as the physical displacement (mobility) increases: students, researchers and professors move now increasingly from one place to another to build new networks. The obvious advantage of this networked, connected perspective is that it immediately transcends traditional boundaries, be they political, institutional or based on disciplines. He concludes: "As space would grow as networks grow, it would also bring us back to de Certeau's notion of a space that develops even as the individual walks and interprets" (Guédon, 2009: 72). Yet, this transcendence raises a new tension: that is the one of local embedding, to which is related the physical place of universities.

The present-day physical emplacement of European universities and its architecture are built on a tradition, which is to a large extent the reflection of the pillar-system of the universities: buildings are organised according to different disciplines, usually each discipline has its own building or floor within a building. The space of a networked university still has to be invented. On the one hand, the university as institution needs architecture, as pointed out by Bart Verschaffel:

> an actual, real space, and bodies who feel they are really in the game because they are in the building. [. . .] These institutional spaces provide—as long as they last—unique conditions to talk and think about what is happening "outside", in the streets, the new virtual communication spaces, and the world.
> *(Verschaffel, 2009: 145–146)*

On the other hand, there is need for a new architecture, where buildings are interconnected, and hubs and meeting places are created across disciplines. There is a need for spaces where researchers belonging to different sciences can encounter each other and exchange forms of "counting and recounting." Universities should make a fresh effort to create new, mobile "spaces of encounter." For instance, one could create new meeting centres to which scholars could be invited to be displaced for the duration of one semester. All participants would have their office and administrative support in that place, while continuing their normal academic activities of teaching and research. However, they could try to share free time together: informal meetings and also formal seminars. In these seminars they could explain to the other members (who are not specialised in their own field) in a comprehensible way their research and the methodology required for it. This might be a creative way of travelling through the landscape of knowledge. Thus by moving to new places within a given university, participants would create new spaces of interaction. It is to be expected that this is a way in which new networks are likely to be formed, which possibly might result in new insights.

Conclusion: Open Space

Central in this chapter has been the use of metaphors. They are mobile forces of imagination that displace us and that make educational creativity and scientific development possible. Thus metaphors also help to stimulate reflection on the possibilities facing the university in the twenty-first century. In contrast with the present-day tendency that expects concrete results on the basis of preset objectives and clear benchmarks, also in universities, the image of a networked university still needs to be discovered, by slowing down, by being hesitant, by becoming attentive to how the network society presents itself. The image of the web shows the open space at the centre of any web: it is the space of the *non-dit* of our hopes, desires and drives. It is the space of what is uncertain, vulnerable, uncontrollable, or incomprehensible that is the mainspring of human action. It is the in-between-ness that makes people to encounter each other and that may constitute an essential part in the search towards a networked university.

Note

1 This is a strongly revised version of my article "Pyramid, Pillar and Web: Questions for Academic Life Raised by the Network Society." I thank Ron Barnett, Carine Defoort and Wim Weymans for their comments on earlier versions of this text.

8

THE UNIVERSITY AS FOOL

Donncha Kavanagh

> The fool doth think he is wise, but the wise man knows himself to be a fool.
>
> *William Shakespeare (1564–1616), As You Like It*

Introduction

If identity is an emergent property in a network of relationships, then the idea of the University is perhaps best understood through analysing its relationship with other *institutions* over time. The central argument in this chapter is that, akin to the Fool's role in the medieval royal court, the University is a "Foolish institution" embedded in a close relationship with various "Sovereign" institutions. The first part of the chapter describes the evolution of the relationships, before proceeding to explore other "foolish" aspects of the contemporary university. The chapter concludes by reflecting on how the metaphor of the Fool provides a frame for re-thinking the educational practices of the University and its own future.

The University: A Foolish Institution?

The Fool is usually associated with the Middle Ages but is also a feature—in some form or another—of many societies over history (Otto, 2001; Phan, 2001). The Fool has many faces; he is a shape shifter, a chameleon and a trickster, always open to the possibility of transformation. This ambiguity extends to the Fool's own sexuality—the Fool is usually male but female Fools were not uncommon—as demonstrated by the Fool's enduring penchant for cross-dressing. Perhaps the best-known representation is in Shakespeare's plays which often featured the Fool as a recurring character type, usually based on the jesters employed by the royal courts of his time. The Fool is symbolically linked to the king, and this relationship holds on stage, in the reality of the royal court, and in its metaphorical use in my historical interpretation of the evolution of the University. Saying that the University is a "Foolish institution" means that it is always defined by its unique relationship with another institution, termed the "Sovereign institution." This study of the University's evolution identifies at least five different institutions that realize this Sovereign role—the Church, the State, the Nation, the Professions, and the Corporation—as well as others that partly attain the position.

The first Fool–Sovereign relationship of note emerged in the medieval universities in Italy, France and England around 1100 AD. The medieval universities provided many of the defining features of the contemporary university, including the term university, a system of lectures, examinations, administrative structure (faculties), the residential college, and a central location (i.e. the notion of the University as a place). Typically, these institutions grew out of monasteries or cathedral schools and were tied to a universal, "natural" order—the universal ideology of Christianity—rather than to the State or civic society. While law, arts, medicine and theology were all part of the curriculum, theonomy—government by God—provided the medieval university with a dominant and unifying philosophical principle. Thus, the medieval university might be described as the *University of God*, with the Church taking the role of the Sovereign institution, with its focus on indoctrination, rather than on teaching, living or research.

As a deviant, the Fool is a liminal character, and yet he holds a position at the centre of the royal court. His relationship with the King is equally complex: he is the King's friend and confidant, but he is also a servant and subject to punishment at a whim ("Take heed, sirrah—the whip!" *King Lear*, 1:4:109). In *King Lear*, the Fool seeks to demonstrate to Lear the truth about the people around him, but when Lear goes insane and is unable to heed the Fool's advice and knowledge, the Fool vanishes. Interestingly, the tradition of court jesters ended in Britain less than fifty years after *King Lear* was first performed, as Oliver Cromwell's Puritan republic had no place for such frivolities as professional jesters.

Our Foolish institution, the University, is not dissimilar. By the end of the eighteenth century, the medieval university had become quite isolated from society, oligarchical, rigid, introverted, and reactionary, being largely opposed to the Reformation, unsympathetic to the Renaissance, and antagonistic to the new science of the Enlightenment. In addition, the universities saw their scientific leadership usurped by the scientific academies, such as the Royal Society, that were established all over Europe in the seventeenth and eighteenth centuries. An early lesson that the University learned was that while it should be loyal to the Sovereign institution, this loyalty is not unconditional, and it may align itself to other, more powerful, Sovereigns as these emerge.

The Enlightenment and the Reformation reduced the power of the Church and it was these changes that lay at the heart of the University's strategic realignment in the nineteenth century. An important contribution to this process was Kant's argument, in 1798, that the authority of the three "higher" faculties of theology, law and medicine—around which the medieval universities were centred—was *heteronomous* (i.e. imposed by others), while the authority of the "lower" faculty (philosophy) was *autonomous*, legitimated by reason alone, by its own practice. Kant's argument was tremendously important in providing a conceptual basis for academic freedom, not unlike the freedom afforded the Fool in the royal court. But perhaps the more important part of his thesis was that the State had a *duty* to protect this freedom, which formed the basis for a more complex relationship between the State and the University, with the former protecting the latter in order to ensure the rule of reason in public life, and the latter, via philosophy, providing a counter to the excesses of the State and its desires. Power also shifted to the State as, for instance, during the eighteenth century the German state began to regulate academic behaviour through new bureaucratic and accounting practices which ultimately evolved into the "publish or perish" syndrome (Clark, 2006). Through these conceptual and practical reorientations, the State came to take the Sovereign's role in the evolving story of the Foolish institution.

During the nineteenth century, another realignment emerged as part of modernity's cultural project and its engagement with cultural nationalism. Now, the dominant institution in the University's field was not so much the State, as the *Nation*. While Kant had argued that the State should support and protect the University because this was needed to foster *reason*, the new dispensation positioned *culture* as the University's unifying function. Hence the humanities and literature became central, in contrast to philosophy's pole position in Kant's "university of reason." This concern with culture followed the romantic fascination with subjective *Bildung* (the self-development of man) and is well articulated by Cardinal Newman in his influential book, *The Idea of a University*.

At much the same time a quite different development was taking place in the US where the University was moving away from the Nation and towards the *Professions*. The medical and legal professions had been important stakeholders of the University since medieval times, but developments during the nineteenth century brought the professions, more generally, into a sovereign alignment with the University. In particular, there was a shift from contemplative, idealist philosophies and theories of learning propagated by the Platonic tradition towards real-world, action-orientated, purposeful production of knowledge via a modern experimental science of inquiry. By the mid-nineteenth century the idea was in place in the US that universities were not just to produce "gentlemen," teachers, preachers, lawyers and doctors—as per the Newman model—but were to be actively involved in industrial and agricultural development. The unifying goal of the new form of university was the betterment of *humanity*, in contrast to the "University of Culture" which was centred on nationalism. This idea became institutionalized in the US through the land grant movement (from 1862), in the demands of the time that research be related to the technical advance of farming and manufacturing in service to the political and economic segments of society, and in response to the needs of a new American middle class (Bledstein, 1978: x).

In 1876, Johns Hopkins University was founded and many Americans wanted this to follow the "German" or "Humboldtian" model focusing on graduate work and research. However it soon became clear that a large undergraduate student body was required to support graduate study and scholarship. Hence it effected a superimposition of a Platonic German University (or French *grandes écoles*) on top of a classical English/American liberal arts college. This somewhat contradictory institution became hugely influential and the model for all subsequent American universities and indeed many universities outside the US. The research, graduate component concentrated on increasingly specialized, fragmented scholarship while the college component dedicated itself (at least in theory) to general education, character building, and civic education for a democratic society. Serving the civic community, rather than the State, meant providing "human resources" to the professions and industry—such as engineers, doctors and lawyers. This led to increasing disciplinary specialization and fragmentation with departments reflecting professional associations externally.

This new idea of a university also brought a new pragmatic approach to pedagogy, which stressed developing applicable thought *processes*, rather than just the learning of great books and cultural legacies. Hence, the focus shifted to immediate experience, practical education and useful and instrumental knowledge (i.e. the sciences and professional studies) over the traditional humanities curriculum (philosophy, literature, history, and theology).

Not surprisingly, this new university model was criticized by many. In the early nineteenth century, Veblen was a vocal critic of the attempt to link the College (undergraduate) and the University (graduate), and the training of novice professionals which he dismissed as "vocationalism." Writing in the 1930s, the influential American educationalist, Abraham Flexner, made much the same point, arguing that "Practical importance, is not a sufficient title to academic recognition: if that is the best that can be said, it is an excellent reason for exclusion" (Flexner, 1930: 27). Flexner and Veblen represent one position in a much wider debate about which Sovereign the University should serve—the State, Nation or the Professions—and whether or not research (and/or professional training) should form part of the University's function, or whether this is best left to other institutions. Of course the practical workings through of these issues varied from country to country, but suffice to say that the "pure" liberal University, unsullied by professional schools, did not flourish during the twentieth century.

By the late nineteenth century, a further shift occurred as the University commenced a more explicit engagement with business and commerce. A first sign that the *Corporation* was becoming the new power was the widespread substitution of "laymen" (i.e. businessmen) in place of clergy in the governing boards of US undergraduate colleges. As the University shifted its gaze to the Corporation, it increasingly came to adopt organizing principles from the business world, which again affected the nature of the institution. We can, indeed, speak of the emergence of the "Entrepreneurial University." As mass education developed, universities grew and became more powerful, bringing increasing demands for accountability. This justified the diffusion of management discourse and technologies into the university where, increasingly, the administrator took the central position, a role previously occupied by the professor. The pace and nature of this diffusion differed from country to country, but the trend followed a general pattern. As night follows day, faculty resisted and criticized the advent of managerialism, the perceived corporatization of the University, the de-professionalization of academic work, the rise of consumerism, the discourse of "excellence," and the commodity (versus community) model of the University.

The Fool's Many Faces

During the nineteenth century, the University demonstrated a remarkable ability to align itself with different sovereigns and to institutionalize organizing practices that at once enabled transformation and yet sustained a meaningful link with tradition. The institution, in the guise of the new American university model, flourished during the twentieth century, although a confused identity emerged as different actors fought for the already contested position of Sovereign.

After the Second World War, it became clear, at least in the United States, that university research had played a vital role in the war effort and that universities were more than simply teaching institutions. Thus the Military wrested the Sovereign's role, at least in some parts of the University, as US universities came to be seen as the primary locus for the research that would underpin that country's military and industrial dominance. At the same time, there was a long-standing view—going back at least to pivotal thinkers like John Dewey and William James—that education was a tool for progressive social change. Thus, the University wasn't just there to serve a Sovereign (be it the Church, State, Nation, the Corporation, Professions, or Military), but its primary role should be a promoter-cum-architect of emancipation and social justice. In other words, the new Sovereigns should be the ideals of Justice and Emancipation.

But all of these competing Sovereigns led to confusion, tension and finally violence. As early as 1930, Flexner was complaining that universities were too many things: they were "secondary schools, vocational schools, teacher-training schools, research centers, 'uplift' agencies, businesses—these and other things simultaneously" (Flexner, 1930: 179). But by the early 1960s, Clark Kerr's idea of a "multiversity" reflected the reality if not the aspiration of higher education in the US and beyond. For Kerr (1963/2001), the multiversity is a large, inconsistent, bureaucratic institution with fuzzy boundaries, made up of and serving many communities, functions and interest groups and articulating quite different traditions. The multiversity is paradoxical in that it presents itself as a radical institution, when often its conduct is quite conservative. Likewise, it happily depicts itself as a cloister, an ivory tower aloof from the world and yet it readily embraces the desires and wishes of external groups, such as the Church, State, Professions, and Military.

One way of capturing the confused nature of the University is to leverage tropes favoured by the "postmoderns" that seem especially applicable to the contemporary institution. It is at once virtual, reflexive, fragmented, ambiguous, de-centred, contradictory, devoid of fundamentals, inconsistent, and multifaceted (see, for instance, Smith & Webster, 1997). It is also a corporate conglomerate that is embedded in, dependent on, and constituted by information and communication technologies. And the postmoderns have burrowed away at the institution's foundations and traditions, raising profound questions about ideas such as the canon as "self-evident repositories of enlightenment" (Aronowitz & Giroux, 1991: 15), and the notion that intellectual knowledge, as interpreted by the academy, should be privileged over other types of knowledge (such as practical knowledge, gossip and folk wisdom).

Other metaphors also describe the nature of the "postmodern" university and how it differs from earlier visions. If the liberal university espoused by Newman was akin to a village with its priests, and Flexner's vision of a modern university was analogous to a one-industry town with an intellectual oligarchy, the multiversity is a city of infinite variety, in which there is a lower sense of community but also less sense of confinement. And if there is a diminished sense of purpose, there are also more ways to excel. Another way of understanding the postmodern university is to see it as a maze of major fault lines: student v. faculty, professors v. non-professorial teaching staff, academics v. administration, full-time v. part-time, humanists v. scientists, research v. teaching, production v. consumption of knowledge, liberal education v. vocational training, radical thought v. conservative practice.

The university as a "Foolish" institution neatly captures this heterogeneity and confusion. Throughout history and across cultures the Fool has used masks and masquerade, costumes and Carnival to play with (mis)representation and dissimilitude. With the Fool, you may not get what you see. The Fool as trickster is "the mythic embodiment of ambiguity and ambivalence, doubleness and duplicity, contradiction and paradox" (Hyde, 1998: 7), providing a dynamic in a sea of apparent order, a mischievous willingness to contemplate and provoke an alternative state of affairs even at some risk to its own status. Thus, while some might pine for Kant's university of reason, or the University of Culture, the contemporary university is perhaps better understood as the institutional manifestation of modernity's ontological uncertainty, insecurity and ambiguity.

Making Meaning: The Fool as Normative Narrator

Thinking of the University as a Foolish institution helps clarify the essence of what it has been doing in the past and its challenges into the future. For instance, the Fool is a story-teller, telling stories that are always embedded in a framework of norms and values that connect the moment into longer conversations over time and space. In considering this story-telling role, the metaphor of Shakespeare's Fool suggests parallels to how we see the University: the Fool has *audiences* (plural) rather than a single audience. First and primarily, the Fool speaks to his king, his Sovereign. Second, he also addresses other characters in the play. Third, he has conversations essentially with himself, about his own position, and the Fool's role in the world. Fourth, he routinely makes witty remarks about topical issues engaging the viewing audience of the time but which have nothing whatsoever to do with the play.

Likewise, the Foolish institution (the University)—which shares the Fool's fetish for garish costumes—addresses four different audiences. First, the University directs much of what it says to its Sovereign institution, whether this is the Church, the State, the Nation, the Professions, the Corporation, the Military, or the ideals of Emancipation and Justice. For instance, as the Nation became the University's Sovereign, professors became indispensable "interpreters" of the Nation giving them a powerful and privileged position in society. This is why, in the nineteenth century, universities garnered a crucial role in promoting national languages, codifying national literatures and geography, and providing repositories of national culture. Likewise, business schools provide a mechanism whereby the University can speak to its new Sovereign, the Corporation, as an institution. In this regard, university research tries to be purposeful, working to deepen and consolidate the Sovereign's power and position.

Second, it also addresses other institutions within its compass, such as "marriage" and the "family." This constituency includes aspiring and declining Sovereigns. Third, the University has conversations with itself about the nature of the University and its role in the world. Finally, the University engages in "idle" speculation and basic research that have no immediate practical relevance.

Akin to the medieval Fool, who is not there to merely tell stories, the University is expected to provide a *normative* narrative, or a critical interpretation of the world. From the seventeenth century, this was enacted through the theatrics of the public academic lecture and performed disputation—though these modes declined as Enlightenment rationality marginalized dissimulation and role-playing (Clark, 2006)—and through the University's long tradition of academic freedom. The University does not just (re-)tell stories, parables, and proverbs. Its power also comes about from its material ability to *sort things out* (Bowker & Star, 1999); it is a *sorter par excellence*. While the medieval Fool does this discriminating through an observant eye, quick wit and an agile ability to voice distinctions, the University relies on a set of material and writing practices embedded in lecture and library catalogues, grading schemes, charts, tables, classification systems and such like. These "little tools of knowledge" (Becker & Clark, 2001) provide a formidable sorting ability that underpins the university's epistemic power and also its administrative competence in making decisions about who to appoint, which course to run, who to promote, and so forth. And this ability to "sort things out" will become even more important in a world overwhelmed by information, chatter and trivia.

Through these twin processes of normative narrating and sorting, the university constructs and maintains what I term the *semiotic nexus*. The semiotic nexus gives meaning to an institution—be it the University, its Sovereign or one of the other institutions in the realm—through telling a multi-part, compelling, value-laden tale about the institution and its place in the world. The university is not the only institution engaged in this process of "making meaning"—narrating is a form of theorizing that everyone engages in—but it plays a central role in determining what counts as knowledge, as well as defining what is valuable, peripheral, obscene, sacred, profane, reputable, opinion, or fact. The University, like the Fool, personifies truth and reason, in that it is *required* to tell the truth, to abolish myth, and to distinguish fact from mere opinion. In other words, the University's normative story-telling ability allied to its sorting practices and technologies are basic to how the University realizes its imagined community of academics, how it at once becomes an institution itself, and also how it maintains and sustains the semiotic nexus underpinning other institutions. In other words, these practices play a significant role in the *process* of institutionalization.

These processes work largely at the level of the *institutional complex*, which I define as a network of identifiable institutions that interact with one another and with, in particular, a focal institution, which in our case is the University.

Play in the Fool

The Fool is a ludic spirit within the institutional complex, and play—a free activity standing outside of and opposed to the seriousness of ordinary life (Huizinga, 1955)—is its *modus operandi*. As with the child, the Fool is allowed, expected and given time and space to play. Through playing with language, the Fool sparks a new (yet old) understanding of the here and now. This incandescent quality at once makes events alive—giving them immediate meaning—while simultaneously framing them within a longer temporal structure or *longue durée* that articulates the empirical with a transcendent truth. Each "play" then endures as a new mental creation, to be repeated and retained in memory, echoing older refrains of truth and tradition. Following Huizinga, play is primordial and because of its close links with the sacred, it works to keep old norms and beliefs alive. The Fool as playmaker *extraordinaire* is central to this continual process of institutional re-creation through which an institution breathes, lives and renews itself.

Yet, because it takes work to create order within play, play always (subliminally) reminds us that the world is fundamentally chaotic and that any meaning within this chaos is always provisional and artificial. The Fool's work of play then is to institutionalize order and at once to open up order to de-institutionalization. Through its role as playmaker, the Fool puts an institution "into play," which means that work must be done either to re-create or to de-stabilize the institution. In this way, the Fool's ability and license to play is paradoxically central to both institutionalization *and* de-institutionalization.

While the Fool is a liminal entity that is encouraged to play, its role is not without boundaries. Indeed, delimiting social positions is central to its own (liminal) role. And the Fool must also be careful not to transgress this role, as may happen, for instance, if it appropriates the position of Sovereign or becomes an agent of the Sovereign. In both cases, it forgets to "play the fool." This perhaps has happened to the University as it grew into a "multiversity" wherein (a) "foolish" intellectuals ceded power and status to earnest "academic workers," and (b) the multiplicity of Sovereigns in the institutional complex led to profound confusion about the University's own identity. Another transgression occurs when the Fool cannot see beyond the play-making; that is when the Fool becomes a Trickster, a Lucifer figure working solely to undermine and destroy order. This happens when the Fool forgets that part of the Fool's role is sustaining order in the institutional complex. Within the university setting, the decline of the academic lecture into public farce during the eighteenth century, the excesses of postmodern self-indulgence, and the careerism underpinning much statistical and interpretative sophistry are perhaps good examples of this kind of transgression.

Yet another transgression occurs when the Sovereign itself becomes a Fool or Trickster, which can happen when the Sovereign forgets that its power is ultimately derived from a primordial sovereign, namely the People.

Using Meaning: The Fool as Educator

Pursuing the metaphor of the Fool presents an interesting perspective on the University as an educational institution. While the Fool is an educator of sorts, she does not really "own" knowledge that she "passes on" as per our conventional understanding of pedagogy. Unlike the teacher who is usually cast as the learner's caring coach, the Fool is an irritant, a provocateur, whose *modus operandi* is to provoke new wisdom in others. The Fool's approach is, quite literally, to play the fool, acting as a lucid and ludic lens through which others perceive and recognize profound truths, truths that indeed may be lost in the conventions of learning and scholarship. The fool (like the child) is not expected to "know" anything and is therefore free to act the fool, because she cannot, by definition, "know any better." Paradoxically, this epistemic vacuum is also a potential source of great wisdom, which is why the idea of the "wise fool" has such a long tradition. Moreover, the oxymoron "wise fool" is also reversible: he that believes himself to be wise is necessarily foolish. For the Fool also reminds us that knowledge of the mystery of life is always beyond even the wise; at best we can only know that there is much of which we are and can only be ignorant. And in recognizing this, the highest wisdom is perhaps to do nothing other than to play the Fool, as

Erasmus wickedly pointed out in his seminal satire, *The Praise of Folly* (Erasmus, 1511/2005).

The Praise of Folly was hugely influential in the sixteenth century and perhaps its central message can continue to map out a positive path for the University, an institution that is bedevilled by angst about its role in the world. The central character in Erasmus's masterpiece is Stultitia, the goddess of Folly, who advocates that *nature* is the primordial life-force of the universe and that all manifestations of institutionalization, all civilizing enterprises, laws, customs and traditions, are but foolish attempts to contain nature. The University, from this perspective, must continue to live with its role as an institutionalizer *and* de-institutionalizer. It must be a dependent, loyal subject to its Sovereign(s) and yet it must also be a promiscuous charlatan. It must be caring and yet it must be fearlessly critical. It must be central yet at the same time liminal. It must advocate reason and yet always celebrate and recognize that folly is foundational. In short, it must be the institutional manifestation of an *oxymoron*, remembering that this word comes from the Greek, *oxumōrone*, meaning "pointedly foolish."

Conclusions

The University as Fool, dancing with and between a constellation of powerful Sovereigns, also provides a useful perspective on local practices and disputes in universities, on the contemporary role of academics, and on the nature of theorizing and learning. And while the Fool's role is traditionally understood in terms of its relationship with the State, it is clear that the University has partly escaped its subservience to the State through engaging with and being funded by other Sovereigns, such as the Professions. This has implications in terms of how the University engages with its Sovereigns, and again the metaphor provides an enduring trope to guide the nature of this engagement. Here, we are at one with Dahrendorf (1969) for whom the fools of modern society are the intellectuals who "have the duty to doubt everything that is obvious, to make relative all authority, to ask all those questions that no one else dares to ask" (Dahrendorf, 1969: 51). While this role was traditionally conferred on and appropriated by the academic, this is less so today. For instance, the sociologist of science, Steve Fuller, has observed that academia "increasingly looks like a state of exile from the intellectual world" (Fuller, 2005: 2), probably because academic freedom diminished in significance once a general right to free speech became institutionalized. However, there is an historical and social onus on the university to not only house but to actively *foster* intellectuals that question and play with society's institutions. In this context, it is important to reassert and re-invigorate the academic's role as Fool (*qua* Intellectual), which can only be secured through engaging distinctively, closely, and *critically* with the various Sovereigns in the University's institutional complex. Finally, the perspective enunciated in this chapter requires that distinctive virtues and practices be celebrated within the

University, with consequential implications for how the institution should be funded, assessed and organized.

Acknowledgements

This chapter is based on: Kavanagh, Donncha (2009) "Institutional Heterogeneity and Change: The University as Fool." *Organization*, 16(4): 575–595, which includes a more extensive bibliography.

9

RE-IMAGINING THE UNIVERSITY

Developing a Capacity to Care

Gloria Dall'Alba

Introduction: The University as a Social Institution

What contributions do universities make to society? What contributions could they make? As policy decisions in many countries have seen universities move from targeting a selected elite towards educating a substantial proportion of populations, governments have recognised the increased potential of the university to contribute to economic development and prosperity. As a result, contributions of the university through education, research and engagement with the broader society are increasingly presented in terms of knowledge and skills enhancement for economic prosperity. This policy context impacts upon higher education curricula (see, for example, Barnett, Parry & Coate, 2001), the research priorities of governments and funding bodies, and forms of engagement between universities and their communities.

However, the economic cost to societies of higher education for larger numbers of citizens, as well as provision of funding for research and community engagement, presents, in turn, a challenge to universities. When the costs of this expansion in provision are considered, policymakers commonly attempt to re-coup some of the costs, such as through encouraging recruitment of fee-paying international students and by presenting the benefits of university education primarily in terms of economic gains for the individual. A consequence of the reasoning that university education is an individual benefit is that individuals are expected to make a substantial contribution to funding their education, although there are notable exceptions, especially in some European and Middle Eastern countries. While the importance of personal economic benefits or public productivity gains cannot be dismissed, such a bifurcation misses the point that the university potentially contributes to *both* individual and collective benefits, for personal *and* for public gain.

Conceiving the purpose of the university in terms of knowledge and skills enhancement has left it open to being coopted within this largely instrumental agenda. While knowledge and skills enhancement is necessary, it sells the university short on achieving a broader contribution it potentially can make—and, in some instances, does make—to society itself. The benefits of university education, research and engagement with society are not limited to economic gains. These benefits also include the provision of services that enable societies to function in our complex world, enhanced awareness and capability, achievement of potential, and enriched social and cultural life. Construing the purpose of the university primarily in economic terms limits a wider contribution it can make as a *social* institution to framing and forming futures.

Despite the prevailing policy context, however, there are currently efforts within universities to overcome a narrowly economic agenda and make a broader contribution to addressing contemporary issues. These efforts are being made in teaching, research and social engagement, as well as through calls by university leaders. For instance, Steven Schwartz (2010), the Vice-Chancellor of Macquarie University in Sydney, Australia has argued for practical wisdom to be featured as a means of broadening the education of university students for the twenty-first century. In addition, during her installation speech as President of Harvard University in the USA, Drew Faust (2007) argued as follows:

> We are asked to report graduation rates, graduate school admission statistics, scores on standardized tests intended to assess the "value added" of years in college, research dollars, numbers of faculty publications. But such measures cannot themselves capture the achievements, let alone the aspirations of universities. . . . A university is not about results in the next quarter; it is not even about who a student has become by graduation. It is about learning that molds a lifetime, learning that transmits the heritage of millennia; learning that shapes the future. . . . Education, research, teaching are always about change—transforming individuals as they learn, transforming the world as our inquiries alter our understanding of it, transforming societies as we see our knowledge translated into policies.

These arguments imply a need to re-consider not only *what* students and staff in universities know or can *do*, but also how we are learning to *be*. In contrast, conceiving the purpose of the university in terms of somewhat narrowly construed knowledge and skills enhancement implies new learning can largely be incorporated into existing ways of being in the world, rather than contributing to transformation where this is needed.

This chapter argues for re-framing debate about the purpose of the university through a shift in focus from knowledge and skills to possibilities for being, as these relate to higher education, research and engagement with society. A key argument here is that the university has the potential to *open and interrogate possibilities for being*, at individual and collective levels, *in ways that promote attuned responsiveness* to questions and issues in our contemporary world. The remainder of the chapter explores what this might mean for a university of the future.

Re-imagining Ourselves in the University: Care for Others and Things

The current emphasis on knowledge and skills enhancement sees the purpose of the university increasingly defined in terms of outcomes to be achieved when educating students, conducting research and engaging with society beyond the university, in the way that Drew Faust describes above. This emphasis can be clearly seen in accountability measures and associated "reward" mechanisms. Nel Noddings points out that when we value students according to what they achieve, "they become resources" in an instrumental sense (1992: 13). The same argument can be made about university staff when they teach and research, as well as when they engage with society in other ways.

Foregrounding readily identifiable achievement and outcomes has become so pervasive in our contemporary world within and without the university that other contributions are at risk of being overlooked or overshadowed. Martin Heidegger (1993/1954) highlighted a similarly instrumental view in the ways in which technologies are increasingly used in human endeavours. He expressed disquiet about the way in which such a view frames human being and nature, as resources to be used and exploited. Heidegger warned of a danger that the pervasiveness of such an instrumental, exploitative view may eventually mean we are unable to understand ourselves in any other way.

In countering such an instrumental view, we can re-imagine the way we understand ourselves, which also enables us to re-frame the idea and purpose of the university. In contrast to an exploitative, technologised understanding of ourselves, Heidegger develops a concept of care, which he regards as a necessary feature of being human (1962/1927: 84). His notion of care means concerning ourselves with people and things that matter to us, which includes being absorbed in the various activities, projects and things in our world. It also involves being with others, which can take a range of forms from domination to liberation, although it is often somewhere in between.

Drawing on Heidegger's concept of care and relating it to formal education, Nel Noddings challenges the "deadly notion that the . . . first priority should be intellectual development" (1992: 12). Privileging the intellect in this way occurs at the expense of attending to broader features of what it means to be human. Noddings argues for an alternative focus for education upon developing the capacity to care. She argues that such a focus is not anti-intellectual (*ibid.*: 19), but "if we decide that the capacity to care is as much a mark of personhood as reason or rationality, then we will want to find ways to increase this capacity" (*ibid*: 24). She points out that "people have various capacities for caring—that is, for entering into caring relations as well as for attending to objects and ideas" (*ibid.*: 18).

In line with Martin Heidegger's notion, this concept of care includes care for both others and things in our world. Conceiving education in terms of care for others and things turns attention differently towards education. Not only does it feature what students are expected to know and be able to do (an epistemological dimension), but also who students are becoming or, in other words, how they are learning to be (an ontological dimension). For instance, students can be educated to care for ideas, nature and built environments, as well as caring for clients, colleagues and others in encounters with them. As students are educated about how to do this, their learning also contributes to forming and shaping the ways in which they relate to others and things in the world, in other words, who they are becoming as professionals, citizens, persons. In this way, ontology is integrated with epistemology through developing the capacity to care "as a mark of personhood." Expanding this capacity to care promotes an interweaving of what students know and can do with how they are learning to be, such that neither an epistemological nor an ontological dimension is privileged.

A capacity to care for others and things has relevance not only for education, but also for the research and social engagement in which the university is involved. Similar to educational endeavours, there is a risk that research and engagement with society can be exploitative in a manner that undermines or dominates others and things in our world. Alternatively, research and social engagement can be directed to caring for ideas, nature and built environments, as well as supporting and enabling achievement of potential in each area of human endeavour. It is important to note that caring for *both* others *and* things are necessary to developing and expressing the capacity to care; one is not an alternative to the other. Care for others and things are demonstrated in what we investigate or promote in our research and engagement with society. They are also expressed in how we carry out these activities and how we relate to others when we do so.

Care for others and things can provide a positive alternative to an instrumental approach that readily leads to exploitation in our world, with its high cost of war between peoples, financial collapse and damage to the environment. For Patricia Huntington, "Heidegger supplies a rich vocabulary for reconceptualizing human nature as care—custodian for what appears—rather than as the rational animal who lords over the earth" (2001: 27). Developing the capacity to care is arguably more complex and intellectually challenging than settling for improved rationality or readily measurable outcomes. Indeed, such short-sightedness would not be valued, as we strive for responsible care in our actions and interactions. Importantly, care for others and things can contribute constructively to the natural environment, social organisation and achievement of human potential in ways that strengthen the ethical bases of our societies, as we take responsibility for our ways of being in the world.

Taking Responsibility in Care for Others and Things

Inherent in the notion of care for others and things, then, is responsibility. While this is not a feature of care that is explicitly highlighted by Martin Heidegger, taking responsibility for our actions and interactions is implicit in Heidegger's (1962/1927) concept of authenticity (see, for example, Vu & Dall'Alba, 2011), which is closely related to his concept of care. The importance of responsibility is evident in the part that universities play in educating students to be professionals. In some instances, education for responsible practice is a requirement of university programmes, especially where these are overseen or approved by a regulatory body or professional association. But educating students about responsible care arguably extends further, to caring for others and things in all aspects of preparing for life beyond the university. Programmes that prepare students for contributing to society after their university studies, but which undermine or neglect their capacity to care for others and things in our world could hardly be described as educative.

In educating students to care responsibly for others and things in the world, then, we must demonstrate this care convincingly in our encounters with our students and surroundings. These encounters can play a vital role in deepening students' understanding of what it means to care for others and things. As Nel Noddings points out, "caring is a way of being in relation, not a set of specific behaviors . . . or an individual attribute" (1992: 17). When we fail to demonstrate the care for others and things that we espouse, students are typically astute in identifying double standards and hypocrisy. At best, our efforts will be undermined; at worst, our students may become skilled in emulating our hypocrisy.

Not only is responsibility of relevance in educating students, but also in our research and engagement with society—which can also have an educative role outwards beyond the university and inwards toward the university. When we take responsibility, the kinds of research and social engagement in which we become involved—as well as the way in which we do so—would place high value on the social and ethical bases for these endeavours. Taking responsibility also entails paying careful attention to the anticipated consequences of our research and engagement for society and the surrounding environment.

If we are concerned to develop the capacity to care for others and things in our world, then the way we teach, research and engage with others outside the university would demonstrate this sense of responsibility. It is important to point out here, however, that taking responsibility does not entail that we "take away 'care' from the Other" (Heidegger, 1962/1927: 158). In other words, it does not include controlling or displacing others' efforts to engage with the people and things that matter to them, such as through indoctrination, exploitation or other forms of domination. Instead, developing the capacity to care for others and things can open possibilities for being, in ways that contribute to framing directions and forming futures.

Opening and Interrogating Possibilities for Being

The introduction to this chapter pointed to a need for a shift in focus in the way the university is currently conceived, from enhancing knowledge and skills to opening and interrogating possibilities for being. Such a shift is needed across the areas of endeavour within the university, including teaching, research and engagement with society. Although this shift does not mean discarding all current goals and practices, it does involve re-thinking the purpose and character of what we do in the university. A shift in focus from knowledge and skills to possibilities for being can broaden, clarify and give direction to the contribution the university makes as a social institution into the twenty-first century.

A shift of this kind re-imagines the purpose of the university in a way that no longer primarily looks back: Have the desired knowledge and skills been identified, acquired or applied? Somewhat paradoxically, rapid technological and social change has not yet prompted universities to direct attention forward to an unknowable future, while drawing upon what has been learned from the past. A focus on possibilities for being, however, serves to direct our attention forward: What possibilities have been opened and do they provide a strong basis for addressing both the anticipated and unknown challenges to be faced? In other words, a shift in focus to possibilities for being involves asking what ways of being in the world are opened and supported by the university through higher education, research and engagement with the broader society.

How, then, can the university open possibilities for being? As we experience the familiar in new ways or come into contact with the unfamiliar through education, research or engagement with others, this opens new possibilities, or other ways of being. Similarly, being with others can also extend our possibilities for being through broadening our perspectives. When we call into question and revise taken-for-granted assumptions or perspectives, other ways of being are made possible. For example, the advent of new technologies, such as the internet, not only challenge our understanding of what it means to communicate but, in some respects at least, also change the way we relate to one another as citizens, researchers, teachers. Similarly, each time that university staff and students travel to vulnerable areas, using their expertise to provide secure housing, reliable sources of clean water or improved literacy and numeracy, new possibilities are opened to those who live in these areas. When students are transformed into historians, biotechnologists or occupational therapists, new ways of being in the world are opened to them. In ways such as these, the university as a social institution contributes to framing and forming futures.

When possibilities are opened, we press ahead into an emergent possibility, thereby negating and foreclosing other possibilities. This is often not an entirely deliberative or rational process, but we actualise one of the available possibilities by enacting it. In this way, individual teachers, students, researchers and support staff press ahead into realising one possibility among several. So, too, do collectives, such as research teams, groups involved in social engagement and whole professions. At times, this can take us in unexpected directions, which once again opens further possibilities.

Opening possibilities always occurs within constraints, however. For instance, transforming students into skilled professionals is constrained in some ways by the practices they seek to enter. The resources that are available affect the scope of engagement with communities outside the university, at least to some extent. New directions in research are necessarily limited by the sophistication of tools and technologies to support the research. At the same time, opening possibilities for some can mean constraining them for others. For example, awarding funding to one team denies or reduces it for another, in ways that may not always be equitable. Nonetheless, constraints on opportunities also open their own possibilities, which can lead us to direct our attention and energies in new directions. Moreover, when we scrutinise the way that constraints operate in specific situations, this sometimes opens possibilities about which we were previously unaware.

While the university can create the conditions for new possibilities to emerge through engagement with society, research and higher education, it can play an additional part in discerning what those possibilities might be. For instance, what are the available options for addressing the needs of a specific community beyond the university? What are the possible directions that could further a particular programme of research? In what ways can learning during professional practice be directed to the service function of the profession?

In addition to assisting in the discernment of possibilities, the university can also promote thoughtful interrogation of the appropriateness of various possibilities for charting and sustaining a desired direction. For example, how could a specific community benefit from, or be harmed by, various forms of engagement with the university? What are the strengths and limitations of conducting research within parameters that have been proposed? What are the likely consequences of particular ways of enacting professional practice? To the extent that the university assists in discerning and interrogating available possibilities, to that extent it can enable more informed judgements about how to proceed and why it is valuable to adopt one approach or course of action over another. It can thereby support the process of pressing ahead in an informed way in line with a desired direction.

Determining a desired direction, in itself, contributes to framing and forming futures. We can simply be carried along with the way things are usually done or fall in with what would most readily advance our own interests. Alternatively, we can continually differentiate a direction for our work through taking a stand on our becoming; on how we are to be with others and things. Indeed, each of us is called to care (Heidegger, 1962/1927: 322). However, who and what we are in "the publicity of the everyday world is mercilessly ignored and passed over in the call," depriving us of our usual means of escape from responding to this call (King, 2001: 164). The call to care does not provide us with clarity on how we are to proceed in any given situation. The call "is not to tell us *what* we are to *do*, but *how* we are to *be*" (*ibid.*).

Through a focus on possibilities for being, then, the university can encourage thoughtful—and, at times, courageous—responses to the call to care. It can promote the development of the capacity to care as an integral part of higher education, research and social engagement. In so doing, the university is ideally placed to challenge and support a continuing process of taking a stand on our becoming, on how we are learning to be. For example, educational programmes could regularly prompt students to adopt an informed and critical stance on what they are learning and who they are becoming. A university climate that supports development of the capacity to care would encourage researchers to be ethical in their practice, as well as acutely attuned in their research to potential short- and long-term consequences for society and the surrounding environment. Engagement that contributes to society in meaningful ways would be fostered and highly valued as a key function of the university.

Through aiding in opening, discerning and interrogating possibilities, then, the university can contribute to framing directions and forming futures, for both individuals and collectives. A focus on possibilities for being can inform us as we enact emergent opportunities in higher education, research and engagement with society. It can also encourage critical reflection about the university's contribution to society and, indeed, about its own purpose.

Promoting Attuned Responsiveness

When we foreground the contribution the university can make to possibilities for being in a manner that frames and forms futures, responsibility is once again highlighted. Taking seriously our responsibility—literally, our ability to respond—requires that we strive to be attuned to that to which we are responding. Martin Heidegger argues that our very openness to the world is made possible by attunement (1962/1927: 176; see King, 2001: 55–59 for elaboration). Through attunement, we are able to respond in ways that are appropriate to the situations we encounter.

Developing attunement requires particular care in attending to others and things in ways that give us insight into their specific conditions and requirements. It entails a yielding; an effort to understand others and things on their own terms. Such attuned dwelling with others and things provides openings for revising taken-for-granted assumptions and perspectives, so that other ways of understanding, of acting and of being become evident. Attunement with the particulars of a situation allows us to discern possibilities; to posit ways in which things could be otherwise. It also offers a firmer basis on which to make informed judgements about action to be taken or avoided, as well as desired directions in which to move forward. Attunement provides us with ways of proceeding that address the conditions and requirements of the situations we encounter.

Becoming attuned enables us to be responsive to—or choose to be neglectful of—the conditions and needs we encounter as we go about in the world. For example, we can engage with communities beyond the university in identifying how we can assist in addressing their specific requirements and needs. Through our research, we can sharpen our awareness in ways that enable us to respond appropriately to conditions in our world. Our teaching and educational programs can promote a responsiveness which is attuned to each new situation that our students and graduates encounter. Attuned dwelling with others and things, which enables us to be responsive to their conditions and needs, affords us a basis upon which to challenge and support others in their becoming. In this way, our capacity to care can also be enhanced. Or, failing this, we can impose our own priorities and preferences in our engagement with society, research and teaching in ways that lack responsiveness to need or fail to be attuned with the requirements of particular situations.

A key part the university can play, then, is in promoting and supporting responsiveness that is attuned to the particular conditions and requirements in each situation. In other words, the university can encourage attuned responsiveness to both others and things in the situations encountered in our contemporary world. Indeed, this is a responsibility the university has acquired by virtue of its social mandate to educate, research and engage with society. Where these endeavours are neither attuned nor responsive to conditions and needs in the situation, their relevance and social contribution is undermined. At the same time, attuned responsiveness requires agency and some degree of autonomy on the part of the university, as well as on the part of those individuals and teams who teach, research and engage with communities beyond the university.

Challenges to Promoting Possibilities for Being

There is currently a range of challenges for the university in promoting possibilities for being that are attuned and responsive to contemporary issues in our world. One of these challenges relates to what Martin Heidegger referred to as human being's "average everydayness" (1962/1927: 69) or, in other words, our tendency simply to allow ourselves to be carried along with the way things are done by those around us. "Falling in" with others in this way is convenient and necessary for accomplishing our many tasks and projects, but it can run counter to both attunement and responsiveness to others and things in specific situations. As the shift in focus for higher education, research and social engagement that is argued for in this chapter requires attuned responsiveness, average everydayness is not adequate for accomplishing such a shift. Concerted and continuing efforts are necessary to achieve this shift, which amounts to a re-imagining of the purpose and character of what we do in the university.

A second challenge, related to the first, is the current policy context within which universities operate in many countries. As noted, construing the purpose of the university primarily in terms of knowledge and skills enhancement for economic prosperity threatens to limit unduly the way in which we imagine our purpose and ourselves within the university. In order to gain or secure funding, universities commonly fall into line with demands from governments that foster an instrumental focus on readily measurable outcomes when educating students, conducting research and engaging with society. These efforts to obtain funding are often occurring in a context of diminishing funding relative to the costs associated with higher education, research and social engagement. Re-imagining our purpose and ourselves in the university in a way that is not consistent with the current policy context requires courage and leadership. It entails taking a stand in working to educate governments and policymakers about the broader contributions the university can make to society.

A third challenge to achieving a shift in focus to possibilities for being is the difficulty of revising familiar and ingrained ways of understanding, of acting and of being, both within the university and among its stakeholders. Transforming understanding, acting and being entails commitment and risk. Transformations such as these unsettle and potentially threaten our sense of ourselves, even when we are willing to consider making such a shift. However, they can also provide a means by which we can work towards realising a better future.

Despite these challenges to promoting possibilities for being, there is cause for hope and optimism. Some efforts within universities indicate that the present path is seen as unduly narrow, such as Steven Schwartz's endeavours to promote practical wisdom and Drew Faust's argument above that universities have a part to play in transforming individuals, the world and societies. Some of the efforts towards change have resonances with the ideas put forward in this chapter. There is recognition within universities, then, of the need to construe the purpose of the university differently in line with how we are learning, and encouraging others, to be.

Concluding Remarks

While several of the proposals for opening and interrogating possibilities for being identified in this chapter are consistent with some existing and emerging university practices, the purpose of the university is not commonly conceived in terms of possibilities for being. This chapter has argued that the university can make a valuable contribution to addressing questions and issues in our contemporary world through a focus on possibilities for being, at individual and collective levels. This focus has the potential to enhance the ethical bases of our endeavours through promoting care for others and things in tangible ways across higher education, research and social engagement. It would secure a continuing contribution for the university into the twenty-first century.

A forward-looking focus on possibilities for being would enhance learning from higher education, research and engagement with society, while re-imagining ourselves in the university through care for others and things. Opening and interrogating possibilities for being involves substantial responsibility. In taking seriously our responsibility in framing and forming futures through a focus on possibilities for being, the university can promote freedom in, and for, becoming. Consistent with a call to care, the chapter has not primarily featured "*what* we are to *do*, but *how* we are to *be*." More particularly, it has proposed how we can re-envision our purpose and being in the university.

Acknowledgements

This chapter has benefitted from thoughtful comments provided by Ronald Barnett, Rachel Parker, Jörgen Sandberg and Steven Schwartz.

10

CREATING A BETTER WORLD

Towards the University of Wisdom

Nicholas Maxwell

Introduction

We urgently need to bring about a revolution in universities so that problems of living are put at the heart of the academic enterprise, and a basic aim becomes to help humanity make progress towards as good a world as feasible.

From the past we have inherited a kind of academic inquiry that seeks to help promote human welfare by, in the first instance, acquiring knowledge and technological know-how. First, knowledge is to be acquired; then it can be applied to help solve social problems. Inquiry of this type is still dominant in universities today.

But, judged from the all-important standpoint of promoting human welfare, this kind of inquiry—which I shall call *knowledge-inquiry*—is grossly and damagingly irrational. Three of the four most elementary rules of rational problem-solving are violated in a wholesale, structural way. This long-standing, massive, institutionalised irrationality in our universities, widely overlooked, is in part responsible for the development of our current global problems, and our current inability to tackle these problems intelligently, effectively and humanely.

Modern science and technological research have, of course, produced immense benefits. They have made the modern world possible. But science and technological know-how make possible modern industry and agriculture, modern hygiene and medicine, which in turn lead to population growth, destruction of natural habitats and rapid extinction of species, pollution of earth, sea and air, the lethal character of modern war and terrorism, vast differences in wealth and power around the globe—and, above all, global warming. In a perfectly respectable sense of "cause," modern science and technology are, indeed, the *cause* of these things.[1]

Some blame science for our problems, but this profoundly misses the point. Where we have gone wrong is to pursue scientific and technological research *dissociated from a more fundamental concern with problems of living.* We urgently need to bring about a revolution in science, and in academic inquiry more generally, so that the basic aim becomes to seek and promote wisdom—wisdom being the capacity to realize what is of value in life, for oneself and others, thus including knowledge and technological know-how, but much else besides. This revolution would affect every branch and aspect of academia, and how it is related to the rest of the social world.[2]

In what follows, I distinguish two kinds of inquiry, which I shall call *knowledge-inquiry* and *wisdom-inquiry*. At the core of knowledge-inquiry there is a philosophy of science which I shall call *standard empiricism*; the corresponding philosophy of science at the core of wisdom-inquiry being *aim-oriented empiricism*. Standard empiricism and knowledge-inquiry are what we have inherited from the past, and what we still have, by and large, today. Aim-oriented empiricism and wisdom-inquiry are what emerge when knowledge-inquiry is modified just sufficiently to ensure elementary rules of rational problem-solving and aim-pursuing are implemented, granted that the basic aim is to help promote human welfare, help people realize what is of value in life.

There are two arguments. The first appeals to *problem-solving rationality*, the second to *aim-pursuing rationality*. These establish that knowledge-inquiry is indeed damagingly irrational—three of the four most elementary rules of rational problem-solving are violated—wisdom-inquiry being what emerges when knowledge-inquiry is modified just sufficiently to cure it of its grave rationality defects.

First Argument: Problem-Solving Rationality

Knowledge-inquiry demands that a sharp split be made between the social or humanitarian aims of inquiry and the *intellectual* aim. This latter is to acquire knowledge of truth, nothing being presupposed about the truth. Only those considerations may enter into the intellectual domain of inquiry relevant to the determination of truth—claims to knowledge, results of observation and experiment, arguments designed to establish truth or falsity. Feelings and desires, values, ideals, political and religious views, expressions of hopes and fears, cries of pain, articulation of problems of living: all these must be ruthlessly excluded from the intellectual domain of inquiry as having no relevance to the pursuit of knowledge—although of course inquiry can seek to develop factual knowledge about these things, within psychology, sociology or anthropology. Within natural science, an even more severe censorship system operates: an idea, in order to enter into the intellectual domain of science, must be an empirically testable claim to factual knowledge.

For a much more detailed exposition of knowledge-inquiry see my (1984 or 2007: chapter 2). For evidence that knowledge-inquiry prevails in academia, see my (*ibid.*: chapter 6). I do not claim that everything in academia accords with the edicts of knowledge-inquiry. My claim is, rather, that this is the only candidate for rational inquiry in the public arena; it is the dominant view, exercising an all-pervasive influence over academe. Work that does not conform to its edicts has to struggle to survive. But this may be about to change, as we shall briefly see below.

This is the conception of inquiry which, I claim, violates reason in a wholesale, structural and damaging manner.

What do I mean by "reason"? As I use the term here, rationality appeals to the idea that there are general methods, rules or strategies which, if put into practice, give us our best chance, other things being equal, of solving our problems, realizing our aims. Rationality is an aid to success, but does not guarantee success, and does not determine what needs to be done. (For further details, see my 1984 or 2007: chapters 4 and 5.)

Four elementary rules of reason, alluded to above, are:

(1) Articulate and seek to improve the articulation of the basic problem(s) to be solved.
(2) Propose and critically assess alternative possible solutions.
(3) When necessary, break up the basic problem to be solved into a number of *specialized* problems—preliminary, simpler, analogous, subordinate problems—(to be tackled in accordance with rules (1) and (2)), in an attempt to work gradually toward a solution to the basic problem to be solved.
(4) Inter-connect attempts to solve the basic problem and specialized problems, so that basic problem-solving may guide, and be guided by, specialized problem-solving.

Two preliminary points now need to be made.

First, granted that academic inquiry has, as its fundamental aim, to help promote human welfare by intellectual and educational means,[3] then the *problems* that inquiry fundamentally ought to try to help solve are problems of living, problems of action. From the standpoint of achieving what is of value in life, it is what we *do*, or refrain from doing, that ultimately matters. Even where new knowledge and technological know-how are relevant to the achievement of what is of value—as they are in medicine or agriculture, for example—it is always what this new knowledge or technological know-how enables us to *do* that matters. All the global problems indicated above require, for their resolution, not merely new knowledge, but rather new policies, new institutions, new ways of living. Scientific knowledge, and associated technological know-how have, if anything, as we have seen, contributed to the creation of these problems in the first place.

Second, in order to achieve what is of value in life more successfully than we do at present, we need to discover how to resolve conflicts and problems of living in, progressively, less violent, more *cooperatively rational* ways than we do at present.

Granted this, and granted that the above four rules of reason are put into practice then, at the most fundamental level, academic inquiry needs to:

(1) Articulate, and seek to improve the articulation of, personal, social and global problems of living that need to be solved if the quality of human life is to be enhanced (including those indicated above).

(2) Propose and critically assess alternative possible solutions—alternative possible *actions, policies, political programmes, legislative proposals, ideologies, philosophies of life.*

In addition, of course, academic inquiry must:

(3) Break up the basic problems of living into subordinate, specialized problems—in particular, specialized problems of knowledge and technology.

(4) Inter-connect basic and specialized problem-solving.

Academic inquiry as it mostly exists at present puts (3) into practice to splendid effect. The intricate maze of specialized disciplines devoted to improving knowledge and technological know-how that go to make up much of current academic inquiry is the result. But, disastrously, what we have at present, academic inquiry devoted primarily to improving knowledge, fails to put (1), (2) and (4) into practice. In pursuing knowledge, academic inquiry may articulate problems of knowledge, and propose and critically assess possible solutions, possible claims to knowledge—factual theses, observational and experimental results, theories. But, as we have seen, problems of *knowledge* are not (in general) problems of *living*; and solutions to problems of *knowledge* are not (in general) solutions to problems of *living*. In so far as academia does at present put (1) and (2) into practice, in departments of social science and policy studies, it does so only at the periphery, and not as its central, fundamental intellectual task.

In short, academic inquiry devoted primarily to the pursuit of knowledge, when construed as having the basic humanitarian aim of helping to enhance the quality of human life by intellectual means, fails to put the two most elementary rules of reason into practice (rules (1) and (2)). Academic inquiry fails to do (at a fundamental level) what it most needs to do, namely (1) articulate problems of living, and (2) propose and critically assess possible solutions. And, as a result of failing to put (1) and (2) into practice, knowledge-inquiry fails to put (4) into practice as well. As I have remarked, *three* of the four most elementary rules of rational problem-solving are violated. (For a much more detailed exposition of this argument see my 1984 or 2007.)

This gross structural irrationality of contemporary academic inquiry has profoundly damaging consequences for humanity. In giving intellectual priority to problems of knowledge, academia fails to do what it most needs to do: articulate our problems of living, individual, social and global, and imaginatively develop and critically assess possible solutions—possible *actions*, policies, political programmes, institutional innovations, philosophies of life—designed, if adopted, to help us realize what is of value in life, make progress towards a better world. Again, in devoting itself to acquiring knowledge in a way that is unrelated to sustained concern about what humanity's most urgent problems are, as a result of failing to put (1) and (2) into practice, and thus failing to put (4) into practice as well, the danger is that scientific and technological research will respond to the interests of the powerful and the wealthy, rather than to the interests of the poor, of those most in need. Scientists, officially seeking knowledge of truth *per se*, have no official grounds for objecting if those who fund research—governments and industry—decide that the truth to be sought will reflect their interests, rather than the interests of the world's poor. And priorities of scientific research, globally, do indeed reflect the interests of the first world, rather than those of the third world. In this respect, funds devoted to military research, in the US, UK and some other wealthy countries, are especially disturbing: see Langley (2005) and Smith (2003).

Knowledge and technology successfully pursued in a way that is not rationally subordinated to the tackling of more fundamental problems of living, through the failure to put (1), (2) and (4) into practice, is bound to lead to the kind of global problems discussed above, problems that arise as a result of newly acquired powers to act being divorced from the ability to act *wisely*. The creation of our current global problems, and our inability to respond adequately to these problems, has much to do, in other words, with the long-standing, rarely noticed, structural *irrationality* of our institutions and traditions of learning. Knowledge-inquiry, because of its irrationality, is designed to *intensify*, not help *solve*, our current global problems.

Wisdom-Inquiry: Problem-Solving Version

At once the question arises: What would a kind of inquiry be like that *is* devoted, in a genuinely rational way, to promoting human welfare by intellectual means? The answer is *wisdom-inquiry*.

As a first step at characterizing wisdom-inquiry, we may take knowledge-inquiry (at its best) and modify it just sufficiently to ensure that all four elementary rules of rational problem-solving, indicated above, are built into its intellectual and institutional structure: see figure 1.

The primary change that needs to be made is to ensure that academic inquiry implements rules (1) and (2). It becomes the fundamental task of social inquiry and the humanities (1) to articulate, and seek to improve the articulation of, our problems of living, and (2) to propose and critically assess possible solutions, from the standpoint of their practicality and desirability. In particular, social inquiry has

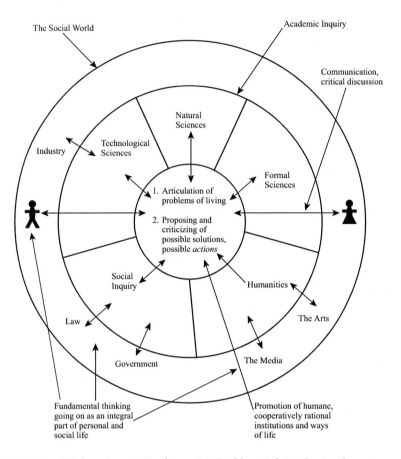

FIGURE 10.1   Wisdom-Inquiry Implementing Problem-Solving Rationality

the task of discovering how conflicts may be resolved in less violent, more cooperatively rational ways. It also has the task of promoting such tackling of problems
of living in the social world beyond academe. Social inquiry is, thus, not primarily
social *science*, nor, primarily, concerned to acquire knowledge of the social world;
its primary task is to promote a more cooperatively rational tackling of problems
of living in the social world. Pursued in this way, social inquiry is intellectually
more fundamental than the natural and technological sciences, which tackle subordinate problems of knowledge, understanding and technology, in accordance
with rule (3). In figure 1, implementation of rule (3) is represented by the specialized problem-solving of the natural, technological and formal sciences, and more
specialized aspects of social inquiry and the humanities. Rule (4) is represented by
the two-way arrows linking fundamental and specialized problem-solving, each
influencing the other.

One can go further. According to this view, the thinking that we engage in as we live, in seeking to realize what is of value to us, is intellectually more fundamental than the whole of academic inquiry (the latter having, as its basic purpose, to help cooperatively rational thinking and problem-solving in life to flourish). Academic thought emerges as a kind of specialization of personal and social thinking in life, the result of implementing rule (3). This means there needs to be a two-way interplay of ideas, arguments and experiences between the social world and academia, in accordance with rule (4). This is represented, in figure 1, by the two-way arrows linking academic inquiry and the social world.

The natural and technological sciences need to recognize three domains of discussion: evidence, theory, and aims. Discussion of aims seeks to identify that highly problematic region of overlap between that which is discoverable, and that which it is of value to discover. Discussion of what it is of value to discover interacts with social inquiry, in accordance with rule (4).

Second Argument: Aim-Oriented Rationality

So much for my first argument in support of wisdom-inquiry. I come now to my second argument, which appeals to, and modifies, the Enlightenment programme of learning from scientific progress how to achieve social progress towards an enlightened world.

In order to implement this programme properly, it is essential to get the following three steps right.

1. The progress-achieving methods of science need to be correctly identified.
2. These methods need to be correctly generalized so that they become fruitfully applicable to any human endeavour, whatever the aims may be, and not just applicable to the endeavour of improving knowledge.
3. The correctly generalized progress-achieving methods then need to be exploited correctly in the great human endeavour of trying to make social progress towards an enlightened, wise, civilized world.

Unfortunately, the *philosophes* of the eighteenth century Enlightenment got all three points wrong. And as a result these blunders, undetected and uncorrected, are built into the intellectual-institutional structure of academia as it exists today.

First, the *philosophes* failed to capture correctly the progress-achieving methods of natural science. From D'Alembert in the eighteenth century to Popper in the twentieth century (Popper, 1959, 1963), the widely held view, amongst both scientists and philosophers, has been (and continues to be) that science proceeds by assessing theories impartially in the light of evidence, *no permanent assumption being accepted by science about the universe independently of evidence.* Preference may be given to simple, unified or explanatory theories, but not in such a way that nature herself is, in effect, assumed to be simple, unified or comprehensible. This orthodox view, which I call *standard empiricism* is, however, untenable. If taken literally, it would instantly bring science to a standstill. For, given any accepted theory of physics, T, Newtonian theory say, or quantum theory, endlessly many empirically more successful rivals can be concocted which agree with T about observed phenomena but disagree arbitrarily about some unobserved phenomena. Physics would be drowned in an ocean of such empirically more successful rival theories.

In practice, these rivals are excluded because they are disastrously disunified. *Two* considerations govern acceptance of theories in physics: empirical success and unity. In demanding unity, we demand of a fundamental physical theory that it ascribes *the same* dynamical laws to the phenomena to which the theory applies in addition to empirical success. (For details of this account of theoretical unity see my 1998: chapter 4, 2004: appendix, section 2, 2007: chapter 14, section 2 or 2010: chapter 5.) But in persistently accepting unified theories, to the extent of rejecting disunified rivals that are just as, or even more, empirically successful, physics makes a big persistent assumption about the universe. The universe is such that all disunified theories are false. It has some kind of unified dynamic structure. It is physically comprehensible in the sense that explanations for phenomena exist to be discovered. (For a fuller exposition of this argument see my 1984: chapter 9, or 2007: chapters 9 and 14, and especially 1998, and 2004: chapters 1 and 2 and appendix.)

But this untestable (and thus metaphysical) assumption that the universe is physically comprehensible is profoundly problematic. Science is obliged to assume, but does not know, that the universe is comprehensible. Much less does it know that the universe is comprehensible in this or that way. A glance at the history of physics reveals that ideas have changed dramatically over time. In the seventeenth century there was the idea that the universe consists of corpuscles, minute billiard balls, which interact only by contact. This gave way to the idea that the universe consists of point-particles surrounded by rigid, spherically symmetrical fields of force, which in turn gave way to the idea that there is one unified self-interacting field, varying smoothly throughout space and time. Nowadays we have the idea that everything is made up of minute quantum strings embedded in ten or eleven dimensions of space-time. Some kind of assumption along these lines must be made but, given the historical record, and given that any such assumption concerns the ultimate nature of the universe, that of which we are most ignorant, it is only reasonable to conclude that it is almost bound to be false.

The way to overcome this fundamental dilemma inherent in the scientific enterprise is to construe physics as making a hierarchy of metaphysical assumptions concerning the comprehensibility and knowability of the universe, these assumptions asserting less and less as one goes up the hierarchy, and thus becoming more and more likely to be true, and more nearly such that their truth is required for science, or the pursuit of knowledge, to be possible at all: see figure 2. In this way a framework of relatively insubstantial, unproblematic, fixed assumptions and associated methods is created within which much more substantial and problematic assumptions and associated methods can be changed, and indeed improved, as scientific knowledge improves. Put another way, a framework of relatively unspecific, unproblematic, fixed *aims* and methods is created within which much more specific and problematic aims and methods evolve as scientific knowledge evolves. (A basic aim of science is to discover in what precise way the universe is comprehensible, this aim evolving as assumptions about comprehensibility evolve.) There is positive feedback between improving knowledge, and improving aims-and-methods, improving knowledge-about-how-to-improve-knowledge. This is the nub of scientific rationality, the methodological key to the unprecedented success of science.[4] Science adapts its nature to what it discovers about the nature of the universe (see Maxwell, 1974, 1976, 1984 or 2007, 1998, 2004, 2010: chapter 5).

This hierarchical conception of physics, which I call *aim-oriented empiricism*, can readily be generalized to take into account problematic assumptions associated

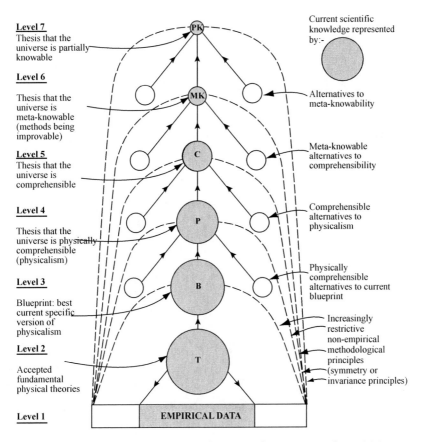

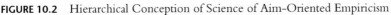

FIGURE 10.2 Hierarchical Conception of Science of Aim–Oriented Empiricism

with the aims of science having to with *values*, and the *social uses* or *applications* of science. It can be generalized so as to apply to the different branches of natural science. Different sciences have different specific aims, and so different specific methods, although throughout natural science there is the common meta-methodology of aim-oriented empiricism (Maxwell, 2004: 41–7).

So much for the first blunder of the traditional Enlightenment, and how to put it right.

Second, having failed to identify the methods of science correctly, the *philosophes* naturally failed to generalize these methods properly. They failed to appreciate that the idea of representing the problematic aims (and associated methods) of science in the form of a hierarchy can be generalized and applied fruitfully to other worthwhile enterprises besides science. Many other enterprises have problematic aims—problematic because aims conflict, and because what we seek may

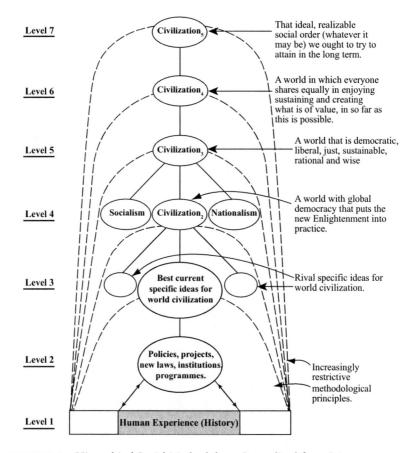

FIGURE 10.3 Hierarchical Social Methodology Generalized from Science

be unrealizable, undesirable, or *both*. Such enterprises, with problematic aims, would benefit from employing a hierarchical methodology, generalized from that of science, thus making it possible to improve aims and methods as the enterprise proceeds. There is the hope that, as a result of exploiting in life methods generalized from those employed with such success in science, some of the astonishing success of science might be exported into other worthwhile human endeavours, with problematic aims quite different from those of science.

Third, and most disastrously of all, the *philosophes* failed completely to try to apply such generalized, hierarchical progress-achieving methods to the immense, and profoundly problematic enterprise of making social progress towards an enlightened, wise world. The aim of such an enterprise is notoriously problematic. For all sorts of reasons, what constitutes a good world, an enlightened, wise or civilized world, attainable and genuinely desirable, must be inherently and permanently problematic.[5] Here, above all, it is essential to employ the generalized version of the hierarchical, progress-achieving methods of science, designed specifically to facilitate progress when basic aims are problematic: see figure 3. It is just this that the *philosophes* failed to do. Instead of applying the hierarchical methodology to *social life*, the *philosophes* sought to apply a seriously defective conception of scientific method to *social science*, to the task of making progress towards, not a *better world*, but to better *knowledge* of social phenomena. And this ancient blunder, developed throughout the nineteenth century by J.S. Mill, Karl Marx and many others, and built into academia in the early twentieth century with the creation of the diverse branches of the social sciences in universities all over the world, is still built into the institutional and intellectual structure of academia today, inherent in the current character of social science (Maxwell, 1984 or 2007: chapters 3, 6 and 7).

Wisdom-Inquiry: Aim-Pursuing Version

Properly implemented, in short, the Enlightenment idea of learning from scientific progress how to achieve social progress towards an enlightened world would involve developing social inquiry, not primarily as social *science*, but rather as social *methodology,* or social *philosophy*. A basic task would be to get into personal and social life, and into other institutions besides that of science—into government, industry, agriculture, commerce, the media, law, education, international relations—hierarchical, progress-achieving methods (designed to improve problematic aims) arrived at by generalizing the methods of science. A basic task for academic inquiry as a whole would be to help humanity learn how to resolve its conflicts and problems of living in more just, cooperatively rational ways than at present. This task would be intellectually more fundamental than the scientific task of acquiring knowledge. Social inquiry would be intellectually more fundamental than physics. Academia would be a kind of people's civil service, doing openly for the public what actual civil services are supposed to do in secret for governments. Academia would have just sufficient power (but no more) to retain its independence from government, industry, the press, public opinion, and other centres of power and influence in the social world. It would seek to learn from, educate, and argue with the great social world beyond, but would not dictate. Academic thought would be pursued as a specialized, subordinate part of what is really important and fundamental: the thinking that goes on, individually, socially and institutionally, in the social world, guiding individual, social and institutional actions and life. The fundamental intellectual and humanitarian aim of inquiry would be to help humanity acquire wisdom—wisdom being the capacity to realize (apprehend and create) what is of value in life, for oneself and others, wisdom thus including knowledge and technological know-how but much else besides.

One outcome of getting into social and institutional life the kind of aim-evolving, hierarchical methodology indicated above, generalized from science, is that it becomes possible for us to develop and assess rival philosophies of life as a part of social life, somewhat as theories are developed and assessed within science. Such a hierarchical methodology provides a framework within which competing views about what our aims and methods in life should be—competing religious, political and moral views—may be cooperatively assessed and tested against broadly agreed, unspecific aims (high up in the hierarchy of aims) and the experience of personal and social life. There is the possibility of cooperatively and progressively improving *such philosophies of life* (views about what is of value in life and how it is to be achieved) much as *theories* are cooperatively and progressively improved in science. In science, ideally, theories are critically assessed with respect to each other, with respect to metaphysical ideas concerning the comprehensibility of the universe, and with respect to *experience* (observational and experimental results). In a somewhat analogous way, diverse philosophies of life may be critically assessed with respect to each other, with respect to relatively uncontroversial, agreed ideas about aims and what is of value, and with respect to *experience*—what we do, achieve, fail to achieve, enjoy and suffer—the aim being to improve philosophies of life (and more specific philosophies of more specific enterprises within life such as government, education or art) so that they offer greater help with the realization of what is of value in life. This hierarchical methodology is especially relevant to the task of resolving conflicts about aims and ideals, as it helps disentangle agreement (high up in the hierarchy) and disagreement (more likely to be low down in the hierarchy).

Wisdom-inquiry, because of its greater rigour, has intellectual standards that are, in important respects, different from those of knowledge-inquiry. Whereas knowledge-inquiry demands that emotions and desires, values, human ideals and aspirations, philosophies of life be excluded from the intellectual domain of inquiry, wisdom-inquiry requires that they be included. In order to discover what is of value in life it is essential that we attend to our feelings and desires. But not everything we desire is desirable, and not everything that feels good is good. Feelings, desires and values need to be subjected to critical scrutiny. And of course feelings, desires and values must not be permitted to influence judgements of factual truth and falsity.

Wisdom-inquiry embodies a synthesis of traditional Rationalism and Romanticism. It includes elements from both, and it improves on both. It incorporates Romantic ideals of integrity, having to do with motivational and emotional honesty, honesty about desires and aims; and at the same time it incorporates traditional Rationalist ideals of integrity, having to do with respect for objective fact, knowledge, and valid argument. Traditional Rationalism takes its inspiration from science and method; Romanticism takes its inspiration from art, from imagination, and from passion. Wisdom-inquiry holds art to have a fundamental rational role in inquiry, in revealing what is of value, and unmasking false values; but science, too, is of fundamental importance. What we need, for wisdom, is an interplay of sceptical rationality and emotion, an interplay of mind and heart, so that we may develop "mindful hearts and heartfelt minds" (Maxwell, 1976: 5). It is time we healed the great rift in our culture, so graphically depicted by Snow (1964).

All in all, if the Enlightenment revolution had been carried through properly, the three steps indicated above being correctly implemented, the outcome would have been a kind of academic inquiry very different from what we have at present, inquiry devoted primarily to the intellectual aim of acquiring knowledge.

First Hints of the Revolution

During the last 10–20 years, numerous changes have occurred in academia that amount to a shift towards wisdom-inquiry. In what follows I concentrate on universities in the UK.

Perhaps the most significant of these steps is the creation of departments, institutions and research centres concerned with social policy, development, environmental degradation, climate change, poverty, injustice and war, and other matters such as medical ethics and community health: see Iredale (2007) and Macdonald (2009) for developments of this point.

At Cambridge University, one can see the first hints of the institutional structure of wisdom-inquiry being superimposed upon the existing structure of knowledge-inquiry. As I have emphasized, wisdom-inquiry puts the intellectual tackling of problems of living at the heart of academic inquiry, this activity being conducted in such a way that it both influences, and is influenced by, more specialized research. Knowledge-inquiry, by contrast, organizes intellectual activity into the conventional departments of knowledge: physics, chemistry, biology, history and the rest, in turn subdivided, again and again, into increasingly specialized research disciplines. But this knowledge-inquiry structure of ever more specialized research is hopelessly inappropriate when it comes to tackling problems of living. In order to tackle environmental problems, for example, in a rational and effective way, specialized research into a multitude of different fields, from geology, engineering and economics to climate science, biology, architecture and metallurgy, needs to be connected to, and coordinated with, the different aspects of environmental problems. (For the fundamental importance of interconnecting work on broad and specialized problems, see my 1980.) The sheer urgency of environmental problems has, it seems, forced Cambridge University to create the beginnings of wisdom-inquiry organization to deal with the issue. The "Cambridge Environmental Initiative" (CEI), launched in December 2004, distinguishes eight fields associated with environmental problems: conservation; climate change; energy; society, policy and law; water; waste; built environment; natural hazards; and under these headings, coordinates some 102 research groups working on specialized aspects of environmental issues in some 25 different (knowledge-inquiry) departments: see www.cei.group.cam.ac.uk/, accessed 30 May 2010. The CEI holds seminars, workshops and public lectures to put specialized research workers in diverse fields in touch with one another, and to inform the public.

A similar coordinating, interdisciplinary initiative exists at Oxford University. This is the School of Geography and the Environment, founded in 2005 under another name. It is made up of five research "clusters," two previously established research centres, the Environmental Change Institute (founded in 1991) and the Transport Studies Institute, and three inter-departmental research programmes, the African Environments Programme, the Oxford Centre for Water Research, and the Oxford branch of the Tyndall Centre. The School has links with other such research centres, for example the UK Climate Impact Programme and the UK Energy Research Centre.

At Oxford University there is also the James Martin 21st Century School, founded in 2005 to "formulate new concepts, policies and technologies that will make the future a better place to be." It is made up of fifteen Institutes devoted to research that ranges from ageing, armed conflict, cancer therapy and carbon reduction to nanoscience, oceans, science innovation and society, the future of the mind, and the future of humanity. At Oxford there is also the Smith School of Enterprise and the Environment, founded in 2008 to help government and industry tackle the challenges of the twenty-first century, especially those associated with climate change.

Similar developments have taken place recently at my own university, University College London. Not only are there over 141 research institutes and centres at UCL, some only recently founded, many interdisciplinary in character, devoted to such themes as ageing, cancer, cities, culture, public policy, the environment, global health, governance, migration, and security. In addition, very recently, partly influenced by my own work, the attempt has been made to organize research at UCL around a few broad themes that include: global health, sustainable cities, intercultural interactions, and human wellbeing. This is being done so that UCL may all the better contribute to solving the immense global problems that confront humanity.

On the UCL website, the rationale for the global challenges initiative is spelled out in a way which echoes the case for wisdom-inquiry:

The world is in crisis. Billions of us suffer from illness and disease, despite applicable preventions and cures. Life in our cities is under threat from dysfunctionality and climate change. The prospect of global peace and cooperation remains under assault from tensions between our nations, faiths and cultures. Our quality of life—actual and perceived—diminishes despite technological advances. These are global problems, and we must resolve them if future generations are to be provided with the opportunity to flourish.

(http://www.ucl.ac.uk/grand-challenges/, accessed 29 May 2010)

These developments, echoed in many other UK universities, can be regarded as first steps towards implementing wisdom-inquiry. For further indications that the revolution may be underway see my (2009).

Conclusion

Research in universities has been devoted, primarily, to acquiring knowledge and technological know-how. But knowledge and technological know-how increase our power to act which, without wisdom, can lead to as much harm as benefit. Current global crises, and especially the most serious, global warming, have arisen in this way. We urgently need to bring about a revolution in our universities so that they come to seek and promote wisdom—wisdom being understood to be the capacity to realize what is of value in life, thus including knowledge, understanding and technological know-how, but much else besides. Universities need to take up the task of helping humanity learn how to make progress towards as good a world as possible. This revolution—intellectual, institutional and cultural—if it ever comes about, will be comparable in its long-term impact to that of the Renaissance, the scientific revolution, or the Enlightenment. There are signs that this urgently needed revolution may already be underway. If so, it is happening with agonizing slowness, in a dreadfully muddled and piecemeal way. The underlying intellectual reasons for academic change need to be much more widely appreciated, to help give direction, coherence and a rationale to the nascent academic revolution, and to help ensure that the intellectual value and integrity of science and scholarship are strengthened and not subverted.

Notes

1   It may be objected that it is not *science* that is the cause of our global problems but rather the things that we *do*, made possible by science and technology. This is obviously correct. But it is also correct to say that scientific and technological progress *is* the cause. The meaning of "cause" is ambiguous. By "the cause" of event E we may mean something like "the most obvious observable events preceding E that figure in the common sense explanation for the occurrence of E." In this sense, human actions (made possible by science) are the cause of such things as people being killed in war, destruction of

tropical rain forests. On the other hand, by the "cause" of E we may mean "that prior change in the environment of E which led to the occurrence of E, and without which E would not have occurred." If we put our times into the context of human history, then it is entirely correct to say that, in this sense, scientific-and-technological progress is the cause of our distinctive current global disasters: what has changed, what is new, is scientific knowledge, not human nature. (Give a group of chimpanzees rifles and teach them how to use them and in one sense, of course, the cause of the subsequent demise of the group would be the actions of the chimpanzees. But in another obvious sense, the cause would be the sudden availability and use of rifles—the new, lethal technology.) Yet again, from the standpoint of theoretical physics, "the cause" of E might be interpreted to mean something like "the physical state of affairs prior to E, throughout a sufficiently large spatial region surrounding the place where E occurs." In this third sense, the sun continuing to shine is as much a part of the cause of war and pollution as human action or human science and technology.

2   For a much more detailed account of this revolution, why it is needed and what its implications are, see my (1984 or, better, 2007). See also my (1976, 1980, 1998, 2004 and 2010). For an overview of my work plus critical discussion of it by eleven scholars see McHenry (2009). See also http://www.nick-maxwell.demon.co.uk.

3   This assumption may be challenged. Does not academic inquiry seek knowledge for its own sake—it may be asked—whether it helps promote human welfare or not? Elsewhere (Maxwell, 2007: 17–19, 70–5, 205–13) I argue that wisdom-inquiry does better justice than knowledge-inquiry to *both* aspects of inquiry, pure and applied. The basic aim of inquiry, according to wisdom-inquiry, is to help us realize what is of value in life, "realize" meaning both "apprehend" and "make real." "Realize" thus accommodates both aspects of inquiry, "pure" research or "knowledge pursued for its own sake" on the one hand, and technological or "mission-oriented" research on the other—both, ideally, seeking to contribute to what is of value in human life. Wisdom-inquiry, like sight, is there to help us find our way around. And like sight, wisdom-inquiry is of value to us in two ways: for its intrinsic value, and for practical purposes. The first is almost more precious than the second.

4   Natural science has made such astonishing progress in improving knowledge and understanding of nature because it has put something like the hierarchical methodology of aim-oriented empiricism, indicated here, into scientific practice. Officially, however, scientists continue to hold the standard empiricist view that no untestable metaphysical theses concerning the comprehensibility and knowability of the universe are accepted as a part of scientific knowledge: see Maxwell (2004: 5–6, especially note 5, and 13–14, note 14). As I have argued elsewhere (Maxwell, 1998: 23–33, 2004: chapter 2), science would be even more successful, in a number of ways, if scientists adopted and explicitly implemented the hierarchical methodology indicated here.

5   There are a number of ways of highlighting the inherently problematic character of the aim of creating civilization. People have very different ideas as to what does constitute civilization. Most views about what constitutes Utopia, an ideally civilized society, have been unrealizable *and* profoundly undesirable. People's interests, values and ideals clash. Even values that, one may hold, ought to be a part of civilization may clash. Thus freedom and equality, even though inter-related, may nevertheless clash. It would be an odd notion of individual freedom which held that freedom was for some, and not for others; and yet if equality is pursued too single-mindedly this will undermine individual freedom, and will even undermine equality, in that a privileged class will be required to enforce equality on the rest, as in the old Soviet Union. A basic aim of legislation for civilization, we may well hold, ought to be increase freedom by restricting it: this brings out the inherently problematic, paradoxical character of the aim of achieving civilization.

PART IV
A University for Society

11

UNIVERSITIES AND THE COMMON GOOD

Jon Nixon

How much are we willing to pay for a good society?

(Judt, 2010a: 170)

In this chapter I discuss the idea of "the common good" with reference to the history of higher education over the last sixty years. In doing so I provide little more than a preliminary and no doubt partial account of what is a highly complex economic, social and political history of institutional change. I focus on the expansion of higher education and some of its intended and unintended consequences with a view to highlighting tensions and contradictions implicit in the idea of "the common good." Student learning is one of the areas in which these tensions and contradictions are clearly in evidence: in the supposed interests of widening access, a narrow and restrictive view of student learning has come to dominate higher education. I argue that while this is partly a result of economic factors, it is mainly due to institutional inertia and academic conformity. If the University of the Future is to take seriously its own commitment to the common good, then it will have to reconceptualise student learning and reconstruct itself as, first and foremost, a space for learning.

The Expansion of Opportunity

One of the unavoidable questions facing policy makers over the last fifty years has been how to manage their economies in a period of rapid globalisation. Crucial to any viable policy response to this question has been the development of a workforce with the necessary skills and understandings to face the challenges of late capitalism. The expansion of educational provision generally and of higher education in particular is, it is generally assumed, a necessary component of any such response. Higher education became, of economic necessity, a common good. It held out the promise of excellence fairly distributed and undiluted.

This expansionist trend has been particularly pronounced in the UK and US since the Second World War. In the US, for example, "between 1950 and 2000, the number of degree granting institutions more than doubled, from 1,851 to 4,084 . . . with total enrolment increasing from 2.6 million to 14.8 million students, more than fivefold in the fifty years" (Lazerson, 2010: 14). The Netherlands, too, saw student numbers rise steadily from approximately 50,000 in 1950 to approximately 500,000 in 2006. (See Ritzen, 2010: 162.) In recent decades, many other countries have been seeking to increase educational opportunity at a bewildering pace: Canada, China, Russia, Singapore to name but a few. The idea of "the common good" became associated, almost universally, with policies that promoted the expansion of higher education.

Judt (2010b: 394) highlights the rapidity of that expansion in post–Second World War Europe:

> By the end of the 1960s, one young person in seven in Italy was attending university (compared to one in twenty ten years before). In Belgium the figure was one in six. In West Germany, where there had been 108,000 students in 1950, there were nearly 400,000 by the end of the Sixties. In France, by 1967, there were as many university students as there had been *lycéen* in 1956. All over Europe there were vastly more students than ever before—and the quality of their academic experience was deteriorating fast.

That expansion did not come cheap. "Its cost, to countries not yet recovered from the slump of the thirties and the destruction of the war," notes Judt, "was very considerable." Responses to the soaring costs varied across regions: for example, Ritzen (2010: 133–156), echoing Judt, documents what he terms "the financial suffocation of European universities," while in the US, annual expenditure for higher education went from $2.2 billion in 1950 to $134.6 billion in 1990 (National Center for Education Statistics, 2008, Table 187, quoted in Lazerson, 2010: 14). Where expansion has been matched by expenditure it has been justified on the grounds that universities provide personal advancement and national competitiveness. For the individual, universities were seen as the necessary route to the old and new professions; and, for the state, they provided the resources necessary for keeping ahead in the global markets.

The crucial policy issue was—and is—how, and on what basis, to fund what was considered to be not only a vital but an essential expansion of the university sector. Responses to this policy issue have invariably involved from all sides of the political spectrum an emphasis on increased privatisation and increased profitability. What the "new capitalism" will look like is uncertain. However, as Kaletsky (2010: 274) argues, any new settlement will have to meet "the simultaneous need for more government and smaller government" and must be based therefore on a tough debate about "the balance of responsibilities between government and private enterprise"; or, as Stiglitz (2010: 296) puts it, "between the market and the state, between individualism and the community, between man and nature, between means and ends."

The ends and purposes of higher education are not economically determined, but they are informed and shaped by economic considerations. What began over half a century ago as an egalitarian dream of ever-widening access to educational opportunity, a dream of higher education as an intrinsic component of the common good, had from the start to confront the economic reality. ("There was," as Judt (2010a: 47) comments, "a *moralized* quality to policy debates in those early postwar years.") That reality is harsher now—and the choices starker— than perhaps at any time in the intervening years. But from the outset the ethical impulse towards the common good has required as a necessary condition of its sustainability some hard economic decisions that have in turn raised further ethical choices.

The Consequences of Expansion

The common good, in other words, comes at a cost: someone has to pick up the tab. That goes some way towards explaining why universities are so heavily reliant on semi-private, semi-public modes of funding and why Bok (2003) pointed to the "rapid growth of money-making opportunities provided by a more technologically sophisticated, knowledge-based economy" (15). Commenting specifically on the situation of higher education within the US, he argued that "within a few short decades a brave new world had emerged filled with attractive possibilities for turning specialised knowledge into money" (*Ibid.*:13–14). Within the UK, too, this emergent trend towards turning knowledge into money had brought about a fundamental change in the culture of higher education. "Students," claimed Williams (1995: 177), "have been metamorphosed from apprentices to customers, and their teachers from master craftsmen to merchants."

Competition for funds and for student numbers led to institutional stratification and the self-protective groupings of institutions which lobbied intensively for their market niche. Within this context institutional "prestige" has itself become a marketable commodity. (See Brown, 2011: 25–31.) University rankings have become an increasingly important element within this competitive process. Within the UK, the older universities have almost permanent and undisputed occupancy of the premier league, the post-1992 universities are well represented across the broad span of second league institutions, and the bottom league is occupied almost entirely by institutions that have gained university status more recently. (Reay, David & Ball, (2005: 140) and Shumar (1997: 134) point to a similar situation in the US and Australia respectively.)

"Since the 1980's," writes Lazerson (2010: 84) in his account of higher education as an expression of the American dream, "published rankings of colleges and universities have intensified the competition, in ways similar to various consumer reports on the quality of every item that is available for sale." One consequence of this increased competition, he argues, is that higher education in the US has expanded in a segmented and hierarchical fashion in ways that might well be interpreted as having "preserved the social structure of inequality . . . [T]he overall effect was to leave the nation as socially divided as in the past" (23). Heller (2007: 48–49) adds telling detail to this line of argument in pointing out:

> that 77% of all high income students attended a four-year college, while only 33% of poorer students did. . . . While 62% of the higher-income students went on to complete a bachelor's degree, only 21% of their lower-income peers were able to obtain this level of education.

Ongoing research conducted by the UK Sutton Trust supports the view that institutional differentiation driven by the increasing marketization of higher education has tended to reproduce and reinforce structural inequality. In an analysis covering over one million university student admissions during the period 2002–2006, it documented for the first time the extent to which a few individual schools supply the majority of students to the UK's leading research universities—and with lower academic qualifications. (See Sutton Trust, 2008.) In so doing, it exposed the extent to which a significant proportion of young people from state schools miss out on the opportunity of attending universities to which their peers, with no better or even lower grades at "A" level but educated privately, gain admission. (See, also, Sutton Trust, 2004.)

"The overall conclusion," argues Brown (2011: 34) "must be that, at the very least, marketization has not assisted with widening access; more probably, and in conjunction with privatization, it has set it back." What is increasingly apparent is the widening gap between the reality of expansion and the aspiration towards a fairer and more just society: a society shaped and motivated, that is, by a sense of the common good. It is at this point, then, that the idea of "the common good" requires conceptual explication, given its entanglement in the complex economic, social and political history of the post-Second World War era. The idea itself, moreover, is by no means unitary; it involves contrasting and in some cases mutually exclusive strands.

The Limits of Meritocracy

The idea of "the common good" invariably implies holding something worthwhile in common. However, there are very different interpretations of what that "something" is and in what sense it should be "held in common." The expansion of higher education over the last fifty years originated in the post-Second World

War consensus that education in general and higher education in particular is constitutive of the common good. But that consensus held in tension contrasting and even conflicting views as to how, and in what sense, higher education could be "held in common."

Those tensions surfaced as specific policies relating to the expansion and funding of higher education were implemented by successive governments and variously interpreted across the increasingly diversified university sector. The financial crisis of 2007–2008 and its continuing global aftermath revealed the extent of those tensions and the ideological fault lines that lay beneath them. If the problem is framed insistently as one of budget deficit and the solution is framed equally insistently as one of reduction in public expenditure, then two questions begin to dominate the public debate.

The first question focuses on what constitutes "the common good"—or, more starkly, on which components of "the common good" are dispensable. Since the problem and the solution are framed in terms of cost-effectiveness, then the answer to the question becomes something of a foregone conclusion. Dispensability and indispensability come to be judged increasingly according to the criterion of financial return. In all aspects of university life—from class size, through course provision and pedagogical approach, to student welfare—profitability becomes the decisive factor.

That is the background to Nussbaum's (2010) compelling argument that whatever in higher education is "not for profit" is now seriously at risk. Since it is precisely the "not for profit" component of higher education that Nussbaum sees as indispensable in any serious attempt to educate future generations of "global citizens" for full participation in a mature democracy, then universities are in her view facing an unprecedented crisis. Lazerson (2010), too, argues that what he sees as the over-restrictive emphasis on the technical aspect of "vocationalism" in current higher education policy and practice is resulting in a university system that ill-prepares the vast majority of students for a complex and rapidly changing world of work.

The second question focuses on how whatever is eventually deemed to be indispensible should be "held in common." In the current economic climate there is an easy reversion to a very old and deeply regressive assumption that an elite cadre is best placed, particularly in times of crisis, to hold in trust and on behalf of the citizenry as whole "the common good." The assumption reasserts itself in the acceptance of escalating inequalities of income and lifestyle between the wealthiest and poorest in society—and, more specifically, of the structural inequalities relating to university admissions as alluded to above and tirelessly documented by the Sutton Trust. (See Toynbee & Walker, 2009; Wilkinson & Pickett, 2009.)

Inequality becomes acceptable because it is routinely presented as the inevitable consequence of meritocracy—the inevitable consequence, that is, of a system supposedly based on equality of opportunity. The metaphor of the level playing field is often evoked at this point to suggest the equal terms upon which everyone competes within the meritocratic game. What the image of the level playing field conveniently brackets out is the fact that what happens *off* the field may be as important, if not more important, than what happens *on* the field in determining the outcome of the game.

The common good is not much good at all as long as a significant proportion of the population is unable to take advantage of it. "To pretend," as Hattersley (2004: 12) puts it, "that, because there is no legal prohibition on such activities, the children of the inner cities are free to go to Eton and that their grandparents are free to enjoy Caribbean cruises is a cruel deception." From this perspective the idea of "the common good" implies the capability necessary to make the choices which we wish to make. A meritocracy, even when justified on the basis of equality of opportunity, does not begin to measure up to the enormity of this challenge.

It was Young (1958) (the sociologist, social activist and politician who drafted the Labour Party's manifesto for the 1945 general election) who famously coined the word "meritocracy." Since that first usage the term has become synonymous with the good—or at least "good enough"—society. Jackson and Segal (2007: 124) remind us, however, that the word was coined by Young:

> to illustrate the pernicious consequences of a society stratified according to meritocratic criteria, where material resources and social status were bestowed upon the section of the community who were fortunate enough to possess one particular kind of ability, namely marketable talents.

Far from providing the conditions necessary for sustaining the common good, meritocracy as conceived by Young restricts and actively prevents it. (See Young, 2001.)

This leaves universities that genuinely aspire to contribute to the common good in an awkward position. Not only are they located within a society that characterises itself as meritocratic, but they are the means by which highly influential sets of meritocratic criteria are routinely applied in the interests of social selection. Of course, universities can—and do—operate on the assumption that inequality is inevitable or that (to adopt a more acceptable phraseology) they are scrupulously fair in their application of criteria and in providing the proverbial "level playing field"; and, of course, they may—and indeed frequently do—claim that this "good enough" is as good as it gets in pursuit of the ever-allusive common good.

This still leaves a problem, however, for those who see the future of the university in the context of a more magnanimous and democratically ambitious conception of the common good: a conception based not solely on the provision of equal opportunities (important though these are), but also on the acknowledgement of a universal entitlement (difficult though this is) to the capabilities necessary to realise those opportunities. Expansionist policies are not in themselves enough and can (as argued above) have implications that seriously undermine the impulse towards widening participation. How might the future university find ways through—or round—this impasse?

A Space for Learning

I shall highlight just one possible response to that question by focusing on the responsibility of the university to place student learning at the centre of its concerns: the responsibility, that is, not only to provide a rich and intellectually stimulating learning environment, but also to deepen our understanding of what constitutes human learning and what conditions are necessary to sustain and develop it. Universities of the future will continue to have multiple responsibilities and academics will continue to be involved in a wide variety of practices relating to research, teaching and scholarship. Central to those responsibilities and practices, however, will be a commitment to providing all students with a space within which to develop capabilities necessary to flourish as receptive and critical learners.

Nussbaum (2010: 134–135), in a work already cited above, argues that this commitment has been seriously compromised by the emphasis on economic profitability in higher education. This, she maintains, has had a deleterious effect on the quality of student learning: "curricular content has shifted away from material that focuses on enlivening imagination and training the critical faculties toward material that is directly relevant to test preparation." This shift, she goes on to argue, has been accompanied by "an even more baneful shift in pedagogy: away from teaching that seeks to promote questioning and individual responsibility toward force-feeding for good exam results." A significant driver in effecting both these shifts is the increasing reliance on inappropriately applied forms of standardised assessment that are (as she puts it) insufficiently "nuanced." Curriculum, pedagogy and assessment are now largely determined by the bureaucratic requirement to pre-specify learning outcomes: bureaucratic because the requirement in question has very little to do with what anyone in higher education seriously associates with learning and very much to do with externally imposed systems of accountability.

A great deal of learning undertaken in universities is necessarily characterised by uncertainty of outcome and divergence of viewpoint and values. The learning that is associated with the process of deliberation is one such example. In *The Nicomachean Ethics,* Aristotle (1955: 119) defined deliberative reasoning (*phronesis*) as "that which happens for the most part where the result is obscure and the right course not clearly defined." Whatever learning happens as a result of *phronesis* cannot be pre-specified: if it could, it would not be *phronesis*.

That clause—"where the result is obscure and the right course not clearly defined"—highlights the extent to which deliberation as a mode of human reasoning falls outside the current orthodoxies regarding target setting and the

specification of learning outcomes. It may be appropriate to apply those orthodoxies to reasoning that is directed at coherent explanation (what Aristotle termed
theoria) or to the kind of technical know-how that is directed at producing a
clearly defined end product (what Aristotle termed *techne*). But to apply them to
a mode of reasoning the prime purpose of which is to determine which of several
contested outcomes is the "right" one is a clear case of a category error: a mode of
reasoning the outcomes of which are necessarily indeterminate cannot be defined
in terms of its pre-specifiable outcomes.

Aristotle distinguished deliberation—or *phronesis*—from *theoria* and *techne* in
order to highlight that each of these three forms of reasoning aims at a different
kind of excellence. The excellence to which *phronesis* aspires is the excellence of
right action as determined by the agents of that action in circumstances within
which the action is to be undertaken. It is the mode of reasoning that is required
when collective solutions are sought to collective problems. As such, it is an indispensable resource in an increasingly complex world of global inter-connectivity
and difference where the most pressing problems are collective: global warming,
the protection of the environment, the movement of labour, the protection of
children and women from trafficking, etc. Such problems can only be addressed
through a deliberative and reflexive process, the outcomes of which are necessarily "obscure and the right course not clearly defined."

Yet, the evidence would suggest that (a) we are not very good at this kind of
reasoning and (b) we fail to prioritise it. We have the technical know-how to
produce ever more sophisticated systems of communication, but lack the deliberative capability necessary to achieve shared understanding across ever deepening
ideological and cultural divides. The global consequences of this collective failure
could be catastrophic, since, as Beck (2009: 18–19) puts it, "henceforth, there are
no merely local occurrences." What Beck calls "controlling rationality" cannot
be applied "to the uncertainty of the effects, the side effects and the side effects
of the side effects . . . [since] all attempts at rational control give rise to new 'irrational', incalculable, unpredictable, consequences."

Universities of the future, then, have a vital part to play not only in sustaining and developing modes of practical reasoning or deliberation, but in ensuring that these are not distorted through the imposition of wholly inappropriate
bureaucratic requirements. The problem is not one of inactivity: the "shifts" that
Nussbaum identified in assessment, teaching and curriculum testify to high levels
of activity in all three areas. The problem lies in our understanding of the complexity of these activities and in the extent to which that understanding impacts
upon public policy and practice. As Barnett and Coate (2004: 13) point out, "curriculum" has become a "missing term" in the public debate on higher education:

> a term that speaks of matters that lie right at the heart of higher education
> is hardly, in the UK at least, to be seen or heard in the framing of public
> debate on the future of higher education itself.

It will be the responsibility of the future university to re-instate that "missing term" within the kind of debate that Barnett and Coate are here referring to. A space for learning is necessarily a deliberative space and insofar as universities of the future aspire to become spaces for learning they must also become deliberative spaces. The highly technical, bureaucratic and professionalised language of learning that currently dominates universities militates against that aspiration. For all its insistence on "user relevance," it is an exclusive language of technocrats and bureaucrats, the ideological purpose of which is to endorse technocratic and bureaucratic ways of thinking about higher education.

"It is a language," argues McKibbin (2006: 6), "which was first devised in business schools, then broke into government and now infests all institutions." It purports to be neutral:

> thus all procedures must be "transparent" and "robust," everyone "accountable". It is hard-nosed but successful because the private sector on which it is based is hard-nosed and successful. It is efficient; it abhors waste; it provides all the answers.

It collapses all human reasoning into the kind of reasoning whose "outcomes" can be "pre-specified" with reference to specific "targets." The dominant officialise of "course management" and "quality assurance" ensures that the epistemological premises of deliberative modes of reasoning and the reciprocal learning they generate are denied.

Uncertainty, indeterminacy and irreducible complexity are simply unthinkable from the orthodox epistemological perspective which requires us to know what we will have learnt prior to our having learnt it. Yet, it is precisely the capacity for living and working together in uncertainty, indeterminacy and irreducible complexity that the students of today will require if they are to face the enormous challenges and opportunities of tomorrow. "We need," as Patel (2009: 193–194) puts it, "to see, value and steward the world in more democratic ways, realize that property and government can be much more plastic than we'd ever thought possible." The future of the university lies in its commitment to providing a space for learning within which students can begin to meet that need—and, in so doing, acquire the capabilities necessary for them to benefit from and contribute to the common good.

Costing the Common Good

If we were to take seriously the question posed by Judt at the head of this chapter, we might come up with the following broad categories as a bare minimum of conditions necessary for the sustainability of the common good:

- *Experience of learning.* Students need the opportunity of working in small groups, engaging with tutors on a one-to-one basis, and receiving detailed feedback on their work. If they are studying full-time, they also need to be free of the necessity of taking on onerous paid work to fund their studies. They need an environment in which they can live and work with fellow students thereby gaining some measure of independence from home.

- *Academic identity*. Universities need to be staffed by academics whose sense of professional identity is formed and sustained through their teaching and related scholarship. That in turn requires a career structure that recognises and rewards teaching and related scholarship and that expects all academic staff (non-professorial *and* professorial) to engage fully in teaching and course development. It also assumes a broad definition of what counts as research in order that teaching-related research should enjoy parity of esteem.

- *Shared governance*. Universities need to involve academic staff more fully in a wider range of decisions and at every level of institutional decision making. This would require a new balance between administrative and academic staff and systems of shared governance covering every aspect of institutional life—the aim being to ensure that issues relating to teaching and learning were considered within as broad an institutional context as possible.

- *Cross-institutional provision*. There needs to be a process whereby students are able to transfer across institutions. This implies the need for agreements between institutions, or clusters of institutions, to ensure complementary and flexible modes of provision. A prestige-driven, competitive culture would thereby have to give way to a culture of cross-institutional collaboration and development so that barriers to student movement could be minimized.

Conclusion

What emerges from these illustrative categories is that money matters, but that what matters more is how that money is spent: to what uses it is put and what purposes it serves. If an increasing number of young people are to benefit from an uncompromisingly high quality of university education, then universities will have to change and the sector as a whole will have to shift. Neither universities, their publics, nor the government can have it all ways. If we value the university as a constituent element of our common good, then universities will have to re-order their priorities, the public will have to acknowledge that higher education is to be valued for its social as well as individual benefits, and government will have to ensure a strong public presence in whatever arrangements emerge from the current impasse.

That is a very tall order. But unless it is met, or at least seriously aspired to, the notion of "the common good" as applied to universities will be nothing more than a *memento mori*: a symbolic reminder of a sadly deceased ideal. "It is a truth much forgotten," as Inglis (2004: 23) puts it, "that the point of education is to help ensure that the society which is home to us all is capable of carrying on and will continue into a recognisable future." Either we cling to the idea of the university as bestowing optional individual benefits that must be privately costed, or we work towards the realisation of the idea of the university as providing necessary social benefits that must be publically costed. That is the clear choice.

12

TEACHING IN THE UNIVERSITY THE DAY AFTER TOMORROW

Paul Standish

Introduction

This chapter focuses on the ways that contemporary change in the understanding of the university has inevitable implications for teaching and learning, and in consequence for the substance of what is taught, and I propose to show that this is of significance for the public role of the university in circumstances of democracy. Notwithstanding policy statements in some countries that reaffirm the importance of teaching, in the US and the UK most obviously, the broad trend in higher education has been towards the promotion of learning in such a way as to efface teaching. There are, it is true, some good reasons for the emphasis on learning: first, teaching in the university has sometimes taken complacent and unimaginative forms, with insufficient sensitivity to students' individuality and motivation; second, the extended possibilities of learning that are opened by new technology should indeed be exploited, for they can be an important aid to widening participation; and third, learning must in some sense, to be sure, be the *raison d'être* of teaching. With the fashionable emphasis on "learner autonomy," however, there has been a neglect of the dynamics of teaching and learning. Moreover, in this climate current attempts to enhance teaching, especially through the provision of generic training courses, have in key respects curtailed teaching's possibilities. My purpose, however, is not to detail and to diagnose the current malaise—it is surely a malaise that currently confronts us—but rather to weigh the consequences of this effacement of teaching.

To explore these matters my discussion steps a little outside contemporary professionalised writings on higher education. It reflects on texts, drawn from different decades, which aspire to address a wider educated public and to offer a broader, longer-term vision. The texts in question raise questions about the

tensions between elitism and mass provision. They show some sensitivity to the interconnectedness of teaching, learning and content, and bear witness to the preciousness and the precariousness of good teaching. And they ask questions about the purpose and value of the university. But my discussion will attempt to go further, at least to be more explicit in showing that the teaching relation is crucial to human being, and that its curtailment undermines the political place of the university: it undermines its public importance in a democracy understood in terms of perfectionism. For how else can a democracy worthy of the name properly be understood?

Making History Happen

Looking back on the university life of an earlier generation or of another culture can be curiously disconcerting. Images of teaching and learning quickly date, and what at one time might have passed for sophistication quickly becomes jaded and can seem bogus or sham. Consider the following scene, at the University of Watermouth, some time in the late 1960s. "Classes at Watermouth," we are told,

> are not simply occasions for the one-directional transmission of knowledge; no, they are events, moments of communal interaction, or ... . happenings. There are students from Watermouth who, visiting some other university, where traditional teaching prevails, stare in amazement, as if confronted by some remarkable and exciting innovation; their classes are not like that.
>
> *(Bradbury, 2000: 136)*

It is the start of term, and Howard Kirk has just entered the seminar room to take his weekly class, Socsci 4.17. He sits with the handful of students, frock-coated, bearded, kaftanned, long-haired, as they await the arrival of George Carmody, the student who is to lead this week's seminar. When George arrives, wearing a university blazer and tie, with a white shirt and pressed grey flannels, his shoes as brightly polished as his brief-case, it is clear that his expectations of the class are at odds with those both of the other students and of Howard himself. For George has been studying Mill, Marx and Weber, as prescribed some months before, and he is ready to read a paper. But the "report" that George has ready is not what Howard had intended:

> "I asked you to go away and read their works, over the vacation . . . and then to make a verbal statement to this class, summing up your impressions. I didn't ask you to produce a written paper, and then sit here with your head hanging over it, presenting formalized and finished thoughts. What kind of group experience is that?" "You did say that, sir," says Carmody,

"but I thought I could do something more developed. I've put in so much time on this." "I don't want it developed," says Howard, "I want development to occur in discussion." "I'm sorry, Dr Kirk," says Carmody, "but I felt it was better. I mean, I felt I could sum this stuff up and get it out of the way so we didn't need to spend a lot of time going over and over it." "I want us to go over it," says Howard, "it's called discussion. Now put that script away. . ."

(ibid.: 141)

But after some further acrimonious exchange, in which Howard accuses George of being a "heavy, anal type" who will not risk his mind in the insecurity of discussion, with George acquiescing in this diagnosis of his "mental condition" and offering to seek from the Counselling service a note to that effect, it is agreed grudgingly that George will read his paper. But the paper, ploddingly read, is

dull, dogged stuff, an old scheme of words, a weak little plot, a culling of obvious quotations surrounded by obvious comments, untouched with sympathy or that note of radical fire that, in Howard's eyes, has so much to do with true intellectual awareness . . . It is the epitome of false consciousness; its ideas are fictions or pretences, self-serving, without active awareness; it moves towards its inevitable fate.

(ibid.: 142)

And eventually there is an interruption. An irritable question from a student puts George on the defensive, which prompts an angry complaint from Howard, and with this there is a confrontation ("I mean, are you sociology?" he challenges Howard *(ibid.:* 143))—in the fall-out from which George eventually erupts and leaves, clumsily letting the door bang shut behind him. The circle of people, habitués of Howard's seminar, stare after him and then "resume their eye-to-eye sociological huddle" *(ibid.:* 144).

George is referred to as an "an item, preserved in some extraordinary historical pickle, from the nineteen fifties or before; he comes out of some strange fold in time" *(ibid.:* 140); but in not changing, so Malcolm Bradbury seems to tell us, in this dark satire of the university, he paradoxically changes more than anyone else—that is, he somehow resists or is impervious to the formulaic conversion, the raised consciousness, that for everyone else is *de rigueur*. This is of course a dystopian vision, for Howard Kirk is the eponymous History Man, the man whose radical words and, of course, acts make history happen.

Visions of the University

What interests me in revisiting Bradbury's text, first published in 1975, is how this work can be read today. For the dynamics of the satire, which is given to us in a zesty present tense, with authorial point of view tacitly ceded, as it were, to the all-commanding perspective of Howard, depends upon social relations and politics and pedagogy whose tensions are now strangely remote. True, we can name these tensions easily enough, but it is hard to feel today the bite of Bradbury's satire and the darkness of its vision, without, that is, a certain suspension of disbelief. For we know, do we not, that the axioms of Kirk's world—where class struggle and false consciousness meet the revolutionary zeal of sociology—are no longer a part of ours, and the reasons for this are not difficult to explain (say, Thatcherism, the fall of the Berlin Wall, and 9/11, for a start)? So while there is something timeless and remarkable in Bradbury's dissection of the very ideology that sustains Kirk, with its degeneration into hypocrisy and opportunism, the detailing of this picture scarcely connects with where we are. For example, the bemused experience of Watermouth students on visiting other universities, described above, cannot easily be matched against similar stark contrasts in the contemporary experience of students. This is not to deny that there may be, somewhere or other, classes taking place in the ways described, but neither image provides a compelling picture of what is at stake in teaching and learning today.

The History Man came early in what was a wave of campus novels, the very idea of which soon became a familiar topic for doctoral dissertations. The humour that has typically characterised this genre often has its serious point in forms of satire, as we have seen is the case with Bradbury's book. This enables the projection, usually in tacit ways, of a vision of the university as worth defending and in need of defence typically on multiple fronts—against ideology, to be sure, but also against bureaucratisation or instrumentalisation or philistinism in various forms. And in this vision there is, again typically, some powerful sense of what is at stake in teaching and learning— that is, of their power and importance in a human life, not just as the means to acquiring knowledge and understanding, but as internal to the good life itself. It is this that I shall shortly explain more fully.

But let me move forward now by leaving the 1960s and considering another text written about a decade after Bradbury's: Allan Bloom's *The Closing of the American Mind*. When the book was first published, in 1987, it quickly became a surprise best-seller. Here was a Chicago intellectual—at the time of writing Bloom was a Professor in the Committee on Social Thought and the College and co-director of the John M. Olin Center for Inquiry into the Theory and Practice of Democracy at the University of Chicago, in addition to having been recipient, in 1967, of the Clark Teaching Award—writing a polemic against the contemporary university in a manner that drew much in substance and style from Nietzsche. Bloom's book is calculated to offend, and it does this *inter alia* by blatantly attacking developments in Black Studies, Gender Studies and popular culture, reserving particular venom for the mindlessness, so it seems, of pop music. One finds Baudelaire, Bach and Barthes juxtaposed against the Beatles, and Rawls, Rousseau and Racine against the Rolling Stones. Bloom's plea is ultimately for an education based on the Great Books. He is not blind to the problems associated with this, he assures us, and nor does he think these should be ducked:

> Of course, the only serious solution is the one that is almost universally rejected: the good old Great Books approach, in which a liberal education means reading certain generally recognized classic texts, just reading them, letting them dictate what the questions are and the method of approaching them—not forcing them into categories we make up, not treating them as historical products, but trying to read them as their authors wished them to be read. I am perfectly well aware of, and actually agree with, the objections to the Great Books cult. It is amateurish; it encourages an autodidact's self-assurance without competence; one cannot read all of the Great Books carefully; if one only reads Great Books, one can never know what a great, as opposed to an ordinary, book is; there is no way of determining who is to decide what a Great Book or what the canon is; books are made the ends and not the means; the whole movement has a certain coarse evangelistic tone that is the opposite of good taste; it engenders a spurious intimacy with greatness; and so forth.
>
> *(Bloom, 1987: 344)*

Now certainly this seems a plausible enough rehearsal of the reasonable objections that can be made to Bloom's preferred approach, but his confident claims for the pedagogical success of such a curriculum are perhaps more questionable. He continues:

> But one thing is certain: wherever the Great Books make up a central part of the curriculum, the students are excited and satisfied, feel they are doing something that is independent and fulfilling, getting something from the university they cannot get elsewhere. The very fact of this special experience, which leads nowhere beyond itself, provides them with a new alternative and a respect for study itself. The advantage they get is an awareness of the classic—particularly important for our innocents; an acquaintance with what big questions were when there were still big questions; models, at the very least, of how to go about answering them; and, perhaps most important of all, a fund of shared experiences and thoughts on which to ground their friendships with one another. Programs based upon judicious use of great texts provide the royal road to students' hearts. Their gratitude at learning of Achilles or the categorical imperative is boundless.
>
> *(ibid.)*

Is *this* plausible? Certainly there are many who have been inspired and enthused by the general education Bloom prizes so highly, but how far does this position presume the kind of elite student whom Bloom would typically have encountered at Chicago or Yale or Cornell? To be fair, however, he does not imagine this to be an education for all, however gladly he would extend such provision. And he has nothing against the various forms of technical training that students will receive in other institutions of higher learning. But the university, to be worthy of *its* name, must preserve commitments to the general education he advocates. Without a shared vision of the public good, such as might be engendered by enquiry of this kind, we are at the mercy of the public authority of the entertainment industry (*ibid.*: 73). Without this, democracy declines into a clamour of personal (often commercially driven) preferences, while in the university the central place of philosophy will be ceded to a democracy of subjects, the relativism of which means that philosophy has no greater status than photography or fashion. "As Saul Bellow has put it," Bloom writes, "public virtue is a kind of ghost town into which anyone can move and declare himself sheriff" (*ibid.*: 85).

There is no doubt that *The Closing of the American Mind* had its impact partly because of the time in which it was written—that is, a time of strong conservative governments, when capitalism's successes (and excesses) were burgeoning and communism was everywhere in decay. Hence, the much-criticised elitism of the book was far from a barrier to its success but rather found a ready readership amongst newly confident conservative classes. But Bloom's message is far more sophisticated and responsible in educational terms than such a gloss would allow. For at its heart there is a vision of the essential relationship between liberal learning and the public good, which is realised partly negatively through the exposure of the banality into which democracy can decline. "Neither duty nor pleasure involves students with the political," he writes, "and our lives exhibit in the extreme what Burke and Tocqueville said about the disappearance of citizens and statesmen. The petty personal interests of youth—'making it', finding a place for oneself—persevere throughout life" (*ibid.*). Hence, he appreciates at least the honesty of students in the 1980s who could only laugh when asked to think of themselves as agents in world history. While such cynicism is desirably realistic for the students themselves, it can scarcely be healthy for the public realm or for the democracy that professes to enshrine. Students today have been schooled to be calculated in the education they undertake, with a firm eye on "making it" or finding a place for themselves, and they can scarcely have grounds to be any the less cynical.

In sum, Bloom's book is misunderstood to the extent that it is seen as a reactionary tract pandering to the conservatives of the day. While it surely lapses at times into insufficiently focused polemic, at its best its account of a liberal education is, in the best Nietzschean sense, untimely: that is, it carries a message that the public it addresses is not (yet) ready to hear. At their best, again, books of this kind are not written for a ready-made audience, neatly identified in publishers' lists (Books on Higher Education): they create their own readership; they create new readers.

It is very much with this thought in mind that I want to turn now to a more recent text, this one also by a highly eminent philosopher: Martha Nussbaum's

Not for Profit: Why Democracy Needs the Humanities (2010). In a Foreword, Ruth O'Brien welcomes the book's addition to The Public Square, the series in which it appears, in virtue especially of the fact that it offers readers

> a "call to action" in the form of a plan that replaces an educational model that undercuts democracy with one that promotes it. It builds a convincing, if at first counterintuitive, case that the very foundation of citizenship—not to mention national success—rests on the humanities and arts. We neglect them at our peril.
>
> *(Nussbaum, 2010: xi)*

In these commitments, as well as in Nussbaum's explicit faith in a liberal education, there is much that aligns her position with Bloom's, and both books are written with a visionary zeal that sets them apart from the mainstream of more professionalised writings on higher education. Nussbaum's relatively upbeat subtitle can be paralleled in spirit if not in tone with the darker lament that appears inside the cover of Bloom's book, "How Higher Education has Failed Democracy and Impoverished the Souls of Today's Students"; though certainly Nussbaum can hit a more sombre note too, her last chapter having the title "Democratic Education on the Ropes." In both authors, classic texts hold a prominent place and the salience of philosophical thinking is emphasised. And the parallel extends insofar as both authors write in an agreeably accessible, non-technical style, with ample illustration of the ideas they advance, albeit that this is somewhat anecdotal. But at this point I want to begin to draw out some of the differences between these texts, and in doing this it will be appropriate to keep an eye on the cultural and political differences between the times when they were published—a period of just over two decades.

To begin with, some obvious differences should be noted. Bloom's text is considerably longer, at nearly 400 pages of relatively close print in contrast to Nussbaum's 150-odd pages of generously spaced text, some chapters culminating with sets of bullet-pointed recommendations. While her book is about educational institutions generally, his speaks only of the university. While his style is polemical and virtually affronts the reader, hers, though no doubt impassioned, is more gently accessible and courteous in its address. Her book is apparently supported in part by some non-systematic empirical work, as was the case, more systematically, with her earlier educational text *Cultivating Humanity* (Nussbaum, 1997), while his relies on arm-chair theorising. I shall return to these differences below, but let me first draw attention to three facets of the account of liberal education that she develops: the importance she attaches to classic texts, her faith in Socratic method, and her endorsement of educational progressivism.

Nussbaum's commitment to classical texts is illustrated vividly with her description of a particular student. Thus, we find Billy Tucker strangely moved when he learns in Krishna Mallick's classes about the life and death of Socrates. Mallick is acknowledged to be an inspiring teacher, and we are told how she leads students on the course through the careful analysis of political speeches, eventually requiring them to formulate arguments with which they do not in fact agree. Thus, Nussbaum writes:

> Tucker was surprised to discover that he was being asked to argue against the death penalty, although he actually favored it. He had never understood, he said, that one could produce arguments for a position that one does not hold oneself. He told me that this experience gave him a new attitude toward political discussion: Now he is more inclined to respect the opposing position and to be curious about the arguments on both sides and what the two sides might share, rather than seeing the discussion as simply a way of making boasts and assertions. We can see how this humanizes the political "other", making the mind see the opposing person as a rational being who may share at least some thoughts with one's own group
>
> *(Nussbaum, 2010: 52)*

So far so good. How could anyone committed to higher education, one might think, reasonably take exception to this? For surely this is good teaching and a real contribution to democratic citizenship, and although education should not be primarily directed towards economic growth, it is perfectly reasonable to point out how abilities such as Tucker acquires can contribute to students' working lives in diverse ways. In fact, this extract is taken from "Socratic Pedagogy: The Importance of Argument," the longest chapter in the book, and it is plain that this, also referred to frequently in terms of "critical thinking," is central to Nussbaum's strategy and purpose. The position advanced is recognisable enough, but she extends it imaginatively with reference to the thinking of Rabindranath Tagore—a significant presence in the book as a whole, with education in India forming a welcome counter-balance to the default educational landscape of the USA—and through an acknowledgement of the achievements of progressive education (Rousseau, Pestalozzi, Froebel, Bronson Alcott, Dewey), culminating in a celebration of Matthew Lipman's Philosophy for Children. The animus behind this conjoining of classical influences and progressivism is a strong aversion to rote learning, fact-stuffing and other forms of mindless assimilation. And, once again, who would argue with that?

But while the broad sentiments expressed in the book are surely to be endorsed, it is here that I want to question its discursive place and purpose. Eloquently written, it has the character of good quality journalism. Ostensibly imaginative in its range of reference, and not blinkered by American parochialism, this is a book that will strike a chord with many readers, and for those unfamiliar with more searching literature in the philosophy of education, it will come home as refreshingly original. Indeed it is worth saying in passing that one of the problems with the philosophy of education is that while, on the one hand, it addresses topics about which an educated public will undoubtedly feel qualified and justified in entering into discussion, the inherent philosophical complexity of educational matters means that rigorous enquiry into them is likely to slip off the radar of public awareness. Hence, there is a readership and a demand for books of this genre that Nussbaum's writing is eminently equipped to satisfy. It should be apparent then that this, unlike Bloom's, is anything but an untimely book. In assessing its value a fine line is to be drawn between, on the one hand, its success in expressing to a wider audience the importance of the humanities for democracy, and as a correction to the harm that many of our institutional practices currently inflict, and, on the other, its incorporation into that bourgeois, liberal-secular discourse that has become one of the hallmarks of the contemporary public realm. Indeed some of the recommendations that she offers have about them a lack of precision that descends into blandness. The irritant in the Socratic gadfly can then become less the crisis that is a provocation to think something new and more a means of inoculation against too great a disturbance.

The questions these reflections raise are: What kind of discourse is appropriate to the public discussion of the university, especially insofar as this is to reach beyond the exigencies of today? What kind of philosophical reflection properly supports this? In the penultimate section of this paper I develop a thought that is congruent with the ideas of both Bloom and Nussbaum, as it is with the commitments to the university that motivate Bradbury's satire. I shall argue that any defensible account of the university must take teaching to be at its heart. To make this point is to say something about the very nature of discourse itself, at least insofar as this is appropriate to the university and to democracy.

Teaching in the University the Day After Tomorrow

The book that established Nussbaum's reputation, *The Fragility of Goodness* (1983), is a remarkably rich, imaginative and subtle reading of Ancient Greek philosophy and drama, and it broke new ground in the reading of Plato. Questions of education are never far from that text, and probably these are realised especially in her discussions of Plato's dialogue *The Symposium*. I mention this work not as a prelude to examining her discussion but rather in acknowledgement. My reference to that dialogue, so important for teaching and learning, must needs be more succinct.

The Symposium incorporates an aspect of Plato's vision of education, which casts teaching and learning in erotic terms. The sense of *eros* here is critically different from the modern associations of the term. Yes, it extends from the sexual, but this as a category scarcely figures in the way it does today; it involves a sense of longing for what continues to be beyond one's full or final grasp, with a sense of a good that defies containment or even full specification and that in the end is inexhaustible. Thus, it embodies a conception of education as beyond any merely functional training and reaching towards a higher possibility, a greater good. The path towards such a good is to be found in the dynamic context of human relationships, where a triangle is constituted between the teacher, the learner and what is learned. It is important that none of the three points in this triangle can be removed: the relationship between the people exists in their engagement with the subject matter, such that it is elevated in response to the good that the subject enshrines, but perverted to the extent that the personal relationship is itself the object of attention (say, where the teacher is idolised, where harmful technicised models of the master-teacher prevail, or where the student is sentimentalised as in some versions of progressivism); and the subject matter comes alive in the interaction between teacher and student, which is to say in dialogue or conversation, while it is debased where the content is deadened (say, fetishised or commodified or otherwise turned to stone (see Standish, 2011)). It is in this way that it is appropriate to speak of the erotic charge in learning, where, at its best, a peculiar attraction is experienced by student and teacher alike. This is not to be characterised exclusively in terms of their personal relationship: it exists inasmuch as they are drawn by the value of what is in question or the subject of enquiry, which the Latin *studere* nicely realises—to study is to love. And beyond the immediacy of direct dialogue, such a relationship extends through the various forms of enquiry, in laboratories and libraries, in books and journals, where one continues to be drawn by an affection that is ultimately conditioned or made possible by this triangular relation. In this respect, Michael Oakeshott is right that disciplines are forms of conversation.

If the account is sound, is this just an incidental fact about teaching and learning, something to be compartmentalised within our higher education? I have drawn attention to the fact that many people who have benefited from a university education typically cherish some favourable thoughts of teachers who impressed them, and probably the brief account given here resonates also with other aspects of their experience, whether as students or teachers or in research, in formal education or beyond. To speak of this in terms of *eros* may then be rather more plausible than it seems at first sight. One might want to say, moreover, that the student, the teacher or the researcher who is *not* always drawn towards some further possibility of understanding somehow falls short of the demands of her subject, acquiescing in a kind of complacency or hubris (see Standish, 2005). Thus, there must be something perfectionist about enquiry of this kind, and while this must be true of education generally it is perhaps of most obvious pertinence in what is to be called "higher education."

Nussbaum shows the value of critical, Socratic thinking in humanising the political "other." This is convincing enough, but the limitation of her manner of addressing this lies in the fact that it constructs alterity in a particular way—say, within a politics of different viewpoints and identities. This falls short of the deeper alterity that is realised in the relationships depicted in *The Symposium*. For there it seems that alterity is rather a condition of human relationships, or perhaps a potential within them when they are rightly oriented. The arena of such relationships is then seen less in terms of cooperation amongst equals than as inherently structured by asymmetries. Such asymmetries resound in the words of great thinkers. In an address to students in 1838, Ralph Waldo Emerson declared: "Truly speaking, it is not instruction, but provocation, that I can receive from another soul" (Emerson, 1838). And we can recall also the apparent hyperbole of Emmanuel Levinas's claim, made of our relation to the other human being: the other teaches me, addressing me from an interiority I cannot fathom but to which I must respond.

If a right conception of this erotic, perfectionist dimension of education is plausible, this sequence of remarks can be seen as attempts to disrupt the levelling assumptions that dominate our understanding of human relations. It is important to realise that this is not a matter of social equality, understood, say, in terms of the just distribution of resources or fair access to educational provision: it has to do with human relations themselves and, given that we are always humans-in-relation, with what it is to be a human being. If this is so, it begins to justify the seemingly exorbitant nature of the vocabulary above.

I find a final helpful hyperbole in a phrase from Nietzsche's preface to the 1886 edition of *Human, All Too Human*, later repeated in from *Beyond Good and Evil*, and then again in a new preface to *The Gay Science*, the significance of which Stanley Cavell has elaborated in the title essay to his 2005 collection. The phrase expresses Nietzsche's aspirations for a possibility of the human, perhaps for a possibility of philosophy itself, that is surely appropriate to any conception of the university that is to escape the exigencies of the moment and its functional incorporation as an arm of the state: "A man of tomorrow and the day after tomorrow." In fact, to echo my earlier remarks about the untimely and about the kind of discourse in respect of the university that we should seek, Nietzsche identifies "free spirits" of this kind with what he specifies as the desired audience for his words (see Cavell, 2005: 117). And so, to reiterate my affirmation of the perfectionist longing in teaching and learning, with its necessary avoidance of the allure of decadent self-satisfaction, let me press the significance of the following remarks of Cavell:

> I adapt Nietzsche's characterization of the philosopher—the man of tomorrow and the day after tomorrow—noting that the casual distinction in English between tomorrow and the day after tomorrow translates the German *Morgen* and *Übermorgen*, and I claim (subject to correction, if not to anticipation) that the prefix *Über-*, so characteristic a site of Nietzschean inflection, is in play here, as marking a distinction homologous with that between *Mensch* and *Übermensch*, man and superman, or over-man, or after-man? To what end? Take *Morgen* in its sense of morning, as well as of tomorrow, and we may discern an idea of an after-, or over-, or super-morning.
>
> *(ibid.: 118)*

Let us step aside for a moment to attend to the nature of the language we are presented with here, and let us ponder its demands on the reader: its rendering uncommon what is most common (morning), its foregrounding of differences between languages, its registering of hyperbolic tropes. And, more thematically, let us consider its anticipation of Thoreau's celebrated pun, which highlights the proximity of "morning" to "mourning"; which is to say that the readiness for something new implies a readiness to let go—say, release ourselves from our most comfortable thoughts, unloosen our fixed assurances, be ready to live in a new way. The words here bring us up short, their recalcitrance emphasised when we confront the difficulties of translation, but with an activation of thought that moves in ways beyond predictable linear directions and disturbs the ease we habitually find in our words.

Conclusion

Bloom acknowledges the elitism in his account, but it is right in my view to do something more than acknowledge it. In some ways I regret the prominence of classic texts in the depictions of education that both he and Nussbaum provide. And there is something faintly patronising about Nussbaum's illustration of Billy Tucker's initiation into Socratic pedagogy, however remote this surely is from her intentions. I would rather stress the ways that the insights into teaching and learning that are afforded by *The Symposium* in fact have their relevance well beyond the circumscribed vision of the university that Bloom offers; indeed ultimately, as I have tried to show, these are at the heart of the human condition. To speak in more specifically educational terms, they are to be found in the multiple circumstances in which a teacher leads a student into a practice—whether in the pursuit of the humanities in the university or in the craft activities of the community college, whether at the hands of an expert coach in sport or a gifted teacher of music. Moreover, to the extent that human practices (what other kind are there?) are necessarily rule-governed, and especially insofar as these are the not the tightly formulated rules of games or legal contracts but rather open-ended rules in accordance with which action continually reshapes the practice, there will be some relation to the teacher, not just to a trainer, in virtually all we do. For what is human life outside such practices? It is right to point out that so much more is learned than is taught; but what is learned is conditioned by practices in which teaching necessarily plays a part.

I have tried to demonstrate the interconnectedness of teaching, learning and content in terms of a triangle of relationships, such that over-emphasis on one or the other causes education to become degenerate, and I have claimed that this is crucial not only for academic enquiry but for the sustenance of the public realm. In the process I have drawn attention to the problematic nature of writing about these matters. And I am inclined to add that this discursive difficulty rightly challenges us when we think about education and the public realm. In contrast to the confrontational campuses of the 1960s, which Bradbury depicts, higher education today has assimilated ideological difference to the common measure of audit. It has domesticated and thereby neutralised critique. The eros of *The Symposium* has become "Socratic method," its humour and inspiration dulled, its sting drawn, in the cheery efficiencies of professionalised practice. And it is no longer clear that Bradbury's satire or Bloom's polemic would have purchase here. Are there "free spirits" to read such works? (Are there free spirits still? Are there *yet*?) Is there a language in which such works can now be written? The reading that is required here is precisely what is being lost, and our educational regimes collude in this in various ways—not least in the modelling of effective teaching that increasingly holds sway. This loss is one that afflicts the university, and in doing this it stultifies the public realm. Then the threat to teaching is a threat to democracy. Certainly this can be remedied, but no immediate remedy is in view—not today, and not tomorrow. But the university of the day after tomorrow can be a place where these best possibilities of teaching are recovered, and in the end these will demonstrate its essential public place in the democracy to come.

13

THE UNIVERSITY

A Public Issue

Jan Masschelein and Maarten Simons

Introduction

We are no human capital! This slogan of protesting students in Germany is a rare political articulation (Linksruck 2003). It signals a moment of collective de-identification. Clearly, the capitalization of humanity is an old story. The story of the perverse humanization of capital however is more recent, and students seem to be the first victims. The term "students" has become synonymous with the resources to be exploited, the talents to be mobilized, the object of investment, the guarantee of a country's competitiveness or, when addressing the possible disobedient component of human capital, the customers to be seduced. Their de-identification is at once an affirmation: "we are students!" Despite the long-standing lamenting of academics and all other inhabitants of the institution called "university," it is perhaps the students who really experience what is happening to us and through us today.

Lamenting has become a second nature of many academics; as if resistance in the margins, remembering the good old academic values and ceremonial critique of policy and administration, makes their search for excellence bearable. In fact, nothing seems to be unbearable for academics today. Their search for excellence has become a way of life, their way of life. And students become the victims of this way of life: the victims of a cold war in the name of excellence, of the daily struggles in the war on talent and human capital, and the innovation race associated with academic entrepreneurship. Maybe only in that moment, the moment that students declare themselves to be no human capital, the entrepreneurial academics and the entrepreneurial university become the victims of their own wars of excellence. Looking over the battlefield of human capital, they come to notice that there are no longer students—those who want to study, that is, those who *have* no interest but *are interested* (in a matter) and therefore want to expose themselves beyond any logic of investment or calculation on rates of return.

That moment is also the moment that inaugurated this short essay.[1] The moment that made us start thinking about the institution we call "university" and about what it actually could mean to be "academic" and "student." Perhaps with hesitation, and too hastily and stuttering, this essay seeks to declare affirmatively: we are students, we are academics, we are a university! Indeed, what we want to offer is an exercise of thought that attempts to distil the spirit of the university, to give the university air to breathe, and to give her a voice in the global, European and national wars on excellence. This is not just to say it is an absurd war and not just to question the permanent mobilization of human and other resources, and not only to draw our attention to all the casualties of the academic fights.

The University as a Unique Pedagogical Form

Indeed, as a voice that stems from the university's morphology, our exercise also tells something else: the university has a unique form, or, more particularly, the university constitutes a pedagogical form *sui generis*, and this form articulates a *public* space, a *public* time and a *public* matter. Hence, and contrary to what is often suggested, the uniqueness of the university in our view resides neither in the fact that she combines three (separate) functions or that her staff combines three roles (research, teaching, public service), nor in the fact that her teaching would be research-based. Instead, it resides in its *unique pedagogical form*, a form *sui generis*, which is in itself at once investigation, education and world-making. It is a *form that turns matter into public matter* (into a world) and gathers a public of students and professors, that is, of learners and academics *turned into public figures*. The paradigmatic (not exclusive) figure of this unique pedagogical form, as we will discuss in the essay, is the public lecture.[2]

It is tempting to look back during this discussion, and to reclaim the classic or modern university to oppose its current deformation in the global, competitive arena. However, we read the long history of the university (including the classic or modern university) to a large extent as a history of the taming of the university's public form. Public here[3] refers in a broad sense to what and who is de-appropriated or disconnected from particular interests (of social groups, professions, markets, states . . .) and usages (in the sphere of production and reproduction). This movement of de-appropriation or disconnection can be called also a "profanation" in the precise way that Agamben indicates: "[p]ure, profane, freed from sacred names is that thing that is being replaced in view of the common use by people" (Agamben 2005: 96, our translation). And sacred then means: having a defined, particular use, i.e. a privatized or appropriate(d) meaning.[4] Offering public time, public space and public matter, and hence available for nobody in particular or for anybody, is dangerous in the eyes of all those who want to conserve or protect a particular social, cultural, political or economic order. From that perspective, not only the current war on excellence and the imperative of innovation (reflected in the entrepreneurial university), but also the modern wars on culture and the imperative of reason (modern university), and perhaps the holy wars in the name of divine law (medieval university) neutralized the public form of the university (De Ridder-Symoens, 1992).

There is, indeed, a history to be told about the neutralization of the university, about its deformation. It is however beyond the scope of this essay to present a detailed history of neutralization and taming of the university's public form. Furthermore, we are abstracting from all kinds of cultural differences and specific (national) traditions in higher education. Our main concern instead is to consider some of the major *movements* of *de-identification* during history that preceded the current movement expressed in the statement "we are no human capital." Hence, the first section of this essay offers a short overview of the movements that inaugurated dimensions of the public, pedagogic form of the university. These historical excursions prepare for our articulation of the public form of the university in the second part of the essay.

Movements of De-identication and Profanation

The Profanation of the Book

Universities have been called the most important legacy that the Middle Ages offered us. Their origin lies in a particular gathering which included a particular pedagogical form (a particular kind of study and teaching) and ensured a particular kind of life detached from the immediate demands of the economic and social world and from the orders of the cathedral schools and monasteries out of which they originated (Verger, 1992). The model of this gathering was not Plato's academy, but the medieval associations called "universitas." The term was used to indicate all kinds of associations and therefore needed to be specified: the *universitas magistrorum et scholarium* or the *universitas studii*. It is crucial to note that it was not an association of masters and pupils or apprentices (*operae*), but of masters (later becoming professors) and *students*.

The first movement of de-identification, thus, can be summarized in the declaration: *"We are no pupils, disciples, apprentices, but students—universitas studii."* This declaration involves a de-identification with practices of initiation or preparation to become part of particular social, cultural, vocational or religious groups. What is affirmed is that time for study is "free time" (scholé), that is, time freed from social, religious or economic concerns and free to get involved with the text. And, of course, the de-identification was immediately accompanied with re-identification strategies (e.g. to instaure professions and disciplines) and with new exclusions and seclusions, but what interests us here is precisely the original movement itself which we consider to be the invention of a pedagogic form. The university, then, was a new form of *scholé*, of *public* study (outside the seclusion of the monastery cell) and its inhabitants were masters as well as students for whom the search for truth and knowledge was not a private calling, but a public activity. Its core was a particular form of public lecture which was bound to the birth of the "book-text," which no longer appeared as the symbol of a cosmic and divine reality, but as the materialization of abstractions and concepts, that is, of thoughts.

A major invention of the medieval university is the written text as optical object (and therefore readable—instead of audible—in the sense we are used to today[5]). The book-text indeed is available for *public study,* and makes it actually possible (Illich, 1992). The invention of the readable text allows words to become disconnected from a particular usage by a particular group and no longer "sacred." This book-text asked for interpretation and commentary. The public lecture was a *collegium,* a reading together and the gathering of a thinking public/audience around a common text. And the available book-text includes a profanation, that is, an availability for public use. This public study did not require obedience, but a critical-interpreting attitude related to an *amor veritatis* (love of truth) and *amor sciendi* (love of knowledge) (Verger, 1992). It had no direct use for any profession, but led to the right (and sometimes the duty) to lecture publicly at all European universities (*licentia ubique docendi*). We cannot go into the fortunes of this medieval invention, and it is clear that right from the beginning it went with all kind is of strategies to tame its public form (e.g. by turning the association into a kind of professional guild and by "disciplining" the knowledge) and was bound to a persistent experience of living according to a divine order and its moral law. Obviously, the attempts to neutralize this act of profanation and to tame the perceived religious, social and political dangers of written/readable texts are numerous, but it is a crucial movement in inventing a public, pedagogic form.

The Profanation of Reason

"We are no state officials, no civil servants, no clergymen or appointed teachers, but scholars." This second movement articulates an attempt to invent a public, pedagogic form beyond the nation state and its civic and juridical framing of human affairs. What is claimed for—as Immanuel Kant articulates very strongly—is a public sphere where reasoning is a goal in itself and in view of which the public sphere the state claims for itself is but a place for the private use of reason and obedience. What is at stake in this movement is a de-identification with the private use of reason and all sorts of domestication of reason, but at the same time an affirmation of the public use of reason.

In his famous essay "What is Enlightenment?" Kant relates Enlightenment to freedom in "the most innocuous form of all—freedom to make public use of one's reason in all matters" (Kant, 1784/1977: 55). Kant continues by clarifying that he means by the public use of one's own reason, the "use which anyone may make of it as a *man of learning (Gelehrte)* addressing the entire *reading public*" (*ibid.*: 55). As man of learning one is a world citizen, who, as Kant says, is not *instructing* pupils, but "publicly voices his thoughts," "imparts them to the public" (*ibid.*: 56). A man of learning (a scholar, in the English translation of his text) is "addressing the real public (i.e. the world at large)" and speaks "in his own person" (*ibid.*: 57). Indeed, learned individuals are putting "before the public their thoughts," with "no fear of phantoms" (*ibid.*: 59).

Kant contrasts the public use of one's own reason with its private use. This is the use which one makes of it when one acts in "a particular civil post or office" (*ibid.*: 55) that is "employed by the government for public ends" (*ibid.*: 56). In that case one "acts as part of the machine" (*ibid.*: 56). And as part of a public institution (a machine with public ends) one speaks "in someone else's name" (*ibid.*: 56) and speaking becomes a kind of teaching or instruction. According to Kant, the use which one makes of one's reason as part of a social machine or institution is purely private, since these, however large they may be, are "never any more than a domestic gathering (*häusliche Versammlung*)" (*ibid.*: 57).

Let us try to rephrase what Kant is saying here. The public character of one's speech refers to a certain use of one's capacity to reason, a capacity which, as Kant explains in the beginning of his essay, everybody has, the *only limits*, according to Kant, being laziness and cowardice. The public character, thus, has to do with the particular use itself. Public use, however, refers to the use when we are addressing the public in its truest sense, that is, being constituted by anyone who has the capacity for reasoning, that is, "the public" beyond any machine or institution. Here, Kant locates the figure of the scholar and, as Kant states, *anyone* can be this figure. The figure of the scholar is characterized by an equalizing ethos, addressing the other under the assumption of equality—that is, the profanation of reason as something everybody can use when not lazy or faint-hearted—and speaking in her own name, so demonstrating an ethos to risk oneself. This is at once an *experimental ethos* because the scholar exposes herself to the limits (of the institution or machine) and is transforming the issue one is speaking about into a public issue, that is, making it public.

However, Kant also immediately closed off the opening he made insofar as (1) he confined his public to a *reading* public and insofar as (2) reasoning finally implies for him a very particular judgemental ethos of obedience (see Foucault, 1997). At this point—and by Kant himself—the public use of reason is tamed by outlining the limits within which the correct use of reason should stay—and Kant now starts to address his readers as "judges" (i.e. people who are submitting themselves to a tribunal, in this case, the tribunal of reason). Kant's attempt to define the "right" use of reason is about the taming of the public use of reason and the neutralization of the university's public, pedagogic form.

The Profanation of Culture and of Time

The third movement claims: "*This institution is not the university and we are no generation (no modern subject), but students.*" These claims echo the de-identification

in 1968 with forms of authority based on culture (and all other forms of pater-
nalism) and with a rigid nation-based and bureaucratically organized academic
system. Claiming that the *institution* is not the university, that what it is to be
student should not be equated with the object of the institutionalized pedagogy
of enlightenment means that study and teaching content are disconnected from
the sacred, modern project of cultivation. Being a student is being part of a movement, and hence the inauguration of a present moment and situation in between
past and future. The affirmation of being a student becomes at once the affirmation of a revolutionary event and enthusiasm that transcends history.

As Readings (1996: 147) writes, what matters is:

> that the narrative of *Bildung*—of simple passage from infancy to adulthood,
> from dependency to emancipation (the Kantian narrative of enlightenment
> that characterizes the knowledge process itself in modernity)—has been
> rejected by the students in the name of an uncertainty.

What is broken down is the "arrow of time" (pointing to the enlightened future)
that was institutionalized in the modern university, and what is interrupted is any
teleological understanding of being a student under the sign of cultivation.

Professors can no longer profess in the name of (their) culture or in the name
of the future their knowledge holds for the new generation. Being a student now
is being marked with at once a (revolutionary) enthusiasm and an openness and
uncertainty. What is invented is a new public, pedagogic form to gather students and
professors, and to organize and "live" the university. The involved profanation of
culture and institutions opens up a form for students and professors to imagine collectively the future (and past), and to seek for time and space for study, for research,
for teaching, for public discussion inside or outside the dismantled institutions.

Students and professors do not *have* specific interests, but as part of a public
sphere they *are* interested and attached to a world beyond national culture, rigid
bureaucracy and institutional logic. Clearly, revolutionary enthusiasm is at once
canalized, movements are institutionalized, student leaders turn out to be candidate politicians (for institutionalized parties) and public attachment becomes
reframed in the logic of service for society. The organization of interest groups,
identity projects, public surveys and pedagogies of self-directed and individualized
learning seemed to function as an effective strategy to neutralize the public power
of imagination. Yet, the profanation of the sacred divide between generations, the
sacred character of what should be transmitted (knowledge and culture) and the
sacred arrow of time (time having a defined telos, being "progress") inaugurated
attempts to shape a public, pedagogic form.

The Profanation of Production and Circulation

The declaration in the first line of this essay captures perfectly the final movement:
"*We are no human capital, we are no learners, we are students.*" And perhaps, and this

is the declaration articulated in this essay: "We are no entrepreneurs, no knowledge producers, no knowledge transmitters, no innovators, we are professors." Maybe this articulates indeed the de-identification with the current entrepreneurial university, the profanation of time of investment, calculation and choice and the breaking through one's increasingly individualized circle of learning and the endless accumulation of credits. What is at stake is the profanation of the (productive) *time* of knowledge, transmission and innovation and the (competitive) *space* of environments, circulation and mobilization. But perhaps, we should acknowledge also another profanation. Despite previous movements of profanation, and despite massification and democratization, the academic community kept addressing its public as a public of *readers*, people with erudition, carriers and representatives of culture.

Perhaps today, we witness a profanation of thinking and communication, that is, thinking and speaking become disconnected from cultures, languages and their spatio-temporal fixations. What else does the so-called consumer, network, online student—often criticized or ridiculed by academics who embrace tradition and the idea of cultivation and reason—articulate then but that everyone is able to think, to speak or to communicate? Of course, this democracy in thought and communication—and the clear message "you, academics, do not have to teach us to think, to speak, to communicate"—could be fearfully perceived as undermining the very foundations of the university. This message is particularly fearful for those academics who embrace the idea that thinking and communication cannot be disconnected from culture and language, and that writing and reading books are the obligatory passage points to enter the kingdom of truth. Such a message is specifically a harsh one for those post-modern academics—the last inhabitants of the university of reason or culture—who want to *explain* exactly that and how we are all captured by language, embedded within cultures, trapped within an endless series of representations and sentenced to an endless construction and reconstruction of reality. Isn't the (democratic) message here: "stop thinking about the (im)possibility of thinking, stop talking about the (im)possibility of communication, but start thinking and talking about something"? To assume a radical democracy in thought and communication comes down to assuming everyone is able to communicate and think, and consequently experiencing thinking and speaking, thought and language as "pure means" to be collectively involved with a matter of concern. Indeed, maybe this profanation of communication inaugurates the invention of new pedagogic forms, which are to be welcomed and where students and professors are interested in something and where that thing becomes an issue that gathers a thinking public.

The morphology presented in the next section is in line with this fourth movement, but it draws as well on the inventions of the previous movements, holding to the assumption that a form is an invention and can and should be re-invented. Our attempt to clarify the university's specific form is an attempt to articulate a specific *pedagogic* form, and the "public lecture" is to be conceived as the paradigmatic articulation of this form. We will clarify how, in a specific way and as a particular form, the public lecture integrates what is today differentiated in the so-called teaching/learning, research and service functions. (For how we understand "public lecture," see also endnote 2.)

Articulations of the University Form

A Matter of Public Lecturing

It may sound odd to bring public lecturing today to the foreground again. Max Horkheimer called it already in 1953 a "symptom of archaism" and "a failed secularisation of the sermon," where professors as guardians of the (scientific) truth give students a lecture. Indeed, why are professors still addressing masses of students today in the age of the World Wide Web during a public lecture? And yet, as well as professors holding on to this archaic form of education, students also seem to ask for public lectures and even question the tendency to student-focused/action-oriented forms of education. In line with Horkheimer, one could criticize that students prefer public lecturing because they need transparency and a clear overview, or they are in need of a kind of doctrine to orient them in a world that becomes more and more complex (and therefore rather show a longing for clear guidance, rather than for critical autonomous thought). But it is striking to notice that Horkheimer closes his critical comments on academic education and public lecturing with the idea that perhaps we need these *anachronistic* moments and archaic forms of academic education—which he also calls a *"Refugium"*—that encloses trust among students and professors beyond contractual relationships. The reason is that in the time/space of the lecture one is focused on something common or shared, that is, "a thing" or matter which is put on the table, so to say, and its truth. The thing in common asks for commitment and concern, it shows something about what living and living together is about, and hence it can be inspirational or edifying.

Giving a public lecture actually turns the figure of the academic (the scholar in Kant's terms) into the public figure of the professor. This figure does not enter the lecture hall as a researcher who presents "matters of facts" and how knowledge about these facts was produced. But s/he is also an instructor who turns the lecture hall into a learning environment and who makes a world of learning resources available to students in order to enable them to start their productive, and increasingly individualized and personalized, learning circles. During lecturing a professor puts something on the table, and this act encloses two movements: she/he talks about the things on the table as her/his "matter of concern," but these things and her/his talking and thinking are at once rendered present to an audience that becomes a public, a public of students.[6] Lecturing is a hesitating speech which slows us down and makes us think. It is too much a hesitating speech to be able to gather students around facts and it is too much a concerned speech to instruct students to deal productively with resources.

Contrary to teaching (a lesson), the professor addresses a public and he/she looks at him/herself as not essentially different from the gathered public. During the lecture, the professor indeed puts him/herself at the disposal of the matters of concern he/she presents and invites the students, as Goffman (1981) stresses, to get involved with something, assuming they are all equal in giving meaning and valuing what is put on the table. Indeed, putting something on the table includes an act of profanation. Facts and resources turn into issues and possible matters of concern by disconnecting words and things from particular usages and specific interests, and by "making them free for common use" so to speak. During lecturing, and to put it in a very broad way, something reveals its "issue-ness," that is, it reveals to us the question about how we are going to live with it.

In the lecture hall, the world is turned into a real and common issue and people into a concerned public. For the latter, we want to reserve the term students as far as studying implies to be devoted to think in the presence of an issue or common concern. In that way, becoming a student is always also being carried away beyond the lecture hall, beyond the lecturer, and towards the issue, towards the world. What is actually at stake is a form of public thinking (the public use of reason). The lecture hall and the public lecture, in the particular sense we want to understand it, are the place and time where people are placed out-of-position, in a position of exposure, outside the time of production and mobilization, because they are slowed down by a provocation to think, that is, to become attached to the issue, and to question it (Stengers, 2005). This provocation *finds its place* by putting a matter on the table and by making its protection and appropriation (for instance, as matters of facts "protected" by the particular use of methods and theories, or as the matter appropriated by a particular discipline) undone.

In sum, lecturing is about giving things the power to provoke students (and the professor him/herself) to think, instead of pointing students at the facts that should be known or the resources to be used in productive learning. Hence, the unique pedagogic form of the university is the form that makes thinking public and gathers a public around thoughts.

A Space and Time of Public Lecturing

Given this account the specificity of the public role of universities resides mainly with the professor's public thinking (study) and public speech, in lecture halls, auditoria, and seminar rooms. And we should certainly not forget the particular architecture of these places. Lecture halls or seminar rooms are often designed to gather people around some*thing*, to make things public and allow for a public to come into existence. These places could be described, drawing upon Foucault, as particular *heterotopia*, "a place without a place," as a kind of sanctuary that suspends the existing social distribution of spaces and division of places. In his famous essay *Of other spaces* Foucault (1986) claims that even in our time, there are still spaces, heterotopia, that are in certain way "sacred." In our terminology, these "sacred places" are precisely places where everyone and everything is profanated and de-appropriated (see above). They are places that become public places, and where the sacred in the more classical sense, referring to a place which acquires its meaning from a particular religion, is actually inoperative. A *heterotopia* is a "place without place," a *"lieu sans lie,"'* a place which in a way escapes the usual order of places—and sites—although it is still a concrete "place" or "location" with its own order, its own technologies, rituals, ways of speaking and its own discipline. According to Foucault (1986: 3), it is a place where we are exposed, that is to say "drawn out of ourselves, in which the erosion of our lives, our time and our history occurs."

In this line of thought, the lecture hall can be described as a heterotopia. It is a place where *we* are exposed to a thing-in-common and engaged in public thinking. The relation of exposure is a relation of provocation, and takes place as an event that gathers a thinking public around a matter of concern. As a heterotopia, the lecture hall includes strategies of *com-munization,* that is, strategies that enable an audience to share or take part in the *munus* of an issue (i.e. the burden or questioning that an issue poses to us) (Masschelein & Simons, 2002). An issue that provokes thinking, and turns something into a matter of public thought, indeed raises at once the question about how to live together in the face of the issue. An issue is not an object, it is something turned into what matters, and hence, an issue poses questions about relations, doing justice and living together in its presence. Strategies of im-munization, on the contrary, install clear divisions, hierarchies, positions and roles and prevent someone to become exposed or something to become an issue (to become com-munized). Objects, facts, resources cannot gather a public, cannot provoke thinking. Drawing upon Stengers (2005), we could say that in a heterotopia something really happens—the lecture hall is somehow a "magic place" and lecturing a "magic ritual." The magic moment is when something becomes an issue, and public thinking actually takes place. The lecture, as a kind of magic ritual, "sparks a public into being," that is, it gathers people as equals in "the presence of" and slows them down, make them hesitate, makes them think (again) (Marres, 2005: 208).

The lecture hall is not only an "other space" but also an "other time." As a *heterochronia,* it is an event-space, that is, a place where something happens, takes/finds (its) place. Public lecturing gathers people in the breach between past and future, breaking the arrow of time, turning time into "free time" or *scholé.* Free time however is not leisure time, but is beyond occupied time (time of cultivation, production, mobilisation, circulation): it becomes time of study and thought, of hesitation and slowing down in the presence of something. Different from the time of isolation in a secluded study room, something does not just turn into an issue of concern but an issue of public concern. The lecture hall is the event-space of public study and public thought.

We want to stress again that the region of thought is, to make use of Hannah Arendt's (1968/1983: 3) words, "the gap between past and future." But this gap, another name for the present, "is not the present as we usually understand it," as a point in a continuous "flow of uninterrupted succession." The "exercise of thought" involves an experience of oneself as somebody who is "able to," suspending historical time (and historical necessity), suspending biographical time (and psychological necessity), suspending social time (and sociological necessity). It is ageless, as Arendt says. But this suspension is at the same time an attachment, an attachment to the present, to the issue that is presented and hence an engagement in public thought.

Public lectures thus are associated with the emergence of a new consciousness, or an overtaking of the self that extends one's own, private affairs by making things into a public affair (cf. Rancière, 2008). Perhaps, the magic of lecturing comes close to what Latour (2004) calls a "*collective* experiment." During a lecture, and in the face of the issue that is present, who we are and what we think is put to the test. It is not an experimental situation where the professor and students are detached observers, but they are part of it, or more precisely, one becomes a professor and student exactly by partaking in the collective gathering around issues of concern. As a public event it actually inaugurates a question about how we are going to live together with something that turned out to be an issue. Indeed, in the public event of the lecture something turns into a *res publica*.

The Ethos of the Professor and the Student

The professor can be described as a concerned "truth teller" or *parrhesiast* (Foucault, 1989). To be a professor then means to profess. In line with its original meanings, to profess is a mode of speech that adds something to the world, and therefore actually also creates a world leading to an invocation/convocation of thought. The professor gives his/her voice to a thing, articulates a matter, puts it on the table and makes it present, and by doing this creates a power that makes us think and gathers us around the matter as a public. What the professor is saying always implies a declared commitment or attachment (cf. Derrida, 2001). To profess mathematics or literature is not simply to teach mathematics or literature, but it involves a commitment of oneself in a public promise to dedicate or devote oneself (and to have been dedicated, devoted) to the matter. The professor is not just talking about something, about objects and facts, but always also expressing his/her dedication to that "some thing." For him/her, it is always an issue of concern. In a way, he/she is always a kind of amateur, that is someone who to a certain extent "loves"—or at least "cares" about—what he/she is presenting.

The professor's public use of reason includes an experimental and equalizing ethos. In the lecture hall one is not a student in terms of intelligence, prior qualification, level of cultivation or learning capacities. An issue that provokes thinking equalizes at the level of care, concern and indeed, perhaps the courage to partake in public thinking and to face the question—raised in even a specific issue—on how we are going to live together with. To be a student then is to enter the gap between past and future, an "other place" and "other time" and to dedicate time to what should be taken care of. To be a student is always to be a student of "some thing," of an issue or common concern. For that reason university study is always collective study and being a student is always carrying the mark of a public.

The time of study is the time of weakening oneself and losing oneself in front of for instance "a text" or in front of "things." The time of experimentation that includes an exposition is in fact what characterizes every genuine "time of study." The texts or things are not just a playground to project one's thoughts and actions, or resources to be exploited in an entrepreneurial spirit, but become actually something to what people are exposed and in the presence of which they can and have to think. Clearly, this kind of exposition through study is uncomfortable, not just because in this experimental situation there are no longer criteria or rules to judge the things one is confronted with, but also because one's own position is always at stake in the presence of something.

Perhaps today, we should try to find out what helps to make academics to become professors (again) and learners to become students. We should think again about how to turn a text, a virus or a river into a cause for thinking? How to design the scene in such a way that the thinking proceeds in the presence of the issue or thing? How to conceive of the scene of lecturing for example, its architecture (the inside and outside of the habitat), its technology of speech, its material way of bringing together students? How to avoid that a lecture becomes a merely performance or spectacle, and that it remains a public act of truth telling? How to construct a certain closeness or nearness (both spatially and temporally) in order to be able to think "in the presence of"? How to get time and space to become concerned and engaged in collective study? How to use new information and communication technologies to provoke public thinking and collective study? These are specific questions on the "architecture and didactics of the world university" which we cannot discuss in further detail here. But we do want to stress that perhaps one of the important things to do is to slow down today's learner centred and demand-driven teaching discourses, and the related mobilizing discourses and technologies on instructional quality and excellence. We could start by recalling Humboldt's (1810) statement that the professor is not there for the student, and that the student is not there for the professor; at the university both are there for the truth, and from our perspective, have to be concerned about an issue.

Concluding Thoughts: The University and Its Public

This morphology has constituted an attempt to articulate the unique public form of the university. As such we hope it functions as well as an attempt to transform the current gathering around the university itself from a discussion concerning matters of performance (output, indicators, rankings), needs (assessments, satisfaction rates, responsiveness) and resources (available human capital, financial resources) into a matter of public concern. We do not attempt to modernize or innovate the university, but to turn the university itself into a public issue that makes us think, and hesitate. We want to try to give the university again some "presence." Not so much as an ideal, but as an idea that could "slow down" our reasoning and create an opportunity for a slightly different awareness of the problems and situations that are mobilizing us today. Hence, in order to reaffirm the role of the university, we should perhaps put the practices that are called research, teaching and service today to the test of the unique pedagogic form of the university.

But for who is the university and her unique pedagogic form an issue? In the ongoing academic war and the permanent mobilisation of academics and students, this question is perhaps a waste of time and a waste of resources, perhaps even the expression of naive longing for peace. We hope this essay however contributes to turning the university again into a public concern—the university and its public. Or to put it differently: perhaps today, especially today, the shared assumption "we are no human capital, not a community of learners, not entrepreneurs, but students and professors" articulates a unique com-munitas of students and professors.

Notes

1   This essay draws upon ideas elaborated in more detail in: Simons and Masschelein, 2009; Masschelein and Simons, 2009; Masschelein and Simons, 2010.
2   In a certain way we continue upon the studies of Illich (1992) and Kittler (1987) who pointed to the practice of lecturing as the founding gesture of the (medieval) university and upon Readings (1996) who also refers to the "scene of teaching" and the "time of study" as a resource for resistance to the university of excellence. However we emphasize rather and especially their public dimension. We should already indicate that we will use the notion "public lecture" in a particular way throughout the text for the practice where professors are addressing a gathering of students in a lecture hall. (In German we speak of "Vorlesungen"—which could be literally translated in "reading before."
3   This is how we mostly use the notion of "public" throughout the text, in some contexts we use it as synonymous with a "gathering of people," or "audience."
4   We will use the terms "profanation" and "sacred" in the way we just explained. What could be confusing is that sometimes sacred is used in literature and ordinary language not to denote a time/place with a particular value (e.g. the place of God and his laws and hence having a definite meaning), but a place/time where laws are suspended (e.g. the laws of politics, religion and the economy, state, market and the church) and in that sense is a free or public time/space. This last understanding of "sacred," then, comes close to what we will call here "profanation."
5   As Illich explains, before that time there existed no real "book-pages" (texts were written without separations between words and between sentences, there was no ordering, indexing, etc . . .), in the scriptoria texts had to be voiced ("sung" in Illich's phrase) in order to be copied (they could not be read—one can easily control this by trying to read on your screen a text without separations). Scriptoria were very noisy places (and totally different from the later libraries). (See Illich, 92.)
6   For the notions "matter of fact," "matter of concern," "(public) issue," "things" and "making things public": Latour, 2005.

14

THE FUTURE OF UNIVERSITY RESEARCH IN AFRICA

Berte van Wyk and Philip Higgs

Introduction

In this chapter, we draw on the resources of philosophy (particularly African philosophy) to re-imagine the future university in South Africa. One of the consequences of the democratisation of South African society is a renewed focus on aspects of a distinctly African origin, and this chapter explores ubuntu and communality as two concepts significant for the university's African origin. We discuss ubuntu and communality in relation to two distinct but related contexts ("African" and "South African"), and we briefly explain these two contexts. Although the literature sometimes uses these terms interchangeably, they are distinct because South Africa is a sovereign state on the continent of Africa, with its own historical, political, social, national, economical and cultural context, which sets it apart from the rest of Africa. It is interchangeable at times because South Africa is part of the African continent and many South Africans regard themselves as African, thus associating themselves with the geographical and cultural criteria listed above. Our discussion speaks to African universities within the context of a post-modern society; in this sense the university faces challenges similar to that of universities elsewhere in the world. As such it is a modern university which is expected to work towards many different goals (see Husén, 1994: 22) which are far from compatible with each other. Some are in direct conflict, such as competence and quality with participation, or equality with quality.

The Concept of "African"

The question of what meaning we attach to the adjective "African" when we talk about African philosophy is a crucial debate in attempts at establishing a uniquely

African order of knowledge. Some African philosophers, for example Mudimbe (1988) and Hountondji (1985), regard an intellectual product as African simply because it is produced or promoted by Africans. They, therefore, adopt a *geographical criterion* in their definition of the term "African" in "African philosophy" in that they regard African philosophy as the contributions of Africans practising philosophy within the defined framework of the discipline and its historical and geographic traditions. But then another criterion, referred to as the *cultural criterion*, is also used to determine what is meant by "African" in African philosophy. According to this criterion, a philosophical work is "African" if it directs its attention to issues concerning the theoretical or conceptual underpinnings of African culture. Such a view is presented by Gyekye (1987: 72) when he writes: "Philosophy is a cultural phenomenon in that philosophical thought is grounded in cultural experience." According to this view then, the study of the traditional African world in terms of views, ideas, and conceptions represents the unique substance of African philosophy and legitimates reference to what is referred to as "African."

Kaphagawani and Malherbe (2003: 224) argue that the concept of "African" may become contentious when people want to apply or withhold the description "African" for political reasons, as when people or customs originating in cultures which are not indigenous lay claim to being African or when alien innovations for modern Africans (e.g. those who are urbanised and do not follow customs closely) are advocated as being preferable to the traditional ways of their people. The concept "African" is derived from "Africa," where the latter refers to the continent, and African can also refer to a person, and as a signifier not just of geographical origins, but also of race/ethnicity, as Outlaw (1996: 71) suggests. Thus, Africans are comprised of many cultures and languages, and the concept of African is thus a collective one, and applies to many nationalities on the continent, and even to those who descended from slaves taken from the African continent, such as African Americans.

The difficulties in the attempt to illustrate the meaning of the concept "African" makes it even more imperative to develop an understanding of who we are, where we come from historically, and where we can go as a people with due consideration to our culture, our heritage and our contribution to the elevation of humanity. Being African can also be linked to the process of "Africanisation" (which is an attempt to bring about synchronisation and harmony between nature and the Africa people). Africanisation (Teffo, 1999) would be the infusion of humanness, the transformation and shaping of the world in the image and interests of the African people and "africanness" which encompasses the history and experience of economic, political, social, educational, psychological and philosophical subordination of the African masses by imperialism and western cultural hegemony (Nekwhevha, 2000). We also note that African history and experiences have been shaped by its own multi-cultured traditions and forms of life.

Having attempted to clarify the concept of "African," we now argue that discourses in higher education in Africa stand in need of liberation from ideological hegemony, which derives its power from the hegemony of Western Eurocentric forms of knowledge. The ideal of an African discourse in higher education is for an epistemologically rich society of multiple sets of conceptual schemes, each giving us an entry into reality and maximising a many sided understanding of whatever education issues are at question.

Ubuntu

Ramose (2002: 230) describes ubuntu as the root of African philosophy, and he contends that ubuntu underlines and is consistent with the philosophical understanding of being. Ramose further argues (*ibid.*: 231) that ubuntu can be understood as be-ing human (humanness) and can be expressed as a humane, respectful, and polite attitude towards others. For Ramose, being human is not enough; one is enjoined, commanded as it were, to actually become a human being. Pityane (1999) suggests that ubuntu is perhaps the most abiding principle of value in African thought and system of morality. He posits that ubuntu refers to human solidarity for it suggests that one achieves true humanity through other people. Also, the principle of ubuntu is considered to be the organising principle of African morality. Mokgoro (in Pityane, 1999: 144) states that the value of ubuntu is its basis for a morality of co-operation, compassion, communalism, concern for the collective interest, respect for the dignity of personhood, with emphasis of that dignity in social relationships and practices. We suggest that ubuntu should be an important attribute of the future role of the university.

Ubuntu is already viewed as one of the founding principles of a democratic South Africa. Archbishop Desmond Tutu (in Battle, 1997) explained ubuntu as follows:

> a person with ubuntu is open and available to others, does not feel threatened that others are able and good, for he or she has a proper self-assurance that comes from knowing that he or she belongs in a greater whole and is diminished when others are humiliated or diminished, when others are tortured or opposed.

Ubuntu is used to define just redress so as, in Tutu's words, to go "beyond justice to forgiveness and reconciliation" (Wilson, 2001: 9–11). Ubuntu implies both "compassion" and "recognition of the humanity of the other" (Asmal, K., Asmal, L. & Roberts, 1996: 21). Finally, ubuntu as a concept and experience is linked epistemologically to *umuntu* (Ramose, 2002: 324). Umuntu is the specific entity that continues to conduct an inquiry into being, experience, knowledge and truth; this is an activity rather than an act.

Ubuntu and the University in the Twenty-First Century

The question arises: what specific contribution can ubuntu make to universities in the twenty-first century in Africa? The report to UNESCO of the International Commission on Education for the 21st Century, commonly known as the Delors Report (Delors & Muftu, 1998), articulates four pillars of learning (namely: learning to know, learning to do, learning to live together, and learning to be). Jansen (2007) observes that South African schools need to improve on teaching students to learn to live together. This brings us to the main argument of this section: that ubuntu can make a significant contribution in enabling Africans to live together. While there have been considerable successes in providing increasing access to (South) Africans to universities, this has not yet happened to the extent that Africans can claim that they have learned to live together. Thus, the third pillar of learning of the Delors Report remains elusive in African society.

On learning to live together, the Delors Report (1998) suggests that education should adopt two complementary approaches. The first stage of education should focus on the discovery of other people. In the second stage of education and in lifelong education, the educational process should encourage involvement in common projects; this seems to be an effective way of avoiding conflict or resolving latent conflicts. The university of the twenty-first century should then teach students about human diversity and instil in them an awareness of the similarities and interdependence of all people. From early childhood, the school should seize every opportunity to pursue this two-pronged approach. Some subjects lend themselves to this—human geography in basic education, foreign languages and literature later on. Moreover (Delors Report, 1998), whether education is provided by the family, the community or the school, children should be taught to understand other people's reactions by looking at things from their point of view. Where this spirit of empathy is encouraged in education, it has a positive effect on young persons' social behaviour for the rest of their lives. For example, teaching students to look at the world through the eyes of other ethnic or religious groups is a way of avoiding some of the misunderstandings that give rise to hatred and violence among adults. Thus, teaching the history of religions or customs can provide a useful reference tool for moulding future behaviour.

We argue for an African perspective of ubuntu which relates to forgiveness, recognition, humanness, to be respectful, to be polite, and consistent with the philosophical understanding of being (human). Two incidents further convince us that ubuntu can make a significant contribution to the future university in Africa. First, the world-wide showing of a shocking video in 2007, in which four white male Afrikaner students of the Reitz Hostel at the University of the Free State initiated black female residence cleaners comes to mind. Amongst others, the video showed the students urinating on food which they made the cleaners to eat. The fact that such a racist incident could happen on a university campus convince us that ubuntu has to become part of the fabric of South African society, as ubuntu foregrounds the humanness of others. Then, in May 2008, the country witnessed xenophobic attacks against citizens from other African countries. We see it as a priority of universities to teach their students about democratic citizenship, and how to deal with racism, sexism, and diversity. We contend that ubuntu can be a key concept to deal with the challenges highlighted by these two incidents. Also, as universities are centres of learning, ubuntu can help Africans learn to live together.

Communality

A conceptualisation of ubuntu as a person who achieves true humanity through others lead us to explore a second African value, that of communality. According to Letseka (2000: 181) the importance of communality to traditional African life cannot be overemphasised. This is because community and belonging to a community of people constitute the very fabric of traditional African life. Unlike the Anglo-Saxon, liberal notion of the individual as some sort of entity that is capable of existing and flourishing on its own, unconnected to any community of other individuals, not bound by any biological relationships or socioeconomic, political and cultural relationships, obligations, duties, responsibilities and conventions that frame and define any community of individuals, the communal conception of the individual in most traditional African settings is described by Mbiti (1970: 108) in the following way:

> Whatever happens to the individual happens to the whole group, and whatever happens to the whole group happens to the individual. The individual can only say: I am, because we are; and since we are, therefore I am.

This, Mbiti (1970: 109) claims, is a cardinal point in the understanding of the African view of man. Commenting on traditional life in Kenya, Kenyatta (1965: 297) echoes similar views:

> According to Gikuyu ways of thinking, nobody is an isolated individual, or rather, his uniqueness is a secondary fact about him; first and foremost he is several people's relative and several people's contemporary.

Menkiti (1979: 158) concurs with this observation when he states:

> A crucial distinction thus exists between the African view of man and the view of man found in Western thought: in the African view it is the community which defines the person as a person, not some isolated static quality of rationality, will or memory.

In traditional African life then, a person depends on others just as much as others depend on him or her. In fact, in terms of such a communitarian view, the individual's life and fulfilment is only to be found in community with others. It should be noted, however, that some African intellectuals have challenged this communitarian idea in the discourse on community in Africa. For instance, Hountondji (1996: xviii) responded critically to what he called *unanimism, "*. . . the illusion that all men and women in such communal societies speak with one voice and share the same opinion about fundamental issues."

The slogan "your child is mine, my child is yours" has a particularly African flavour to it. In many ways, it epitomises the sense of community so prevalent in African society. Gyekye (2002: 297) observes that the communal or communitarian (and he uses the two interchangeably) aspects of African socio-ethical thought are reflected in the communitarian features of the social structures of African societies. Communality, according to Dickson (in Gyekye 2002: 297), is a

> . . . characteristic of African life of which attention has been drawn again and again by both African and non-African writers on Africa. Indeed, to many this characteristic defines Africanness.

Communality and Research in Higher Education

Communality as an expression of Africanness also has significant implications for research in higher education. In short, the argument here is one of advocating that research methodologies in an African context should be closely linked to communal values. And for researchers in higher education this means that they should take cognisance of the values that strengthen communal behaviours. In other words, we would argue for the need for a form of African community based research which takes cognisance of values present in the community, for purposes of fostering the communal beliefs of that community. Community based research is, therefore, a kind of research that is conducted by, with and, for the community.

The core characteristic then of African community based research is a form of research that seeks to enhance the capacity of the community members to participate in the process that shapes research approaches and intervention strategies. The active co-operation and participation of members within the community are, therefore, the essential components of African community based research. In African community based research, the community is recognised as a primary stakeholder and actively participates in determining the ends to which research resources are dedicated. That is, the community becomes an active agenda setter for research in higher education rather than just a passive data provider and consumer of research results. In this way, research capacity is applied democratically to respond to local needs in such areas as health, education, natural resources management, and urbanisation. African community based research, therefore, functions to make the research method or system more responsive to the pressing social needs of the community, and in the process, encourages more democratic forms of science and technology. In so doing, African community based research focuses on community social problems and needs, and yields important benefits, such as:

- cost-effective development results
- helping the fabric of grassroots democracy, and
- the opening of educational doors to community knowledge.

Briefly, how does African community based research differ from an approach such as ethno-methodological research? African community based research differs from ethno-methodological research in two fundamental ways:

- Unlike ethno-methodological research, African community based research regards communities and insiders, that is, people in the communities themselves, as both the object and the subject of knowledge. In other words, much of the ethno-methodological research done in communities has tended to be *about,* but not *with* the community. Members of the community appear not as participants in the research, but rather as objects for research. In this regard, African community based research is sensitive to *the double role* of individuals in African societies. Elders and other so-called "epistemic authorities" (Kaphagawani & Malherbe, 1998: 214) in communities should not only be perceived as important informants, but also as research colleagues with critical perspectives on the issues under scrutiny.
- Also, unlike ethno-methodology, which presupposes the existence of a community that thinks "collectively," and thereby ignores the significance of any form of individual consciousness in that community, African community based research takes cognisance of individual thinking and criticism of communal values.

Falling within the scope of African community based research is its *trans-traditional vantage.* By this we mean that African community based research acknowledges the validity of other non-African knowledge systems and the need to integrate indigenous knowledge systems with these. The importance of this *trans-traditional vantage* of African community based research is emphasised by Wiredu (1980), who maintains that the urgent problem facing African intellectuals, in regards to the whole issue of knowledge production in Africa, is the need to address attempts being made to improve the living conditions of people in local communities by means of recourse to indigenous knowledge systems. However, according to Wiredu, African intellectuals who continue to revive and reinstate traditional thinking in Africa without reference to modern ways of thinking, are doing a disservice to Africa by pretending that traditional ways of thinking are still sufficient, useful or even applicable to today's needs in Africa. According to Wiredu, there are new and modern problems and challenges facing Africa, and traditional ways of thinking cannot always cope with these problems and challenges. In the light of Wiredu's remarks, it is important to note that African community based research does not attempt only to revive and reinstate indigenous African knowledge systems while ignoring the impact of modernity and industrialisation.

African community based research will, therefore, give research in Africa a *social basis* by linking research with community needs and experiences. Indeed, we would argue that African community based research plays a significant role in research in an African context, because it forces the inclusion of a grassroots perspective into research. Furthermore, African community based research opens new opportunities, and offers tangible results, for a distinctive form of African research which is characterised by:

- the integration of indigenous and community-based knowledge systems into existing knowledge systems, and
- a recognition of communities as primary stakeholders and active participants in determining the ends to which research resources are dedicated.

The future of university research in Africa should develop appropriate research methodologies based on conceptions of communality, and we argue for community based research. We contend that the future university needs a sense of communality characterised by common interests, goals, values, intellectual, emotional and ideological attachment, interpersonal bonds, grouping of persons, association, communal beings, and interdependence.

Conclusions

Our discussion of ubuntu and communality brings to the fore two additional reflections. First, while ubuntu as an African concept is unique, associated meanings of the concept can be found in other contexts as well. For instance, the emphasis on humanism is found across many cultures; so we find congruence with Western conceptions of humanism. Garfield's (2002) argument that humanism is unavoidable because human beings, qua persons, are committed to self-understanding is applicable to the African context. Thus, the uniqueness of ubuntu shows our independence, and congruence with expressions of humanism in other contexts. At the same time, it also indicates an interdependence on humanistic ideals elsewhere. Second, it also appears that there is an overlap between an African perspective of community and a Western perspective. Kymlicka (2002) uses concepts such as "shared practices," "understandings with each society," "common good," "self-determination," "solidarity," and "attachment." What this overlap shows is that an African community is not isolated from the rest of the world, and that it reflects/contains aspects that are also important to Western communities. What is important is that an African sense of communality is articulated clearly by African scholars; it shows both their independence and their interdependence.

The future of university research in Africa as envisioned in this chapter is located in the transformation of higher education. Our emphasis on ubuntu does not reject European or Western knowledge systems or traditions, but rather believes that African scholars may raise alternative questions and offer a valuable interpretive key, not only to the African experience but the global experience as well. The future university is grounded in African communities and concerns itself with knowledge production that takes the African condition and identity as its central issue—the African condition as historical, not biological—and defines its key task as coming to grips with this condition critically.

15

KNOWLEDGE SOCIALISM

Intellectual Commons and Openness in the University

Michael A. Peters, Garett Gietzen, and David J. Ondercin

Introduction

"Openness" is a central contested value of modern liberalism that falls under different political, epistemological and ethical descriptions. In this chapter, we employ "openness" to analyze the spatialization of learning and education. We discuss dimensions of openness and "open education" (Peters & Britez, 2008), beginning with a brief history of openness in education that focuses on the concept of the Open University as it first developed in the United Kingdom during the 1960s, a development we dub Open University 1.0. We then consider the concept of openness in the light of the new "technologies of openness" of Web 2.0 that promote interactivity and encourage participation, collaboration and help to establish new forms of the intellectual commons, a space for knowledge sharing and collective work. The intellectual commons is increasingly based on models of open source, open access, open archives, open journal systems and open education. We call this model Open University 2.0. Where the former is based on the logic of centralized industrial media characterized by a broadcast one-to-many mode, the latter is based upon a radically decentralized, many-to-many and peer production mode of interactivity. To exemplify the progress and possibilities of Open University 2.0, we focus on Massachusetts Institute of Technology's (MIT's) OpenCourseWare and Harvard's Open Access initiative to publicly post its faculty's papers online. Finally, we look forward to the possibilities of a form of openness that combines the benefits of these first two forms, what we call Open University 3.0, and consider its possibilities for universities in the future. By doing so, we see this chapter as a means to investigate the political economy of openness as it reconfigures universities in the knowledge economy of the twenty-first century and at the same time to suggest a socialized model of the knowledge economy that competes with neoliberal versions.

The underlying argument of the chapter focuses upon the ways in which new forms of technological-enabled openness, especially emergent social media that utilizes social networking, blogs, wikis and user-created content and media, provide new models of openness for a conception of the intellectual commons based on peer production which is a radically decentralized, genuinely interactive, and collaborative form of knowledge sharing that can usefully serve as the basis of "knowledge cultures" (Peters & Besley, 2006; Peters & Roberts, 2011). Openness 1.0 was based on social democratic principles that emphasized inclusiveness and equality of opportunity and was a product of the age of welfarism when higher education was seen as an unqualified public good yet the mechanism of Openness 1.0 followed that of industrial broadcast mass media, which was designed to reach a large audience on a one-to-many logic. In one sense, the technology contradicted the social democratic values permitting only a one-way transfer of knowledge. Openness 2.0 is based on what might be called principles of liberal political economy, particularly intellectual property and freedom of information. This second iteration of openness employs new peer-to-peer architectures and technologies that are part of the ideology of Web 2.0 and given expression in ways that emphasize the ethic of participation ("participatory media"), collaboration and file-sharing characterizing the rise of social media that is interactive and collaborative.

We argue that Open University 2.0 provides the basis for a new social media model of the university that embraces the social democratic articles of the original Open University and that it provides the means to recover and enhance the historical mission of the university in the twenty-first century (Peters, 2007a; 2006a, b). Open University 2.0 provides mechanisms for jettisoning the dominant neoliberal managerialist ideology and returning to a fully socialized view of knowledge and knowledge-sharing that has its roots in Enlightenment thinking about science and its new practices in commons-based peer-production. This position relies on the argument that knowledge and education are fundamentally social activities and that knowledge and the value of knowledge are fundamentally rooted in social relations (Peters & Besley, 2006; Peters, 2007b). At the same time, however, we recognize that any re-theorization of the university must move beyond the limitations of even Open University 2.0, which—despite its logic of openness—often coheres around exclusive institutions such as MIT and Harvard and is correspondingly reliant on factors of exclusivity, including intellectual property and the privileging of "expertise." Consequently, the development of openness as it relates to the university must move from the social democratic model of Open University 1.0, and the liberal political economy model of Open University 2.0, to a new version of openness based on "knowledge socialism." Only through such a development might this new Open University 3.0 achieve its potential as a locus of true inclusion and social and economic creativity.

Media and Education: The Promise of Web 2.0

With Web 2.0, there is a deep transformation occurring wherein the Web has become a truly participatory media; instead of going on the Web to read static content, we can more easily create and share our own ideas and creations. The rise of what has been alternately referred to as consumer—or user-generated media (content) has been hailed as being truly groundbreaking in nature. Blogging and social networking with the facility of user-generated content has created revolutionary new social media that characterize Web 2.0 as the newest phase of the Internet. New interactive technologies and peer-to-peer architectures have democratized writing and imaging and, thereby, the conditions for creativity itself, enabling anyone with computer access to become a creator of their own digital content. Writers and video-makers as "content creators" are causing a fundamental shift from the age of information to the age of interaction and recreating themselves in the process. Sometimes this contrast is given in terms of a distinction between "industrial media," "broadcast" or "mass" media which is highly centralized, hierarchical and vertical based on a one-to-many logic versus social media which are decentralized (without a central server), non-hierarchical or peer-governed, and horizontal based on many-to-many interaction.

Forms of industrial mass media including the book, newspapers, radio, television, film and video broadcast media were designed to reach very large audiences within the industrializing nation-state. The major disadvantage of this media form is the criticism of manipulation, bias and ideology that comes with a one-to-many dissemination, its commodification of information, and its corporate method of production and distribution (Thompson, 1995). Mass media communication is a one-way transmission model where the audience is reduced to a passive consumer of programmed information which is suited to mass audiences. Both industrial and social media provide the scalable means for reaching global audiences. The means of production for industrial media are typically owned privately or by the state and require specialized technical expertise to produce and payment to access. Social media, by contrast, is based on the Internet as platform, and tend to be available free or at little cost, requiring little or no technical operating knowledge. There are also profound differences in production and consumption processes, in the immediacy of the two types of media and in the levels and means of participation and reception.

Even so it is not a question of straightforward replacement. Many of the industrial media are rapidly adopting aspects of social media to develop more interactive capacity. CNN, for instance, has introduced its blogs with viewer participation and interaction and encourage viewers to follow stories on Twitter and Facebook. This means that new media will not simply replace old media, but rather will learn to interact with it in a complex relationship that Bolter and Grusin (2001) call "remediation" and Henry Jenkins (2006) calls "convergence culture." Jenkins argues that convergence culture is not primarily a technological revolution but is more a cultural shift, dependent on the active participation of the consumers working in a social dynamic. Douglas Kellner and George Kim (2009) theorize YouTube as the cutting edge of ICTs and characterize it as dialogical learning community, and for learning-by-doing, learning as communication, learning through reflection on the environment, learning as self-fulfillment and empowerment, learning for agency and social change.

We accept the idea that the advances in information and communication technologies provides the means to expand the community of higher education beyond the traditional campus, creating opportunities for increased openness in access to education. Rather than using the terminology from software development, however, we wish to ground the definition of this openness within the tradition of critical spatiality. Through doing so, we will problematize the notion that the campus is the natural boundary of the higher education experience—a notion which inherently perpetuates pedagogies of inequality and elitism—and suggest that openness offers a new critical relationship between advanced learning and the community beyond the walls of the college.

The socially networked universe has changed the material conditions for the formation, circulation, and utilization of knowledge. "Learning" has been transformed from its formal mode under the industrial economy, structured through class, gender and age to an informal and ubiquitous mode of learning "anywhere, anytime" in the information and media-based economy. Increasingly, the emphasis falls on the "learning economy," improving learning systems and networks, and the acquisition of new media literacies. These mega-trends signal changes in both the production and consumption of symbolic goods and their situated contexts of use. The new media logics accent the "learner's" *co-production* and the active production of meaning in a variety of networked public and private spaces, where knowledge and learning emerge as new principles of social stratification, social mobility and identity formation.

New media technologies not only diminish the effect of distance but they also thereby conflate the local and the global, the private and the public, "work" and "home." They spatialize knowledge systems. Digitalization of learning systems increases the speed, circulation and exchange of knowledge highlighting the importance of digital representations of all symbolic and cultural resources, digital cultural archives, and *new literacies and models of text management, text distribution and generation*. At the same time, the radical concordances of image, text and sound, and the development of global information/knowledge infrastructures have created new learning opportunities while encouraging the emergence of a global media network linked with a global communications network together with the emergence a global Euro-American consumer culture and the rise of *global edutainment* media conglomerates, where education is reduced to the principles of entertainment. In the media economy, the political economy of ownership become central; who owns and designs learning systems becomes a question of paramount political and philosophical significance.

New models of flexible learning nest within new technologies that are part of wider historical emerging techno-capitalist systems that promote greater interconnectivity and encompass all of its different modes characterizing communication from the telegraph (city-to-city), the media (one-to-many), the telephone (one-on-one), the Internet (one-to-one, one-to-all, all-to-one, all-to-all, many-to-many, etc.), the World Wide Web (collective by content but connective by access), and the mobile/cell phone (all the interconnectivity modes afforded by the web and internet, plus a body-to-body connection). At the same time these new affordances seem to provide new opportunities for learning that reflect old social democratic goals concerning equality, access and emancipation that made education central to both liberal and socialist ideals.

Open University 1.0

Well before the emergence of the Internet and the phenomenon of social networking appeared in the mid 1990s, the model of the "open university" in the United Kingdom was established as a technology-based distance education institution in the 1960s. The Open University was founded on the idea that communications technology could extend advanced degree learning to those people who for a variety of reasons could not easily attend campus universities. The Open University really began when in 1923, the educationalist J. C. Stobart while working for the infant BBC wrote a memo suggesting that the new communications and broadcast media could develop a "wireless university." By the early sixties, many different ideas were being proposed including a "teleuniversity" that would broadcast lectures, as well as providing correspondence texts and organizing campus visits to local universities.

Yet the Open University was not merely an institution that followed from the development of technical mechanisms of openness. From the start the idea of the "open university" was conceived, in social democratic terms, as a response to the problem of exclusion. Michael Young (Baron Young of Dartington, 1915–2002), the sociologist, activist and politician, who first coined the term and helped found the Open University, wrote the 1945 manifesto for the Labor Party under Clement Atlee and devoted himself to social reform of institutions based on their greater democratization and giving the people a stronger role in their governance.[1]

A Labor Party study group under the chairmanship of Lord Taylor presented a report in March 1963 concerning the continuing exclusion from higher education of the lower income groups and they proposed a "University of the Air" as an experiment for adult education. The Open University was established in Milton Keynes in September 1969 with Professor Walter Perry as its first Vice-Chancellor. It took its first cohort of students in 1970 which began foundation courses in January 1971. The 1980s was a decade of growth and consolidation. As the OU website notes "By 1980, total student numbers had reached 70,000, and some 6,000 people were graduating each year. From then on the institution would each year boost new records in the numbers of people applying to study and achieving their degree."[2] During the 1980s and 1990s new faculties of business, management, languages and law were added and the OU expanded into Europe attracting more than 10,000 EU citizens outside the UK. Today the OU has some 180,000 students in the UK (150,000 undergraduate and more than 30,000 postgraduate students) with an additional 25,000 overseas students making it one of the largest universities in the world. Over 10,000 students attending OU have disabilities.

The Open University[3] advertises itself as based on "open learning" which is explained in terms of "learning in your own time by reading course material, working on course activities, writing assignments and perhaps working with other students." It has been immensely influential as a model for other countries and distance education flourished in the 1970s and picked up new open education dimensions with the introduction of local area network environments.[4] The mission of the OU is stated as:

> The Open University is open to people, places, methods and ideas. It promotes educational opportunity and social justice by providing high-quality university education to all who wish to realise their ambitions and fulfill their potential. Through academic research, pedagogic innovation and collaborative partnership, it seeks to be a world leader in the design, content and delivery of supported open and distance learning.
>
> *(http://www.open.ac.uk/about/ou/p2.shtml)*

The OU is explicit in its commitment to equality and diversity:

- Our mission expresses our founding aspiration to provide opportunities to all. As such, equality and diversity have been part of the core values of the Open University since its inception.
- Our continued dedication to social justice and equality of opportunity is embodied in a set of commitments and principles. Through these commitments, we will strengthen our position as a university of choice.

Today there are some 43 open universities in the world based on the British model.[5]

Towards Open University 2.0

MIT's OpenCourseWare 2000

According to MIT, OpenCourseWare (OCW) developed from a consideration of how the Internet might be used to further MIT's mission "to advance knowledge and to educate students" (http://ocw.mit.edu/about/our-history/). MIT anticipated a revenue-generating initiative but exploration led to a different type of program (Abelson, 2008). Officially proposed in 2000, OCW furthers MIT's mission by providing free worldwide access to the "core academic content" of its undergraduate and graduate courses, including syllabi, lecture notes, assignments, exams, and audio and video media. The pilot version of OpenCourseWare went on-line in 2002 with content from 50 courses, including Spanish and Portuguese translations. In 2007, it was launched officially with 500 courses, which expanded to 1,800 courses by 2007. 33 disciplines and nearly all of MIT's curricula are represented, not only engineering and other technical areas, but also the humanities, management and the natural and social sciences. By 2009, OCW had expanded to over 1,900 courses and additional translations into Chinese, Persian and Thai (http://ocw.mit.edu/about/our-history/).[6]

As of October 2009, MIT recorded 86.8 million visits to OpenCourseWare, an average of one million visits each month. Visitors access OCW directly and via 220 mirror sites around the world. 46% of traffic is from the United States, 17% from East Asia, 11% from Western Europe, 9% from South Asia, 4% from Latin America, and the remaining 13% from other parts of the world (Program Evaluation Findings Summary, 2009). Visits are differentiated into four user types: 9% are identified as educators, 42% as students, 43% as self-learners and the remaining 6% as other types (http://ocw.mit.edu/OcwWeb/web/about/stats/index. htm). The educators, students and self-learners who comprise the majority of users identify a range of reasons for accessing OCW:

- Educator uses: enhanced personal knowledge (45%), learning new teaching methods (15%), incorporating OCW materials into teaching materials (14%).
- Student uses: enhancing personal knowledge (44%), complementing a course (39%), planning a course of study (12%).
- Self learner uses: exploring interests outside of professional field (41%), planning future study (20%), reviewing basic concepts in field (17%), keeping current in field (11%).

(Program Evaluation Findings Summary, 2009)

This considerable use demonstrates OCW's significant impact, which is further substantiated by personal testimonials by users of course materials and MIT faculty and administrators.[7] It is clear that OpenCourseWare addresses a wide range of educational needs. It makes academic content accessible to people who might otherwise be denied due to a wide range of factors, including geography, poverty and time or other logistical limitations. It allows MIT to promote knowledge sharing in meaningful ways, thus serving the ideals of openness through the affordances of technology. As former MIT President Charles Vest observed in 2001, OpenCourseWare "combines two things: the traditional openness and outreach and democratizing influence of American education and the ability of the Web to make vast amounts of information instantly available" (http://web.mit.edu/new-soffice/2001/ocw.html).

As impressive as MIT OpenCourseWare may be, MIT makes it explicitly clear that it is "not an MIT education." OCW "does not grant degrees or certificates" or "provide access to MIT faculty"; and the materials provided "may not reflect entire content of the course" (http://ocw.mit.edu/OcwWeb/web/about/about/index.htm). It only provides access to "core academic content," not the university itself. Faculty at other institutions may employ it in their own work, and students and autodictats may use it to learn subject matter of MIT courses, and but neither of these options are the same as real access to MIT. OpenCourseWare does indeed share with the university a role in disseminating knowledge; and like the university, it serves teaching, learning and research. The extent to which OCW can fulfill these roles is limited because it does not provide direct access to faculty who would facilitate the learning process to students, self-learners and other educators, and nor does it provide the infrastructure necessary to most types of research, especially in the sciences. Nevertheless, OCW can indeed make claims in these areas, albeit limited ones.

However, the university is more than a teaching, learning and research mechanism, it also provides credentials that certify skills and legitimate graduates in the job market and professions. These credentials demonstrate that graduates attended a particular institution and therefore accrued cultural capital that provides benefits ostensibly unrelated to employment skills, especially in the social realm.[8] This role in legitimation and cultural capital accrual extends to the teaching and research faculty, which can claim institutional affiliation.

Hence despite that fact that MIT, in calling its initiative "open," is drawing on the terminology of the open-source software movement, it does not, in any profound sense, open the University to those who do not otherwise have access to it. Rather, like open-source software itself, OCW replicates existing patterns of knowledge production in academia and reaffirms the closed relationship of the university community to the world at large. That said, by providing free access to knowledge, it does indeed adhere to some liberal ideals, including scientific knowledge sharing ideals that developed during the Enlightenment. OCM has a great deal of similarities with the UK's Open University, an example of what we are describing as "Open University 1.0." *That* Open University relied on technologies to bridge distance and by doing so increase inclusion. OpenCourseWare relies on today's far more sophisticated technologies, as well as the attraction of free content which is accessible to all regardless of academic background, to reach a greater number of people. In this respect, OpenCourseWare is even less elitist than the Open University, an institution known for its accessibility. However, the original Open University is differentiated by its ability to provide substantial institutional support to its students and, perhaps more importantly, the legitimating credentials and cultural capital which are accorded its graduates.

OpenCourseWare follows a model with a one-to-many logic that has more in common with Open University 1.0 than its 2.0 iteration. "Core academic content" travels unidirectionally from the MIT campus to educators, students, self-learners and others around the world. Given the high prestige of MIT among the world's universities, and its geographical location in Cambridge, Massachusetts, also home to Harvard University, the relationship of MIT to the recipients of OpenCourseWare content can be seen as one of centre-periphery. That said, by distributing content worldwide, MIT can also be seen as a mechanism for destabilizing the localization that has traditionally promoted university elitism.

MIT designed the OpenCourseWare model to be replicable, thus facilitating its expansion to other institutions of higher education (Carson, 2009: 26). The legacy of this replicability, the OpenCourseWare Consortium, founded in 2005, now includes member institutions from 36 countries around the world. Spain is the most significantly represented of the top ten countries, with 39 institutions, followed by United States (22), Japan (18), Taiwan (14), South Korea (11), Venezuela (7), Brazil and Saudi Arabia (6), Colombia and United Kingdom (4). Highest institutional concentrations are in Asia, Europe, and Latin and North America; Africa is most poorly represented with only one institution (http://www.ocwconsortium.org/members/consortium-members.html). Like MIT, the Consortium reports a large number of available courses and a high rate of visitor traffic. In a 2008 study, the then 200 members provided more than 6200 courses and over 2.25 million visits per month, not including the traffic generated by more than 1600 courses offered by the China Quality OpenCourseWare program (Carson, 2009: 23).

The growth of the OCW Consortium further destabilizes the localization of the traditional university, moving knowledge distribution away from a one-to-many to a many-to-many model. This process moves university development closer to what we have described as Open University 2.0, a model characterized as diffuse and based on a socialized understanding of knowledge and knowledge-sharing. At this point, the OCW Consortium, with MIT OpenCourseWare, have not become a truly interactive and collaborative form of intellectual commons where content is user-created in meaningful ways. Perhaps the university, given its privileging of expert—and legitimated—knowledge cannot accommodate user-created content to the extent possible in other areas, such as entertainment media. Nevertheless, MIT OpenCourseWare and the OCW Consortium are opening greater social, cultural and technical affordances that may, in time, realize the ideals of Open University 2.0.

Harvard's Open Access

Harvard University followed MIT's embrace of openness, but developed a quite different approach. Harvard's creation and implementation of the model of the Open University had its creation with its faculty making their scholarly articles available to everyone while maintaining copyright protection. Harvard became the first university in the US to embrace an Open Access authorization for its faculty. In the creation of the policy, the faculty was concerned that there could be copyright predicaments and the provisions to maintain ownership of the information was important to some faculty members and the fear was that the policy would take control and would not serve their best collective interests. This Open Access policy and philosophy was faculty-driven which became the first to impose the requirement upon itself instead of having the request coming from the administration. In keeping with the policy/philosophy, faculty members have the right to remove themselves from the contract in which specific cases would be troublesome. The policy requires all faculty members to provide electronic copies of their articles to the Provost's Office (Peek, 2005).

The strength of the policy is that the faculty does not sacrifice anything by sharing the publication rights with Harvard. In doing so, this policy forms a united authority of Harvard if they decide to turn down a journal's request for exclusive publishing rights. Harvard University designed a legal memorandum, which reinforces their negotiations with commercial publishing companies. A distinctive feature of the Open Access policy is that the policy agreement is not coercive from the faculty senate or the university administration. Harvard's Library created a special office that ensures that Open Access information is accessible across the institution's many departments, which contributed to Harvard's goal of a unified institutional atmosphere. A rule in the policy asks the faculty and the administration to review the Open Access policy with the hope of ensuring that everyone who is participating is still content (Peek, 2005).

If other universities choose to follow Harvard's endeavor into Open Access, it will create serious problems for major publishers involved in higher education. The publishing conglomerate Wiley & Sons is composed of sixteen separate publishing houses that deal with education alone. The Open Access policy might create a chain of negative reactions that could force profits to slow. Consequently, the Open Access movement suggests dramatic changes are coming to the journal marketplace. Publishers benefit from the ownership rights that they protect on behalf of both the authors and themselves. Harvard's Open Access policy threatens the traditional way of conducting business with scholars and publishing houses. Scholars and researchers have long been willing to sign contracts that provide all copyrights to publishers instead of retaining their own respective rights. With the creation of the Open University 2.0, it will force the scholarly community to break with tradition and require the open sharing of research, software, and data (Orsdel & Born, 2008).

Harvard will continue to have the traditional educational structure of one to one transference of scholarly information. This application of openness allows Harvard and other institutions of higher education to rethink their respective approaches to knowledge and information systems. This new concept of information of a one-to-many method will reshape the scholarly community that currently exists in higher education. Harvard's Open Access to scholarly articles incorporates the fundamental principle of the new technology of openness as it relates to Open University 2.0. The users and distributors of scholarly information may promote collaboration and establish new forms of the intellectual commons (Peters & Besley, 2006; Peters & Roberts, 2011). Harvard's Open Access provides the basis for a new educational framework and challenges the concept of what constitutes a university that embraces the social democratic ideas of the original concept of the Open University 1.0 (Peters, 2006a, b).

This Open Access to large repositories of information creates a new and global university. Harvard's Open Access policy provides a vision of open education, and a possibility for maximizing educational opportunities for individuals. The scholarly collection available through Harvard University provides an opportunity for individual and communal education. Harvard's Open Access policy benefits the independent learners. These learners can be educated in many subjects just by clicking on a link and studying at their leisure. Individuals who have a wide range of educational goals and desires will facilitate the development of educational information by universities. It is because of these diverse interests that the Open Access policy promotes curricular creativity for both the learner and the institution. The learner has the ability to seek and find what is of interest to him or her and learn the information at his or her own pace. In turn, the faculty has the ability to present their scholarly works in an online format that may be different from their traditional classrooms.

In agreement with MIT's OpenCourseWare, the content from the Harvard university courses and degree programs to being a self-directed learner will become a more serious form of education. For the new type/form of learner, institutions will cultivate the emergence of new persons who will become participants in the creation of open education environments. Harvard's Open Access policy helps inaugurate a new type of educator who is part scholar and part information librarian. The quasi scholar-librarian will be concerned with the content of the information that will serve as a way for individuals to be oriented to the appropriate forms of information. In this new educational environment, learning communities will desire to utilize the informational resources, which is available because of the Open Access policy. These quasi scholar-librarians will form new teaching communities not in the traditional sense of scholar to student, but rather having a linear form of sharing valued information. In doing so, the nontraditional classroom environment in which the scholar and student work allows individuals interested to share and submit their own works (Lynch, 2008).

Despite the promise of Harvard's Open Access policy, it shares many of the limitations of MIT's OpenCourseWare. As with MIT's initiative, Harvard is changing from an elite and exclusive institution, located in what is arguably the world's most elite academic center, from where it diffuses content in a one-to-many relationship to institutions and individual peripheral learners. Furthermore, the education provided by the reading of faculty articles is informal, undirected and uncredentialled. The factors that may be problematic for some who have concerns pedagogically, but also educationally, are recognized and situated in the educational marketplace.

Yet, as with MIT's OpenCourseWare, Harvard's Open Access policy does provide possibilities for bringing Openness 2.0 and the Open University 2.0 to fruition.

Harvard's challenge to a long dominant model of academic publishing promises to benefit all academic institutions by shifting control of knowledge from publishers to the institutions where knowledge is generated. A shift like this might make knowledge more accessible, making it cheaper or even free, but also by undermining the proprietary rights ensured by exclusive information architectures delimited by licensing, passwords, and other mechanisms. The achievement of openness of this sort has the potential to provide academic papers from multiple institutions, in a many-to-many logical framework to people around the world, which facilitates research, scholarship, and learning in truly significant ways.

Looking Forward: Openness 3.0, Open University 3.0 and Knowledge Socialism

The first and second iterations of university openness have provided significant benefits to society. The social democratic character of Openness 1.0 promoted inclusion and opportunity for a wider range of people than would have been traditionally enrolled in university. Knowledge exclusivity was challenged by the institutional assertion that knowledge is a public good. Openness 2.0, with its confluence of freedom of information and technological affordances, further provides a freedom to use, share and improve knowledge. However, both of these forms of openness are necessarily restricted: the first by technical infrastructure limitations, and the latter by resource imbalances and the exclusivity necessary to intellectual property.

The next version of openness, which we call Openness 3.0, combines aspects of the two earlier forms to maximize their respective benefits, while reducing limitations. In this model of openness, education is placed at the center of global society and human rights. In this sense, Openness 3.0 shares similarities to Openness 1.0 and its social democratic goals although it is committed to the promotion of forms of free global science, research and learning. At the same time, it also shares with Openness 2.0 a culture of social, ICT-driven knowledge sharing and innovation. However, Openness 3.0 differs because its ideological foundations are not social democratic, nor—like 2.0—that of liberal political economy. Instead, Openness 3.0 is based on what can be called "knowledge socialism."

Knowledge socialism provides an alternative to the currently dominant "knowledge capitalism." Whereas knowledge capitalism focuses on the economics of knowledge, emphasizing human capital development, intellectual property regimes, and efficiency and profit maximization, knowledge socialism shifts emphasis towards recognition that knowledge and its value are ultimately rooted in social relations (Peters & Besley, 2006). Knowledge socialism promotes the sociality of knowledge by providing mechanisms for a truly free exchange of ideas. Unlike knowledge capitalism, which relies on exclusivity—and thus scarcity—to drive innovation, the socialist alternative recognizes that exclusivity can also greatly limit innovation possibilities (see "Introduction," Peters, Murphy & Marginson, 2009). Hence rather than relying on the market to serve as a catalyst for knowledge creation, knowledge socialism marshals public and private financial and administrative resources to advance knowledge for the public good.

Consequently, the university, as a key locus of knowledge creation, becomes—in Openness 3.0—the mechanism of multiple forms of innovation, not merely in areas with obviously direct economic returns (such as technoscience), but also in those areas (such as information literacy) that facilitate indirect benefits not merely beholden to concern for short-term market gains. Positioning the university in this way might seem overly idealistic, perhaps even disconnected from the tremendous financial realities facing universities, and higher education in general, in much of the world. Reactions of this sort, however, rely on the assumption that the current neoliberal model of higher education, with primacy placed on selling educational "products" to "consumers," is the best remedy to diminishing funding. Furthermore, although individual economic actors maximize personal benefits through their consumption choices, these choices frequently do not correspond to broader societal needs. Free exchange of knowledge in higher education, for instance, does more than provide economic returns to individual actors and institutions. Post-industrial nations, for example, can maximize their place in the global knowledge-based economy by collective, education-based, innovation. Perhaps more importantly, a broader and more social approach to higher education, both in terms of investment and return, provide better means for addressing truly wide-ranging problems such as climate change. The extent to which Openness 3.0, and therefore the Open University 3.0, are practicable remains unclear, but the technical affordances and social needs allow and demand an approach to higher education that moves beyond the limited models still dominant.

Notes

1 See the website of the UA3 at http://www.u3a.org.uk/.
2 See The History of the Open University at http://www.open.ac.uk/about/ou/p3.shtml on which this section is based.
3 See http://www.open.ac.uk/.
4 See, for example, the Indian Open Schooling Network (IOSN) at http://www.nos.org/iosn.htm, the National Institute of Open Schooling at http://www.nos.org/, and Open School BC (British Columbia) at http://www.pss.gov.bc.ca/osbc/.

5   See http://en.wikipedia.org/wiki/Category:Open_universities.
6   http://ocw.mit.edu/OcwWeb/web/about/history/index.htm. For a more detailed history of OpenCourseWare, see Abelson (2008).
7   See, for instance: "OCW Stories" MIT OpenCourseWare site; and David Diamond, "MIT Everywhere" Wired, November 2009.
8   "Cultural capital" is introduced in Pierre Bourdieu and Jean-Claude Passeron, *Cultural Reproduction and Social Reproduction* (1973) and further articulated in Bourdieu, *The Forms of Capital* (1986).

CODA

Ronald Barnett

Patterns of the University

Inevitably, the structure of this book has had some arbitrariness attaching to it. A different structure could have been adopted for the volume; equally, even within the present structure, some of the chapters could happily have been placed in different parts of the volume. Such a level of openness and choice in the allocation of the chapters is inevitable for all of the chapters embody themes that criss-cross the volume. Just some of the large themes contained in this volume have been the following (the authors cited alongside the themes are simply indicative):

- The dominance of the economic sphere in the contemporary shaping of the university (Morley; Díaz Villa; Dall'Alba);
- The performative turn (Waghid; Masschelein & Simons);
- The university understood as a set of spaces (Standaert; Masschelein & Simons);
- The university as a global phenomenon (Morley; Chen & Lo; Peters, Giertzen & Ondercin; Díaz Villa; Standaert);
- The common good and the public sphere (van Wyk & Higgs; Nixon; Peters, Gietzen & Ondercin; Masschelein & Simons; Chen & Lo);
- Multiple knowledges (Wheelahan; Morley; Díaz Villa; Standaert);
- The need for a theory of knowledge (Kavanagh; Maxwell; van Wyk & Higgs);
- Sacred and profane knowledge (Masschelein & Simons; Morley; Wheelahan);
- Wisdom (Kavanagh; Maxwell; Dall'Alba; Nixon);
- The possibility of a recovery of liberal education (Rothblatt; Wheelahan; Chen & Lo; Standish);

- Critical reason (Waghid; Maxwell; Masschelein & Simons);
- The digital revolution (Rothblatt; Morley; Peters, Gietzen & Ondercin);
- Distributed, networked universities (Rothblatt; Peters, Gietzen & Ondercin; Standaert);
- Openness (Peters, Gietzen & Ondercin; Díaz Villa, Chen & Lo);
- Re-covering teaching (Waghid; Wheelahan; Standish; Nixon; Masschelein & Simons).

This is but an abbreviated list of cross-cutting themes in this volume. The mutuality and interconnections across the chapters are considerable (to which the index is testimony).

There is, it is apparent therefore, a complex patterning to the contributions here. A crude summary might be along the following lines: globally, the university is being incorporated into "knowledge capitalism" (Murphy, 2009), a process that is closing off spaces for the university such that its dominant activities—teaching, research and public engagement—are being steered in that direction. And yet, there remain spaces for more emancipatory and publicly-oriented stances on the part of the university. Wisdom, care, purpose networking, sustainability and openness are just some of the ideas offered here that imply that spaces may even be opening anew for the university in the twenty-first century. The very "hybridity" and "liminality"—to pick up two concepts from this volume—are opening new spaces for the university. It is not necessarily the case that the spaces of the university are being closed; or at least, even amid closure, new spaces may be opening. The university has not yet been suffocated.

Responsible and yet Poetic Anarchism

There is a further theme among the contributors, both explicit and implicit, that of responsibility (especially evident in the chapters by Gloria Dall'Alba and Louise Morley but surely implicit in several of the other chapters). To point to new spaces and the possibilities that they afford could point to an unbridled anarchism that, in turn, could lead to the "callousness of prestige" to which Morley refers (after Bousquet), in which the university sector becomes even more stratified. The entrepreneurial age, the coming of "knowledge capitalism," could seem to invite an academic free-for-all. And this free-for-all would be a global competitiveness, with the academic landscape dominated by universities that were both epistemically and economically powerful. Global inequalities across nations would be not just mirrored but exacerbated by global inequalities across universities.

However, the theme of responsibility pulls the university back, steadies it, and gives it pause for reflection as it ventures forward. "When possibilities are opened, we press ahead into an emergent possibility, thereby negating and foreclosing other possibilities." This reflection of Dall'Alba's is crucial here. There are no value-free or neutral options. In choosing to go in certain directions, some further possibilities are opened but others are truncated and even eradicated. Except at the price of bad faith, of pretending that it has no options, therefore, the university has to choose; and to understand that it chooses among the options before it.

But on what basis is the university to choose between its options? It will do so on the basis of its values. It might be tempting to talk of "the value background" of the university (cf. Barnett, 1990) but now, in an unstable world, with a myriad of challenges befalling the university and options opening for it, we should perhaps rather speak of a "value foreground." That is to say, the values by which a university steers among the thickets and attempts to carve out a line of direction for itself needs—in the twenty-first century—to become much more transparent, both to the university itself and to its hinterland. Here, I think that we are indebted to Mario Díaz Villa who provides us with both a detailed set of axioms that might inform the idea of the university in the twenty-first century and a set of principles that provide a general specification of a university that fulfilled the axioms. I believe, too, that the axioms and the principles reflect much of the spirit of the university that percolates much, if not all, of the contributions to this volume, those axioms and principles reflecting values connected with democracy, pluralism, dialogue, the public realm and openness.

The idea of responsibility, it might be felt, has a particular role to play in curbing the excesses of economic and instrumental reason. And so it has. But it is crucial to notice that it also comes into play here in quite a different way. I stressed in the Introduction that ideas of the university appropriate to the twenty-first century required imagination. Leaping out of the immediate situation in which universities find themselves and fashioning ideas afresh requires bold imagination. The imagination itself needs to be anarchic. But the imagination needs also to be conditioned by appropriate values and principles. The imagination itself needs also to be responsible.

The relationship between the imagination and responsibility takes on no less than three quite different forms, therefore. *In the first place*, imagination can help to furnish possibilities in the situation that is immediately before a university. It can discern possibilities for seizing the moment, for exploiting the moment. Here, as stated, responsibility then becomes a brake, a dampening of the worst excesses of unbridled knowledge capitalism. This university would be realising a soft form of knowledge capitalism. But, then, *and in the second place*, imagination can help in going beyond the surface order of things, to discern possibilities that lie beneath. Here, responsibility becomes a way of the university's flowering. Through imagination and responsibility jointly combined, a new kind of university can be glimpsed that does justice to values that challenge the establish order. *Third* responsibility then comes in to steady the ship, to exert a realism on proceedings. It denies the possibility of an undue fancifullism, avoiding a castles-in-the-air mentality. It becomes quite hard-nosed, as flights of fancy are brought up against the realities of the world. The contributions in the fourth part of the volume are precisely of this character, especially the final chapter—by Michael

Peters, Garett Gietzin and David Ondercin: there one sees a specific vision of possibilities for openness tempered by both an understanding of modern technology and fair rules of the game over intellectual copyright.

The offerings in part four of the book are "simply" indications of this combination of imagination and responsibility at play. And "play" here in two senses: play as in the ludic, in the form of a free roaming of the imagination as it explores the possibilities afforded by the spaces of the webs (Standaert) in which the university now finds itself. Here, there is a playfulness—and even as we might put it, following Kavanagh, a "play*fool*ness" as the university hold new and even awkward possibilities up to society; and play in the sense of a give and take, as there is "play" in the bending of tall structures. Here, their play, their flexibility allows them to survive in the otherwise harsh and very real exigencies of the environment in which they find themselves.

The ideas and the possibilities for the university of the twenty-first century, therefore, call for, as we may put it, *a responsible anarchism*. The university needs desperately a kind of anarchism, able to step outside of its presenting situations and imagine quite new possibilities, even at the risk of offending its sovereigns (Kavanagh). In the process, too, it must allow itself to forge new "conceptual grammars" (Morley) that speak to quite radical ideas and values that disturb the existing order. And that anarchism needs to be carried forward tinged with a due responsibility, lightly anchoring the university in the realities of the day. Then, new concepts may just give rise to new kinds of action in the world that seriously take account of the world; that even disturb the world but yet are feasible *in* the world. Its utopias would be *feasible utopias* (Barnett, 2011). To begin with, however, what is required is the exercise of the imagination. A new poetry of the university is now needed; nothing less. Such an exercise is not easy: it is extremely demanding for poetry comes with its rules and conditions. *At some level*, the poetry has to be intelligible. Even poets have to live in the real world.

CONTRIBUTORS

Ronald Barnett is an Emeritus Professor of Higher Education at the Institute of Education, University of London. His books include *The Idea of Higher Education*, *Realising the University in an Age of Supercomplexity*, *A Will to Learn: Being a Student in an Age of Uncertainty* and (most recently) *Being a University*.

Shuang-Ye Chen is an Assistant Professor in the Department of Educational Administration and Policy, The Chinese University of Hong Kong. Her research interests include higher education marketization, education policy and leadership. She has published several papers in Chinese and English on higher education policy and education leadership development.

Gloria Dall'Alba is Associate Professor in the School of Education at the University of Queensland in Brisbane, Australia. Her recent books are *Learning to be Professionals* and *Exploring Education through Phenomenology: Diverse Approaches*.

Mario Díaz Villa is a retired professor of the Institute of Education, Universidad del Valle, in Cali, Colombia. He is a currently an external advisor at several Colombian and Latin American universities. His main research interests are in the sociology of curriculum and pedagogy in the area of higher education.

Garett Gietzen is a Ph.D. student in Global Studies in Education in the Department of Educational Policy Studies at the University of Illinois at Urbana-Champaign, United States of America. His research focuses on how ideas of the public have changed, and are changing, over time and how this relates to the ways in which public higher education is understood and implemented.

Philip Higgs is a Research Professor in the School of Graduate Studies, University of South Africa. His recent books include *Rethinking our World* and *Rethinking Truth*.

Donncha Kavanagh is a Senior Lecturer in the Department of Management and Marketing, University College Cork, Cork, Ireland. He has published in the fields of management, marketing, organisational studies, and engineering.

Leslie N.K. Lo is Wei Lun Professor of Educational Administration and Policy, The Chinese University of Hong Kong. His research interests are higher education, comparative education, education policy and teacher professional development. He has published widely in Chinese and English.

Jan Masschelein is Professor of Philosophy of Education at the Catholic University of Leuven, Belgium. His primary areas of scholarship are educational theory, critical theory and social philosophy and his publications include, as co-editor, *The Learning Society from the Perspective of Governmentality*.

Nicholas Maxwell is Emeritus Reader in the Philosophy of Science, Department of Science and Technology Studies, University College London, United Kingdom. His books include *What's Wrong with Science?*, *From Knowledge to Wisdom*, *The Human World in the Physical Universe* and *Is Science Neurotic?*

Louise Morley is Professor of Education and Director of the Centre for Higher Education and Equity Research, University of Sussex, United Kingdom. Her publications include *Gender Equity in Selected Commonwealth Universities*, *Quality and Power in Higher Education* and *Organising Feminisms: The Micropolitics of the Academy*.

Jon Nixon is Honorary Professor of Educational Studies, University of Sheffield, United Kingdom, having held professorial posts in four UK institutions of higher education. His publications include *Towards the Virtuous University: the Moral Bases of Academic Practice*, *Higher Education and the Public Good: Imagining the University* and *Interpretive Pedagogies for Higher Education: Arendt, Berger, Said, Nussbaum and their Legacies*.

David J. Ondercin is a third year doctoral student in the Department of Educational Policy Studies at the University of Illinois at Urbana-Champaign. His main research interests include distributed knowledge systems, creative and open knowledge societies, and e-learning. His current research interests include economic development policies, democracies, and open education.

Michael A. Peters is a Professor in the Department of Educational Policy Studies, University of Illinois at Urbana-Champaign, United States of America and Adjunct Professor in the School of Art, RMIT, Australia. His recent books include (with Peter Roberts) *The Virtues of Openness: Education, Science and Scholarship in a Digital Age* (with Tina Besley, Mark Olssen, Susanne Maurer & Susan Weber (eds.)), *Governmentality Studies in Education* (with Gert Biesta), *Derrida, Politics and Pedagogy: Deconstructing the Humanities* and (with Simon Marginson & Peter Murphy) *Creativity and the Global Knowledge Economy.*

Sheldon Rothblatt is Professor Emeritus of History and former Director of the Center for Studies in Higher Education, University of California, Berkeley, United States of America. His books include *The Revolution of the Dons: Cambridge and Society in Victorian England, Tradition and Change in English Liberal Education: An Essay in History and Culture* and *The Modern University and its Discontents.*

Maarten Simons is Professor at the Centre for Educational Policy and Innovation and the Centre for Philosophy of Education, Catholic University of Leuven, Belgium. Together with Jan Masschelein he is the editor of the special issues *The University Revisited: Questioning the Public Role of the University in the European Knowledge Society* (2007, Studies in Philosophy and Education) and *Higher Education and Citizenship in Europe: On the Public Role of the University* (2009, European Educational Research Journal).

Nicolas Standaert is a Professor in the Department of Sinology, at the Catholic University of Leuven (K.U. Leuven), Belgium, where he specialises in the cultural contacts between China and Europe in the seventeenth and eighteenth centuries.

Paul Standish is a Professor and Head of Philosophy of Education at the Institute of Education, University of London, United Kingdom. His recent books include: (with Naoko Saito) *Stanley Cavell and the Education of Grownups* (with John Drummond), *The Philosophy of Nurse Education* and (with Paul Smeyers & Richard Smith) *The Therapy of Education.*

Berte van Wyk is a Senior Lecturer in the Department of Education Policy Studies, University of Stellenbosch, South Africa.

Yusef Waghid is a Professor of Philosophy of Education and Dean of the Faculty of Education at the University of Stellenbosch, South Africa. His research focuses on higher education transformation, democratic citizenship education and ethics.

Leesa Wheelahan is an Associate Professor at the L.H. Martin Institute for Higher Education Leadership and Management, at the University of Melbourne, Australia. She is the author of *Why Knowledge Matters in Curriculum: A Social Realist Argument* and numerous chapters and papers on relations between the sectors of tertiary education.

BIBLIOGRAPHY

Abelson, H. (2008). The creation of OpenCourseWare at MIT. *Journal of Science Education and Technology, 17 (2)*, 164–174.

Agamben, G. (2005). *Profanations*. Paris: Payot.

Altbach, P. (1998). *Comparative higher education: Knowledge, the university, and development.* Greenwich: Ablex Publishing Co.

Altbach, P. G., & Levy, D. C. (Eds.). (2005). *Private higher education: A global revolution.* Rotterdam: Sense Publishers.

Altman Borbón, J. (2009). El alba, petrocaribe y centroamérica. ¿Intereses comunes? Revista *Nueva sociedad*, N° 210, enero-febrero.

Amin S. (1976). *Unequal development: An essay on the social formations of peripheral capitalism.* New York: Monthly Review Press.

Appadurai, A. (2004). The capacity to aspire: Culture and the terms of recognition. In V. Rao & M. Walton (Eds.), *Culture and public action*. Stanford: Stanford University Press.

Archer, L., Hutchins, M., Ross, A., Leathwood, C., Gilchrist, R., & Phillips, D. (2003). *Higher education and social class: Issues of exclusion and inclusion.* London: RoutledgeFalmer.

Archer, M. (2000). *Being human: The problem of agency.* Cambridge: Cambridge University Press.

Ardao A. (1993). *América latina y la latinidad*. México: UNAM-CCyDEL.

Arendt, H. (1968/1983). *Between past and future: Eight excercises in political thought.* New York: Penguin.

Aristotle (1955). *The ethics of aristotle: The Nichomachean ethics* (trans. J. A. K. Thompson and revised by H. Tredennick). London: Penguin Books.

Aronowitz, S., & Giroux, H. A. (1991). *Postmodern education: Politics, culture, and social criticism.* Minneapolis: University of Minnesota Press.

Asmal, K., Asmal, L., & Roberts, R. S. (1996). *Reconciliation through truth*: A reckoning of apartheid's criminal governance. Cape Town & Johannesburg: David Philip Publishers.

Assié-Lumumba, N. T. (2006). *Higher education in Africa: Crises, reforms and transformation.* Dakar, Senegal: Council for the Development of Social Science Research in Africa.

Atcon, R. P. (1961). *La Universidad Latinoamericana,* en *Revista de la cultura de occidente.* Mayo-julio, Tomo VII, Buchholz, Bogotá, 1–169.

Atcon, R. P. (1963). *La Universidad Latinoamericana.* Tomo VII (1-3). Bogotá: Revista ECO.

Balfour, R. (2010). The state of postgraduate research in South Africa (2006-2015). Unpublished paper presented in the Faculty of Education at Stellenbosch University, 20 October. Stellenbosch: Matieland.

Ball, S. (2003). The teacher's soul and the terrors of performativity. *Journal of Education Policy, 18 (2),* 215–228.

Ball, S. (2006). Performativities and fabrications in the education economy: Towards the performative society. In H. Lauder, P. Brown, J.-A. Dillabough, & A. H. Halsey (Eds.), *Education, globalization & social change.* Oxford: Oxford University Press.

Ball, S. J., & Exley, S. (2010). Making policy with "good ideas": policy networks and the "intellectuals" of New Labour. *Journal of Education Policy, 25 (2),* 151–169.

Ball, S. J., & Youdell, D. (2008). *Hidden privatisation in public education.* Brussels: Education International.

Barnett, R. (1990). *The idea of higher education.* Buckingham: The Society for Research into Higher Education & Open University Press.

Barnett, R. (1994). *The limits of competence: Knowledge, higher education and society.* Buckingham: The Society for Research into Higher Education & Open University Press.

Barnett, R. (2000). *Realizing the university in an age of supercomplexity.* Buckingham: The Society for Research into Higher Education & Open University Press.

Barnett, R. (2003). *Beyond all reason: Living with ideology in the university.* Buckingham: The Society for Research into Higher Education & Open University Press.

Barnett, R. (2004). *Los límites de la competencia: El conocimiento, la educación superior y la sociedad.* Barcelona: Editorial Gedisa.

Barnett, R. (2005). Recapturing the universal in the university. *Educational Philosophy and Theory, 37 (6),* 785–797.

Barnett, R. (2007). Wisdom and wit in the study of higher education. *Towards a cartography of higher education policy change.* Enschede, the Netherlands: Center for Higher Education Policy Studies (CHEPS).

Barnett, R. (2009a). Knowledge interests and knowledge policies: Re-thinking the university in the twenty-first century. In R. Barnett et al., *Rethinking the university after Bologna.* Antwerp: UCSIA.

Barnett, R. (2009b). Knowing and becoming in the higher education curriculum. *Studies in Higher Education, 34 (4),* 429–440.

Barnett, R. (2011). *Being a university.* London: Routledge.

Barnett, R., & Coate, K. (2004). *Engaging the curriculum in higher education.* Maidenhead: Open University Press/McGraw-Hill Education.

Barnett, R., Guédon, J.-C., Masschelein, J., Simons, M., Robertson, S., & Standaert, N. (2009). *Rethinking the university after Bologna: New concepts and practices beyond tradition and the market.* Antwerp: UCSIA.

Barnett, R., & Maxwell, N. (Eds.). (2008). *Wisdom in the university.* London: Routledge.

Barnett, R., Parry, G., & Coate, K. (2001). Conceptualising curriculum change. *Teaching in Higher Education, 6(4),* 435–449.

Battle, M. (1997). *Reconciliation: The ubuntu theology of Desmond Tutu.* Cleveland, Ohio: Pilgrim Press.

Bauman, Z. (2000). *Liquid modernity*. Cambridge: Polity Press.

Beck, U. (2009). *World at risk*. Cambridge and Malden, MA: Polity.

Becker, P., & Clark, W. (2001). *Little tools of knowledge: Historical essays on academic and bureaucratic practices*. Ann Arbor, Mich.: University of Michigan Press.

Benhabib, S. (2006). The philosophical foundations of cosmopolitan norms. In J. Waldron, B. Honig, & W. Kymlicka (Eds.), *Seyla Benhabib: Another cosmopolitanism*. Oxford: Oxford University Press.

Berman, M. (1983). *All that is solid melts into air: The experience of modernity*. London: Verso.

Berman, M. (1988). *Todo lo sólido se desvanece en el aire: La experiencia de la modernidad*. México: Siglo XXI.

Bernstein, B. (1998). *Pedagogía, control simbólico e identidad*. Madrid: Ediciones Morata.

Bernstein, B. (2000). *Pedagogy, symbolic control and identity*. Oxford: Rowman & Littlefield Publishers.

Bevis, T. B., & Lucas, C. J. (2007). *International students in American colleges and universities: A history*. New York: Palgrave Macmillan.

Bhaskar, R. (1998). *The possibility of naturalism: A philosophical critique of the contemporary human sciences*. London: Routledge.

Bhaskar, R. (2011). *Reclaiming reality: A critical introduction to contemporary philosophy*. Abingdon: Routledge.

Biesta, G. (2006). What's the point of lifelong learning if lifelong learning has no point? On the democratic deficit of policies for lifelong learning. *European Educational Research Journal, 5 (3 & 4)*, 169–180.

BIS (Department of Business, Innovation and Skills) (2009). *Higher ambitions: The future of universities in a knowledge economy*. London: BIS.

BIS (Department of Business, Innovation and Skills) (2010). *Participation rates in higher education: Academic years 2006/2007–2008/2009 (Provisional)* http://stats.bis.gov.uk/he/Participation_Rates_in_HE_2008-09.pdf

Bjarnason, S., Cheng, K., Fielden, J., Lemaitre, M., Levy, D., & Varghese, N. (2009). *A new dynamic: Private higher education*. Paris: UNESCO.

Bledstein, B. J. (1978). *The culture of professionalism: The middle class and the development of higher education in America*. New York: Norton.

Bloom, A. (1987). *The closing of the American mind*. New York: Touchstone.

Bok, D. (2003). *Universities in the marketplace: The commercialization of higher education*. Princeton, N.J.: Princeton University Press.

Boltansky, L., & Chiapello, E. (2002). *El nuevo espíritu del capitalismo*. Madrid: Ediciones Akal.

Bolter, J. D., & Grusin, R. (2001). *Remediation: Understanding new media*. London: MIT Press.

Borrero Cabal, A. (2008). *La universidad. Tomo I estudios sobre sus orígenes, dinámicas y tendencias. La universidad en Europa desde sus orígenes hasta la Revolución Francesa*. Bogotá: Pontificia Universidad Javeriana.

Boston Globe. (On-line reporting, Breaking News 24/7, July 6, 2010).

Bousquet, M. (2008). *How the university works: Higher education and the low-wage nation*. New York and London: New York University Press.

Bowker, G., & Star, S. L. (1999). *Sorting things out: Classification and its consequences*. London: MIT Press.

Brabazon, T. (2007). *The University of Google: Education in the [post] information age*. Aldershot: Ashgate.

Bradbury, M. (2000). *The history man*. London: Picador.

Bradwell, P. (2009). *The edgeless university: Why higher education must embrace technology*. London: Demos.

Brown, R. (Ed.). (2011). *Higher education and the market*. London and New York: Routledge.

Browne, J. (2010). *Securing a sustainable future for higher education: An independent review of higher education funding & student finance*. London: BIS.

Brunner, J. J. (1992). Entonces, ¿Existe o no la modernidad en América Latina? *Fin de Siglo* N° 2 Revista de la Universidad del Valle.

Bueno Chávez, R. (2004). *Antonio Cortejo Polar y los avatares de la cultura latinoamericana*. Lima: UNMSM, Fondo Editorial.

Burgess, J., & Green, J. (2009). *YouTube: Online video and participatory culture*. London: Polity Press.

Burik, S. (2009). Opening philosophy to the world: Derrida and education in philosophy. *Educational Theory, 59(3)*, 297–312.

Cardoso, F. H., & Faletto, E. (1979). *Dependency and development in Latin América*. Los Angeles: University of California Press.

Carr, N. (2010). *The shallows: What the internet is doing to our brains*. London: W.W. Norton & Co.

Carson, S. (2009). The unwalled garden: growth of the OpenCourseWare consortium, 2001–2008. *Open Learning: The Journal of Open and Distance Learning, 24 (1)*, 23–29.

Castells, M. (1996). *The rise of the network society*. Oxford: Blackwell.

Cavell, S. (1979). *The claim of reason: Wittgenstein, skepticism, morality, and tragedy*. Oxford: Clarendon Press.

Cavell, S. (2005). *Philosophy the day after tomorrow*. Cambridge, Mass.: The Belknap Press of Harvard University Press.

Centro de Desarrollo de la Organización para la Cooperación y el Desarrollo Económicos (OCDE). (2010). Perspectiva económicas de América Latina 2010.

Cerny, P. G. (2000). Restructuring the political arena: Globalization and the paradoxes of the competition state. In R. D. Germain (Ed.), *Globalization and its critics: Perspectives from political economy* (pp. 117–138). Houndmills & New York: Macmilian Press & St. Martin's Press.

Chen, H.-J. (2006). *Deguo gudian daxueguan jiqi dui zhongguo daxue de yingxiang (Die Deutsche klassische universitatsidee und ihre rezeption in China) (The classical German idea of the university and its influence on Chinese universities)*. Beijing: Peking University Press.

Chen, P.-Y. (2009). *Daxue you jingshen (University has spirit)*. Beijing: Peking University Press.

Chen, S.-Y., & Lo, L. N. K. (2004). Zhongguo jiushi niandai yijiang gaodeng jiaoyu gaige zhong de shichang jiaose (The role of market in China's mainland higher education reforms since 1990s). *Educational Research, 10*, 33–37.

Chu, Z.-H. (2006). *Zhongguo daxue jingshen de lishi yu xingsi (History and reflection of the spirit of Chinese universities)*. Taiyuan: Shanxi Educational Publishing House.

Cladis, M. S. (2001). Introduction. In É. Durkheim, *The elementary forms of religious life*. Oxford: Oxford University Press.

Clark, B. R. (1998). *Creating entrepreneurial universities, organizational pathways of transformation*. Kidlington, Oxford: Pergamon Press.

Clark, B. R. (2004). *Sustaining change in universities, continuities in case studies and concept*. Maidenhead: Open University Press.

Clark, W. (2006). *Academic charisma and the origins of the research university*. Chicago: University of Chicago Press.

Clegg, S. (2010). *Academic identities re-formed? Contesting technological determinism in accounts of the digital age*. Paper presented at the ESRC/CHEER Seminar Series, "Imagining the University of the Future" Seminar 5: Who can inhabit the new academic identities of a digital age? Leeds Metropolitan University, 12 January, 2010. http://www.sussex.ac.uk/cheer/esrcseminars/seminar5

Comisión Económica para América Latina, CEPAL. (2008). La transformación productiva 20 años después. Viejos problemas, nuevas oportunidades. Trigésimo segundo período de sesiones de la CEPAL. Santo Domingo, república Dominicana. 9 a 13 de junio 2008. Naciones Unidad-CEPAL.

Comisión Económica para América Latina, CEPAL. (2008a). *Panorama social de América latina 2008*. Santiago: Naciones Unidas-CEPAL.

Commonwealth of Australia. (2009). *Transforming Australia's higher education system*. Canberra: Department of Education, Employment and Workplace Relations.

Cornejo Polar, A. (1994). Mestizaje, transculturación, heterogeneidad. *Revista de Crítica Literaria Latinoamericana* N° 40.

Cornejo Polar, A. (1997). Mestizaje e hibridez: los riesgos de las metáforas apuntes. *Revista de Crítica Literaria Latinoamericana* N° 47.

Corredor, C. (1990). *Modernismo sin modernidad: Modelos de desarrollo en Colombia*. Bogotá: CINEP.

Cortés, F. (2006). Marginalization, the marginality, economic marginality and social exclusion considerations. *Population papers, January-March, 47, Universidad Autónoma del Estado de México*, 71–84.

Costa Bonino, Luis (2001). Democracy in Latin-America: A prospective analysis. Online. http://www.costabonino.com/democracia.htm

Crozier G., Reay, D., Clayton, J., Colliander, L., & Grinstead, J. (2008). Different strokes for different folks: Diverse students in diverse institutions – experiences of higher education. *Research Papers in Education Special Issue on Challenges of Diversity for Widening Participation in UK Higher Education, 23 (2)*, 167–179.

Curtis, P. (2009). "Raise university fees to £5000 a year to tackle funding crisis, says CBI", *The Guardian*, 21 September, p. 2.

Dahrendorf, R. (1969). The intellectual and society: The social function of the "fool" in the twentieth century. In P. Rieff (Ed.), *On intellectuals: Theoretical case studies*. New York: Doubleday.

David, M. (2009). Social diversity and democracy in higher education in 21st century: Towards a feminist critique. *Higher Education Policy, 22 (1)*, 61–79.

de Certeau, M. (1988). *The practice of everyday life*. Trans. Steven Rendall. Berkeley: University of California Press.

Deem, R. (2010). *The 21st century university – dilemmas of leadership and organisational futures*. Professorial lecture, Royal Holloway, University of London, 11 February, 2010.

Delanty, G. (1998). The idea of the university in the global era: From knowledge as an end to the end of knowlege? *Social Epistemology, 12 (1)*, 3–25.

Delors, J. & Al Muftu, I. (1998). *Learning: The treasure within.* Report to UNESCO of the International Commission on Education for the Twenty-first Century/ Jacques Delors, chairman; In'am Al Mufti et al. Paris: UNESCO Publishing.

Department of Education Science and Training. (2002). *Varieties of learning: The interface between higher education and vocational education and training.* Canberra: Department of Education Science and Training.

De Ridder-Symoens, H. (Ed.). (1992). *A history of the university in Europe. Vol.I. Universities in the Middle Ages.* Cambridge: Cambridge University Press.

Derrida, J. (2001). *L'université sans conditions.* Paris: Galilée.

Derrida, J. (2002). The university without condition. In P. Kamuf (Ed.), *Without alibi.* Stanford: Stanford University Press.

Derrida, J. (2004). *Eye of the university: Right to philosophy 2.* Stanford: Stanford University Press.

Dewey, J. (1966 (1916)) *Democracy and education: An introduction to the philosophy of education.* New York: The Free Press.

DFID (Department for International Development). (2008). *Briefing. Higher education.* London: DFID.

Douglas, J. A., & Edelstein, R. (2009). Whither the global talent pool. *Change (July/August, 2009),* 37–44.

Durkheim, É. (2001). *The elementary forms of religious life.* Oxford: Oxford University Press.

Durkheim, É. (2006). *Emile Durkheim selected writings on education. Volume II: The evolution of educational thought. Lectures on the formation and development of secondary education in France.* London: Routledge.

ECU (Equality Challenge Unit). (2010). *Equality in higher education, statistical report 2009.* London: ECU.

Emerson, R. W. (1838). Address delivered before the senior class in Divinity College, Cambridge, Sunday evening, 15 July.

Erasmus, D. (1511/2005). *The praise of folly.* Champaign, Ill.: Project Gutenberg. http://www.gutenberg.org/etext/9371 (accessed on 14 November 14, 2007).

Fallis, G. (2007). *Multiversities, ideas, and democracy.* Toronto: University of Toronto Press.

Faust, D. G. (2007, October 12). *Unleashing our most ambitious imaginings.* Installation address at Harvard University, Cambridge, Mass. Retrieved August 27, 2010, from http://www.president.harvard.edu/speeches/faust/071012_installation.php

Ferrari, C., & Contreras, N. (2008). Universidades en América Latina: Sugerencias para su modernización. *Nueva Sociedad,* 218. Online. http://www.nuso.org

Ffrench-Davis, R. (2001). *El comercio intra-latinoamericano y su base analítica para el nuevo decenio.* Draft.

Flexner, A. (1930). *Universities: American English German.* New York: Oxford University Press.

Foucault, M. (1986). *Of other spaces.* Online. http://www.colorado.edu/envd/courses/envd4114-001/Spring%2006/Theory/Foucault.pdf

Foucault, M. (1989). *Parresia: vrijmoedig spreken en waarheid.* Amsterdam: De Balie.

Foucault, M. (1997). What is enlightenment ? In P. Rabinow (Ed.), *Michel Foucault, the essential works, volume 1, Ethics: Subjectivity and truth.* Harmondsworth: Penguin.

Freire, P. (2004). *Pedagogy of hope.* New York: Continuum.

Fuller, S. (2005). *The intellectual.* Cambridge: Icon Books.

Gan, Y., & Li, M. (Eds.). (2004). *Zhongguo daxue gaige zhidao (The way of reforming Chinese universities)*. Shanghai: Century Publising Group & Shanghai People Publishing House.

García, A. (1985). *La crisis de la universidad: La universidad en el proceso de la sociedad Colombiana*. Bogotá: Plaza y Janés.

García Canclini, N. (1990). *Culturas híbridas: estrategias para entrar y salir de la modernidad*. México, D.F.: Grijalbo.

Garfield, J. L. (2002). Philosophy, religion, and the hermeneutic imperative. In J. Malpas, U. Arnswald & J. Kertscher (Eds.), *Gadamer's century: Essays in honor of Hans-Georg Gadamer*. Cambridge and London: The MIT Press.

Geiser, S. (2010). *Beyond the master plan: The case for restructuring baccalaureate education in California*. University of California, Berkeley: Center for Studies in Higher Education.

Goffman, E. (1981). The Lecture. *Forms of talk* (pp. 160–196). Oxford: Blackwell, .

Grewal, D. S. (2009). *Network power: The social dynamics of globalization*. New Haven/London: Yale University Press.

Grubb, W. N. (2005). Vocationalism in higher education: The triumph of the education gospel. *The Journal of Higher Education 76(1)*, 1–25.

Guédon, J.-C. (2009). Between excellence and quality: The European research area in search of itself. In R. Barnett et al., *Rethinking the university after Bologna*, Antwerp: UCSIA.

Guri-Rosenblit, S. (2009). *Digital technologies in higher education sweeping expectations and actual effects*. New York: Nova Science Publishers.

Gyekye K. (1987). *An essay on African philosophical thought: The Akan conceptual scheme*. Cambridge: Cambridge University Press.

Gyekye, K. (2002). Person and community in African thought. In P. H. Coetzee & A. P. J. Roux (Eds.), *Philosophy from Africa: A text with readings*. (2nd ed). Cape Town: Oxford University Press Southern Africa.

Habermas, J. (1989). *Teoría de la Acción Comunicativa: Tomo I. Racionalidad de la Acción y Racionalización Social*. Madrid: Taurus.

Hall, P. (1997). The university and the city. *GeoJournal, 41*, 301–309.

Harley, D. (2009). Why understanding the use and users of open education matters. In Iiyoshi, T. & Vijay, M. S. K. (Eds.), *Opening up education, the collective advancement of education through open technology, open content, and open knowledge*. Cambridge, MA: MIT Press.

Hattersley, R. (2004). Education and the good society. In F. Inglis (Ed.), *Education and the good society*. Basingstoke, UK and New York: Palgrave Macmillan.

Hayhoe, R. (1999). *China's universities: 1895–1995: A century of cultural conflict*. Hong Kong: The Comparative Education Research Centre & The University of Hong Kong.

Heath, S., Fuller, A., & Paton, K. (2008). Networked ambivalence and educational decision-making: A case study of "non-participation" in higher education. *Research Papers in Education Special Issue on Challenges of Diversity for Widening Participation in UK Higher Education, 23 (2)*, 219–231

Heidegger, M. (1962/1927). *Being and time*. J. Macquarrie & E. Robinson (Trans.). New York: SCM Press.

Heidegger, M. (1993/1954). The question concerning technology. D.F. Krell (Trans.). In M. Heidegger (Ed.), *Basic writings* (2nd ed., pp. 311–341). London: Routledge.

HEFCE. (2009). *The research excellence framework: Second consultation on the assessment and funding of research*. http://www.hefce.ac.uk/pubs/hefce/2009/09_38/. Last accessed 23 July 2010.

Heller, D. E. (2007), Financing public research universities in the United States: The role of students and their families. In R.L. Geiger, C.L. Colbeck, R.L. Williams & C.K. Anderson (Eds.), *Future of the American public research university*. Rotterdam and Taipei: Sense Publishers.

Henríquez Ureña, P. (1978). *La utopía de América*. Caracas: Biblioteca Ayacucho.

HEPI (Higher Education Policy Institute). (2009). *Male and female participation and progression in higher education*. Oxford: Higher Education Policy Institute.

Herrera, F. (1965). *La educación avanzada y el desarrollo de América*. Washington: Banco Interamericano de Desarrollo.

Herrera, F. (1966). Función de la Universidad en el desarrollo de América Latina. *ECO, Revista de la Cultura de Occidente*. Bogota: Buchholz.

HESA (Higher Education Statistical Agency). (2010). *Higher education statistics for the UK*. Cheltenham, Glos: HESA.

Hills Report (2009). *An anatomy of economic inequality in the UK: Report of the National Equality Panel*. London: Government Equalities Office.

Horkheimer, M. (1953). Fragen des Hochschulunterrichts. *Frankfurter Universitätsreden, 8*, 24–40.

Hountondji, P. J. (1985). The pitfalls of being different. *Diogenes, 131*.

Hountondji, P. J. (1996). *African philosophy: Myth and reality*. Bloomington: Indiana University Press.

Huisman, J. (2008). World-class universities. *Higher Education Policy, 21(1)*, 1–4.

Huizinga, J. (1955). *Homo Ludens: A study of the play element in culture*. Boston: The Beacon Press.

Humboldt, von W. (1810). Über die innere und äussere Organisation der Höheren Wissenschaftlichen Anstalten. In E. Anrich (Ed.), (1959), *Die Idee der deutschen Universität*. Darmstadt: Wissenschaftliche Buchgesellschaft.

Humboldt, von W. (2005). Solicitud de Institución de la Universidad de Berlín. *Logos, Anales del Seminario de Metafísica*, vol. 38: 293–299.

Huntington, P. (2001). Introduction – general background: History of the feministreception of Heidegger and a guide to Heidegger's thought. In N. Holland & P.Huntington (Eds.), *Feminist interpretations of Martin Heidegger*. University Park, PA: Pennsylvania State University Press.

Husén, T. (1994). The Idea of the university. Changing roles, current crisis and future challenges. In T. Husén (Ed.), *The role of the university: A global perspective*. Tokyo: The United Nations University.

Hyde, L. (1998). *Trickster makes this world: Mischief, myth, and art*. New York: Farrar, Straus and Giroux.

Illich, I. (1992). *In the mirror of the past. Lectures and addresses 1978–1990*. New York/London: Marion Boyars.

Illich, I. (2010). Le texte et l'université: idée et histoire d'une institution unique. *Esprit* 367, *août-septembre*, 172–184.

Inglis, F. (2004). Education and the good society. In F. Inglis (Ed.), *Education and the good society*. Houndmills and New York: Palgrave Macmillan.

Iredale, M. (2007). From knowledge-inquiry to wisdom-inquiry: Is the revolution underway? *London Review of Education, 5,* 117–29. Reprinted in R. Barnett & N. Maxwell (Eds.), (2008).

Jackson, B., & Segal, P. (2007). Equality. In A.H. Halsey with R. Hattersley and others, *Democracy in crisis: Ethical socialism for a prosperous country.* London: Politico's.

Jansen, J. (2007). Learning and leading in a globalised world: lessons from South Africa. In T. Townsend & R. Bates (Eds.), *Handbook of teacher education: Globalization, standards and professionalism in times of change* (pp. 25–40). Dordrecht: Springer.

Jenkins, H. (2006). *Convergence culture: Where old and new media collide.* New York, NYU Press.

Judt, T. (2010a). *Ill fares the land.* London: Allen Lane

Judt, T. (2010b). *Postwar: A history of Europe since 1945.* London: Vintage

Kaletsky, A. (2010). *Capitalism 0.4: The birth of new economy.* London: Bloomsbury.

Kant, I. (1784/1977). An answer to the question: "What is enlightenment?" In H. Reiss (Ed. and intro.), H.B. Nisbet (Trans.), *Kant's political writings.* Cambridge: Cambridge University Press.

Kaphagawani, D. N., & Malherbe, J. (1998). African epistemology. In P. H. Coetzee & A. P. J. Roux (Eds.), *Philosophy from Africa: A text with readings.* Johannesburg: Thompson Publishers.

Kaphagawani, D. N., & Malherbe, J. G. (2003). African epistemology. In P. H. Coetzee & A. P. J. Roux (Eds.), *Philosophy from Africa: A text with readings* (2nd ed.). Cape Town: Oxford University Press Southern Africa.

Kellner, D., & Kim, G. (2009). YouTube, politics and pedagogy. In R. Hammer & D. Kellner (Eds.), *Media/cultural studies: Critical approaches.* New York: Peter Lang.

Kenway, J., Bullen, E., & Robb, S., (2004). The knowledge economy, the techno-preneur and the problematic future of the university. *Policy Futures in Education 2(2),* 330.

Kenyatta, J. (1965). *Facing Mount Kenya.* New York: Vintage Books.

Kerr, C. (1963/ 2001). *The uses of the university.* Cambridge, Mass.: Harvard University Press.

Kittler, F. A. (1987). *Aufschreibesysteme 1800–1900.* München: Wilhelm Fink.

King, M. (2001). *A guide to Heidegger's being and time.* Albany: State University of New York Press.

Klein, N. (2008). *The shock doctrine: The rise of disaster capitalism.* London: Penguin Press.

Kokotovic, M. (2000). Hibridez y desigualdad: García Canclini ante el neoliberalismo. *Revista de crítica literaria latinoamericana.* Año XXVI. N° 52 Lima-Hannover, 289–300.

Kymlicka, W. (2002). *Contemporary political philosophy: An introduction* (2nd ed.). Oxford: Oxford University Press.

Laclau, E. (2006). *La razón populista.* México: Fondo de Cultura Economica.

Langley, L. (2005). *Soldiers in the laboratory.* Folkstone: Scientists for Global Responsibility.

Lastra, A. (2008). Walter Mignolo y la idea de América Latina: Un intercambio de opiniones. *Tabula Rasa.* Bogotá–Colombia, No.9, 285–310, *julio-diciembre.* Originally published in *La Torre del Virrey. Revista de Estudios Culturales 4,* 68–78.

Latour, B. (2004). *Politics of nature: How to bring the sciences into democracy.* London: Harvard University Press.

Latour, B., & Weibel, P. (Eds.). (2005). *Making things public: Atmospheres of democracy.* Karlsruhe and Cambridge: Zentrum für Kunst und Medientechnologie [Centre for Art and Media] & MIT Press.

Lazerson, M. (2010). *Higher education and the American dream: Success and its discontents.* Budapest and New York: Central University Press.

Leathwood, C., & Read, B. (2009). *Gender and the changing face of higher education: A feminised future?* Maidenhead: McGraw-Hill/Open University Press.

Lechner, N. (1989). Democracia y Modernidad: Ese Desencanto llamado Postmoderno. *Revista Foro N° 10.*

Letseka, M. (2000). African philosophy and educational discourse. In P. Higgs, N. C. G. Vakalisa, T. V. Mda & N. T. Assie-Lumumba (Eds.), *African voices in education.* Cape Town: Juta.

Levin, H., & Xu, Z.-Y. (2006). Issues in the expansion of higher education in the People's Republic of China. In H. Lauder, P. Brown, J-A. Dillabough & A. H. Halsey (Eds.), *Education, globalization & social change* (pp. 909–925). Oxford: Oxford University Press.

Lienhard, M. (1996). De mestizajes, heterogeneidades, hibridismos y otras quimeras. In J. A. Mazzotti & U. Zevallos Aguilar J (Eds.), *Asedios a la heterogeneidad cultural.* Philadelphia: Asociación Internacional de Peruanistas.

Lightman, A. (2005). *A Sense of the mysterious: Science and the human spirit.* New York: Vintage Books.

Linksruck, Nr. 166, 26. November 2003. http://www.linksruck.de/artikel_421.html

Lipovetsky, G. (2002). *La era del vacío.* Barcelona: Editorial Anagrama.

Lipovetsky, G. (2005). *Hypermodern times.* Cambridge: Polity Press.

Lo, L. N. K. (1991). State patronage of intellectuals in Chinese higher education. *Comparative Education Review, 35 (4),* 690–720.

Luo, Y. (2010). Renmin de daxue: 1949 nian xinzhengquan xia zhongguo daxue shenfen zhi jiangou--- yi beijing daxue wei anli (The identity construction of universities in the Chinese mainland under the new regime since 1949: A narrative study on Peking University). *Education Journal, 38 (1),* 71–94.

Lynch, C. (2008). Opening up education: The collective advancement of education through open technology, open content, and open knowledge. In T. Iivoshi & M. S. V. Kumar (Eds.), Cambridge, Mass.: The MIT Press.

Lynch, K. (2009). Carelessness: A hidden doxa of higher education. Presentation to the ESRC/ CHEER Research Seminar 2 on *Disqualified Discourses.* "Imagining the University of the Future" Series, CHEER, University of Sussex. 27 April 2009. http://www.sussex.ac.uk/cheer/esrcseminars/seminar2

Lyotard, J.-F. (1984). *The postmodern condition: A report on knowledge.* Manchester: Manchester University Press.

Macdonald, C. (2009). Nicholas Maxwell in context: The relationship of his wisdom theses to the contemporary global interest in wisdom. In L. McHenry, *Science and the pursuit of wisdom: Studies in the philosophy of Nicholas Maxwell.* Frankfurt: Ontos Verlog.

Marginson, S. (1997). *Educating Australia: Government, economy and citizen since 1960.* Melbourne: Cambridge University Press.

Marginson, S., & Considine, M. (2000). *The enterprise university: Power, governance and reinvention in Australia.* Cambridge, Cambridge University Press.

Marginson, S., Murphy, P., & Peters, M.A. (2010). *Global creation: Space, connection and universities in the age of the knowledge economy.* New York: Peter Lang.

Marres, N. (2005). Issues spark a public into being: A key but often forgotten point of the Lippmann-Dewey Debate. In B. Latour & P. Wiebel (Eds.), *Making things public: Atmospheres of democracy.* Karlsruhe and Cambridge: Zentrum für Kunst und Medientechnologie [Centre for Art and Media] & MIT Press.

Maskell, D., & Robinson, I. (2001). *The new idea of a university.* London: Haven Books.

Masschelein, J. (2009). The world "once more": Walking lines. *Teachers College Record*, art. nr. ID Number: 15647. (http://www.tcrecord.org)

Masschelein, J. (2010). E-ducating the gaze: The idea of a poor pedagogy. *Ethics and Education, 5(1)* 43–53.

Masschelein, J., & Simons, M. (2002). An adequate education in a globalised world? A note on immunisation against being-together. *Journal of Philosophy of Education, 36(4),* 565–584.

Masschelein, J., & Simons, M. (2009a). From active citizenship to world citizenship: A proposal for a world university. *European Educational Research Journal, 8(2),* 237–249.

Masschelein, J., & Simons, M. (2009b). The university as a matter of public concern: Thinking about and of a world-university. In R. Barnett et al., *Rethinking the university after Bologna.* Antwerp: UCSIA.

Masschelein, J., & Simons, M. (2010). *Jenseits der exzellenz: Eine kleine morphologie der weltuniversität.* Zürich: Diaphanes.

Maxwell, N. (1974). The rationality of scientific discovery. *Philosophy of Science, 41,* 123–53 and 247–95.

Maxwell, N. (1976). *What's wrong with science?* (Frome: Bran's Head Books, 2nd ed., 2009). London: Pentire Press.

Maxwell, N. (1980). Science, reason, knowledge and wisdom: A critique of specialism. *Inquiry, 23,* 19–81.

Maxwell, N. (1984). *From knowledge to wisdom: A revolution in the aims and methods of science.* (Oxford: Blackwell, 2nd ed., 2007). London: Pentire Press.

Maxwell, N. (1998). *The comprehensibility of the Universe: A new conception of science.* Oxford: Oxford University Press.

Maxwell, N. (2004). *Is science neurotic?* London: Imperial College Press.

Maxwell, N. (2007). *From knowledge to wisdom: A revolution for science and the humanities.* London: Pentire Press. 2nd ed. (1984), revised and extended.

Maxwell, N. (2009). Are universities undergoing an intellectual revolution? *Oxford Magazine, No. 290, Eighth Week, Trinity Term, June,* 13–16.

Maxwell, N. (2010). *Cutting God in half – and putting the pieces together again: A new approach to philosophy.* London: Pentire Press.

Mbiti, J. S. (1970). *African religions and philosophy.* London: Heinemann.

McHenry, L. (Ed.). (2009). *Science and the pursuit of wisdom: Studies in the philosophy of Nicholas Maxwell.* Frankfurt: Ontos Verlag.

McKibbin, R. (2006). The destruction of the public sphere. *London Review of Books, 28, 1,* 3–6.

McKibbin, R. (2010). Good for business. *London Review of Books,* 25 February, 8–10

Melo, J. O. (1990). Algunas consideraciones globales sobre modernidad y modernización. *Análisis Político* N° 10.

Menkiti, I. A. (1979). Person and community in African traditional thought. In R. A. Wright (Ed.), *African philosophy: An introduction,* Washington: University Press of America.

Miedema, J. (2009). *Slow reading.* Duluth, Minn.: Litwin Books.

Mignolo, W. D. (2007). *La idea de América Latina: La herida colonial y la opción decolonial.* Barcelona: Editorial Gedisa.

MOE (Ministry of Education, China). (2009). *Zhongguo jiaoyu tongji nianjian (China's Educational Census)*. Beijing: People's Education Press.

Monbiot, G. (2010). Plan after plan fails to make Oxbridge access fair. There is another way. http://www.guardian.co.uk/commentisfree/2010/may/24/oxbridge-access-fair-top-universities. Last accessed 20 July, 2010.

Morley, L. (2003). *Quality and power in higher education*. Buckingham: Open University Press.

Morley, L. (2010a). Professorial lecture 'Imagining the University of the Future'. http://www.sussex.ac.uk/newsandevents/sussexlectures/louisemorley.php

Morley, L. (2010b). Gender mainstreaming: Myths and measurement in higher education in Ghana and Tanzania. *Compare: A Journal of Comparative Education, 40 (4)*, 533–550.

Morley, L., Leach, F., & Lugg, R. (2008). Democratising higher education in Ghana and Tanzania: Opportunity structures and social inequalities. *International Journal of Educational Development, 29 (1)*, 56–64.

Morley, L., Leach, F., Lussier, Lihamba, A., Mwaipopo, R., Forde, L., & Egbenya, G., (2010). *Widening participation in higher education in Ghana and Tanzania: Developing an equity scorecard*. Research report. http://www.sussex.ac.uk/wphegt/impact-outputs/report-summary.

Morley, L., & Lugg, R. (2009). Mapping meritocracy: Intersecting gender, poverty and higher educational opportunity structures. *Higher Education Policy, 22 (1)*, 37–60.

Moore, R. (2004). *Education and society: Issues and explanations in the sociology of education*. Cambridge: Polity Press.

Moore, R., & Muller, J. (1999). The discourse of "voice" and the problem of knowledge and identity in the sociology of education. *British Journal of Sociology of Education, 20 (2)*, 189–206.

Morris, H. (2010). *The net generation, the knowledge economy and on-line learning: Who is learning on-line and how?* Paper presented at the ESRC/CHEER Seminar Series, 'Imagining the University of the Future' Seminar 5: Who can inhabit the new academic identities of a digital age? Leeds Metropolitan University, 12 January, 2010. http://www.sussex.ac.uk/cheer/esrcseminars/seminar5

Mudimbe V. Y. (1988). *The invention of Africa*. Bloomington: Indiana University Press.

Murphy, P. (2009). Defining knowledge capitalism. In M. Peters, S. Marginson & P. Murphy. *Creativity and the global knowledge economy*. New York: Peter Lang.

Murphy, P., Peters, M. A., & Marginson, S. (2010). *Imagination: Three models of imagination in the age of the knowledge economy*. New York: Peter Lang.

National Plan for Higher Education. (2001). Ministry of Education, Pretoria: Government Printers. *New York Times* (July 6, 2010), A1 and A15.

Newman, John Henry (1946). *Naturaleza y fin de la educación universitaria*. Part one of *Idea de una Universidad*. Madrid: Ediciones y Publicaciones Españolas. Translated from English by Julio Mediavilla.

Nkwhevha, F. (2000). Educational transformation and the African renaissance in a globalising world. *Journal of Education, 25*, 19–47.

Noddings, N. (1992). *The challenge to care in schools: An alternative approach to education*. New York: Teachers College Press.

Nowotny, H., Scott, P., & Gibbons, M. (2001). *Re-thinking science: Knowledge and the public in an age of uncertainty*. Cambridge: Polity.

Nussbaum, M. (1983). *The fragility of goodness*. Cambridge: Cambridge Univeristy Press.

Nussbaum, M. (1997). *Cultivating humanity: A classical defence of reform in liberal education.* Cambridge, Mass.: Harvard University Press.

Nussbaum, M. C. (2010). *Not for profit: Why democracy needs the humanities.* Princeton and Oxford: Princeton University Press.

Orsdel, L. C. & Born, K. (2008). Global initiatives and startling successes hint at the profound implications of open access on journal publishing. *Library Journal.* At http://www. libraryjournal.com/article/CA6547086.html

Ortega y Gasset, J. (2001). *Misión de la Universidad.* With indications and notes from the courses and conferences of Raul J. A. Palma. Originally Published in 1930. Buenos Aires: 26p. http://www.fvet.uba.ar/rectorado/postgrado/especialidad/mision_universidad. pdf. Last accessed 7 April 2000.

Ortiz, R. (1998). *Los artífices de una cultura mundializada.* Siglo del hombre. Editores, fundación Bogotá.

Otto, B. K. (2001). *Fools are everywhere: The court jester around the world.* Chicago: University of Chicago Press.

Outlaw, L. T., Jr. (1996). *On race and philosophy.* New York & London: Routledge.

Pan, S.-Y. (2009). *University autonomy, the state, and social change in China.* Hong Kong: Hong Kong University Press.

Patel, R. (2009). *The value of nothing: How to reshape market society and redefine democracy.* London: Portobello Books.

Peek, R. (2005). RCUK: Free for all. *Information Today, 22, 8,* 17–18.

Pepper, S. (1996). *Radicalism and education reform in 20th-century China.* Cambridge: Cambridge University Press.

Peters, M. A. (2006a). Derrida and the question of the post-colonial university. *Access: Critical Perspectives on Communication, Cultural & Policy Studies, 24 (1–2),* 15–25.

Peters, M.A. (2006b). Higher education, development and the learning economy. *Policy Futures in Education, 4 (3),* 279–291.

Peters, M.A. (2007a). Higher education, globalization and the knowledge economy: Reclaiming the cultural mission. *Ubiquity, 8, Issue 18, May 8, 2007–May 14, 2007.* At http://www.acm.org/ubiquity/views/v8i18_peter.html. (Reprint).

Peters, M.A. (2007b). *Knowledge economy, development and the future of higher education.* Rotterdam: Sense Publishers.

Peters, M. A., & Besley, T. (2006). *Building knowledge cultures: Education and development in the age of knowledge capitalism.* Lanham, Boulder, NY, Oxford: Rowman & Littlefield.

Peters, M. A., & Britez, R. (2008). (Eds.). *Open education and education for openness.* Rotterdam & Taipei: Sense Publishers.

Peters, M. A., Marginson, S., & Murphy, P. (2009). *Creativity and the global knowledge economy.* New York: Peter Lang.

Peters, M. A. & Roberts, P. (2011). *The virtues of openness: Education, science and scholarship in a digital age.* Boulder, Colo.: Paradigm Publishers.

Phan, P. C. (2001). The wisdom of holy fools in postmodernity. *Theological Studies, 62,* 730–52.

Pityane, N. B. (1999). The renewal of African moral values. In M.W. Makgoba (Ed.), *African Renaissance* (pp. 137–148). Cape Town: Tafelberg Publishers.

Popper, K. (1959). *The logic of scientific discovery.* London: Hutchinson.

Popper, K. (1963). *Conjectures and refutations.* London: Routledge and Kegan Paul.

Program evaluation findings summary (2009). http://ocw.mit.edu/ans7870/global/09_Eval_Summary.pdf

Pryor, J., & Crossouard, B. (2010). Challenging formative assessment – disciplinary spaces and identities. *Assessment & Evaluation in Higher Education, 35(3)*, 265–276.

Qian, G., & Hu, J.-C. (2009). *Daqing liumei youtong ji (Chinese educational commission students)*. Hong Kong: Zhonghua Book Company.

Quijano, A. (1990). *Modernidad, identidad y utopía en América Latina*. Quito: Editorial El Conejo.

Rama, A. (1987). *Transculturación narrativa en América Latina*. México: Siglo Veintiuno Editores.

Ramose, M. B. (2002). The ethics of ubuntu. In P. H. Coetzee & A. P. J. Roux (Eds.), *Philosophy from Africa: A text with readings* (pp. 324–330). Cape Town: Oxford University Press Southern Africa.

Rancière, J. (2008). *Le spectateur émancipé*. Paris: La Fabrique.

Readings, B. (1996). *The University in ruins*. Cambridge, Mass./London: Harvard University Press.

Reay, D., David, M., & Ball, S. J. (2005). *Degrees of choice: Social class, race and gender in higher education*. Stoke-on-Trent: Trentham Books.

Reeves, R. (2009). "Progressive austerity: an agenda to protect the poor". *Financial Times*, 21 May 2009. http://www.ft.com/cms/s/0/bfbf77da-4649-11de-803f-00144feabdc0.html. Last accessed 12 May 2010.

Ricoeur, P. (1991). Narrative identity. In D. Wood (Ed.), *On Paul Ricoeur: Narrative and interpretation*. London & New York: Routledge.

Ritzen, J. (2010). *A chance for European universities. Or: Avoiding the looming university crisis in Europe*. Amsterdam: Amsterdam University Press.

Robertson, S. (2009). "Metaphoric imaginings": Re-/visions on the idea of a university. In R. Barnett et al., *Rethinking the University after Bologna*. Antwerp: UCSIA.

Robins, K., & Webster, F. (Eds.). (2002). *The virtual university: Knowledge, markets, and management*. Oxford: Oxford University Press.

Robson, M. (2009). How teenagers consume media, media and internet. Morgan Stanley [online]. Available at: http://media.ft.com/cms/. Last accessed 2 January 2010.

Rojas Aravena, F. (2009). *IV Report of Flacso's General Secretary integration in Latin America: Actions and omissions; conflicts and cooperation*. San Jose, Costa Rica: FLACSO.

Rothblatt, S. (2008). A note on the "integrity" of the university. In M. Beretta, K. Grandin & S. Lindqvist (Eds.), *Aurora Torealis, studies in the history of science and ideas in Hhonor of Tore Frängsmyr*. Sagamore Beach, Mass.: Science History Publications.

Rothblatt, S., & Wittrock, B. (Eds.). (1993). *The European and American university since 1800, historical and sociological essays*. Cambridge: Cambridge University Press.

Rueda Junguera, F. (2001). Integración económica latinoamericana. Balance y perspectivas. *Boletín económico de ICE, N° 2703*.

Saunders, M. (2010). Capturing effects of interventions, policies and programmes in the European context: A social practice perspective. *Evaluation 17(1)*, 1–14.

Schwartz, S. (2010). Restoring wisdom to universities. Vice-Chancellor's annual lecture, Macquarie University, Sydney. http://www.vc.mq.edu.au/vblog/detail.php?id=35 Last accessed 27 August 2010.

Sennett, R. (2009). *El Artesano*. Barcelona: Editorial Anagrama.

She Figures (2009). Statistics and indicators on gender equality in science. http://ec.europa. eu/research/science-society/document_library/pdf_06/she_figures_2009_en.pdf. Last accessed 20 June 2010.

Shepherd, J., & Vasagar, J. (2010). Graduate tax and private colleges at heart of higher education blueprint: Private universities will flourish and struggling institutions will be allowed to fail, if the coalition has its way with the future of higher education. *http://www.guardian.co.uk/education/2010/jul/15/higher-education-universityfunding*. Last accessed 12 July 2010.

Shumar, W. (1997). *College for sale*. London and Washington, D.C.: Falmer Press.

Simons, M., & Masschelein, J. (2009). The public and its university: Beyond learning for civic employability? *European Educational Research Journal, 8(2)*, 204–217.

Singh, J. K. S. (2008). *Whispers of change: Female staff numbers in Commonwealth universities*. London: Association of Commonwealth Universities.

Singh, M. (2001). Reinserting the "public good" into higher education transformation. *Globalisation and Higher Education—Views from the South*. University of Cape Town, South African Council of Higher Education.

Slaughter, S., & Rhoades, G. (2004). *Academic capitalism and the new economy: Markets, state and higher education*. Baltimore: Johns Hopkins University Press.

Smith, A., & Webster, F. (Eds.). (1997). *The postmodern university? Contested visions of higher education in society*. Buckingham: Open University Press.

Smith, D. (2003). *The atlas of war and peace*. London: Earthscan.

Snow, C. P. (1964). *The two cultures and a second look*. Cambridge: Cambridge University Press.

Somers, M. (1994). The narrative constitution of identity: A relational and network Approach. *Theory and Society, 23*, 605–649.

Standaert, N. (2009). Pyramid, pillar and web: Questions for academic life raised by the network society. In R. Barnett et al., *Rethinking the university after Bologna*. Antwerp: UCSIA.

Standish, P. (2005). Towards an economy of higher education. *Critical Quarterly, 47 (1–2)*, 53–71.

Standish, P. (2011). The ownership of learning. In N. Saito & P. Standish (Eds.). *Stanley Cavell and the education of grownups*. New York, Mass.: Fordham University Press.

Stengers, I. (2005). The cosmopolitical proposal. In B. Latour & P. Wiebel (Eds.), *Making things public: Atmospheres of democracy*. Karlsruhe and Cambridge: Zentrum für Kunst und Medientechnologie [Centre for Art and Media] & MIT Press.

Stiglitz, J. E. (2010). *Freefall: Free markets and the sinking of the global economy*. London: Allen Lane/Penguin Books.

Sunkel, O. (1969). The structural background of development problems in Latin America. In C. T. Nisbet (Ed.), *Latin America, problems in economic development*. New York: The Free Press.

Sunkel O. (1973). *El subdesarrollo Latinoamericano y la teoria del desarrollo*. México: Siglo Veintiuno Editores, 6° Edición.

Sutton Trust. (2004). *The missing 3000: State school students under-represented at leading universities*. London: The Sutton Trust.

Sutton Trust. (2008). *University admissions by individual schools*. London: The Sutton Trust.

Teferra, D., & Altbach, P. (2003). Trends and perspectives in African higher education. In D. Teferra, & P. Altbach (Eds.), *African higher education: An international reference handbook*. Bloomington & Indianapolis: Indiana University Press.

Teffo, L. (1999). Moral renewal and African experience(s), in M. W. Makgoba (Ed.), *African renaissance*. Cape Town: Tafelberg Publishers.

Teichler, U. (2008). Diversification? Trends and explanations of the shape and size of higher education. *Higher Education, 56 (3)*, 349–379.

Thompson, J. (1995). *Media and modernity*. London: Polity Press.

Touraine, A. (1988). Modernidad y especialidades culturales: Modernidad e identidad: Un simposio. *Cultura, Economía y Desarrollo* 118. UNESCO.

Toynbee, P., & Walker, D. (2009). *Unjust rewards: Ending the greed that is bankrupting Britain*. London: Granta Books.

Trow, M. (1974). Problems in the transition from elite to mass higher education. *Policies for Higher Education*. Paris: OECD.

Trow, M. (2005). *Reflections on the transition from elite to mass to universal access: Forms and phases of higher education in modern societies since WWII*. Berkeley, Calif.: Institute of Governmental Studies, University of California.

Trow, M. (2010). From mass higher education to universal access: the American advantage. Reprinted in M. Burrage (Ed.), *Martin Trow: Twentieth-century higher education, elite to mass to universal*. Baltimore: The Johns Hopkins Press.

UNESCO. (2009). *Global education digest 2007: Comparing education statistics across the world*. Montreal: UNESCO Institute of Statistics http://www.unesco.org/fileadmin/MULTIMEDIA/HQ/ED/ED/pdf/WCHE_2009/FINAL%20COMMUNIQUE%20WCHE%202009.pdf

United Nations. (1995). *Beijing declaration, fourth world conference on women*. http://www.un.org/womenwatch/daw/beijing/platform/declar.htm Last accessed 17 October 2010.

Universities UK (UUK). (2010). Manifesto for higher education http://www.universitiesuk.ac.uk/ParliamentaryActivities/generalelection/Pages/ManifestoTranscript.aspx. Last accessed 26 July 2010.

Van Orsdel, L. C., & Born, K. (2008). Embracing openness. *Library Journal, 133(7)*, 53–58.

Varghese, N. V. (2004). *Private higher education in Africa*: Paris: IIEP/ADEA/AAU.

Vasagar, J. (2010). Cut student places not funding, says university chief: Protect research even if second rate colleges have to close, says UCL head. http://www.guardian.co.uk/education/2010/jul/13/cut-student-places-university-funding. Last accessed 23 July 2010.

Verger, J. (1992). Patterns. In H. De Ridder-Symoens (Ed.), *A History of the university in Europe. Vol. I. Universities in the Middle Ages*. Cambridge: Cambridge University Press.

Verschaffel, B. (2009). Semi-public spaces: The spacial logic of institutions. In R. Geenens & R. Tinnevelt (Eds.), *Does truth matter?* Dordrecht: Springer.

Vest, C. M. (2005). What we don't know. In C. Vest, *Pursuing the endless frontier: Essays on MIT and the role of research universities*. Cambridge, Mass.: MIT Press.

Virno, P. (2004). *Palabras con palabras: poderes y límites del lenguaje*. Buenos Aires: Paidós Ibérica.

Vu, T. T., & Dall'Alba, G. (2011). Becoming authentic professionals: Learning for authenticity. In L. Scanlon (Ed.), *'Becoming' a professional: An interdisciplinary analysis of professional learning*. Dordrecht: Springer.

Wallerstein, I. (2005). After developmentalism and globalisation, what? *Social Forces,* March 2005.

Wang, R.-Q. (2007). *Bainianlai Zhongguo Xiandai Gaodeng Jiaoyu (Chinese modern higher education in a hundred years).* Taipei: Center for China Studies, NCCU.

Welsch, W. (1998). Rationality and reason today. In D. R. Gordon & J. Niznik (Eds.), *Criticism and defense of rationality in contemporary philosophy.* Amsterdam: Rodopi.

Weymans, W. (2009). From coherence to differentiation: Understanding (changes in) the European area for higher education and research. In R. Cowen & A. M. Kazamias (Eds.), *International handbook of comparative education.* Dordrecht: Springer.

Wheelahan, L. (2010). Tertiary education as insurance against risk – what are the outcomes? For whom? In G. Marston, J. Moss & J. Quiggin (Eds.), *Risk, welfare and work.* Melbourne: Melbourne University Press.

White, H. (1987). The value of narrativity in the representation of reality. In H. White, *The content of the form: Narrative discourse and historical representation.* Baltimore, Md.: Johns Hopkins University Press.

Williams, G. L. (1995). The "marketization" of higher education: reforms and potentials in higher education finance. In D. D. Dill & B. Sporn (Eds.), *Emerging patterns of social demand and university reform: Through a glass darkly.* Oxford, New York and Tokyo: Pergamon for the International Association of Universities Press.

Wilkinson, R., & Pickett, K. (2009). *The spirit level: Why more equal societies almost always do better.* London: Allen Lane

Wilson, R. A. (2001). *The politics of truth and reconciliation. Legitimizing the post-apartheid state,* Cambridge: Cambridge University Press.

Wiredu, K. (1980). *Philosophy and African culture.* Cambridge: Cambridge University Press.

World Economic Forum. (2009). *The global gender gap report 2009.* Geneva: The World Economic Forum.

Xiao, H.-T. (2001). *Daxue de linian (The idea of the university).* Wu Chang: Central China Science & Technology University Press.

Yang, D.-P. (Ed.). (2000). *Daxue jingshen (University spirit).* Shenyang: Liaohai Press.

Yang, R., Vidovich, L., & Currie, J. (2007). Dancing in a cage: Changing autonomy in Chinese higher education. *Higher Education, 54 (4),* 575–592.

Yin, Q., & White, G. (1994). The "marketisation" of Chinese higher education: A critical assessment. *Comparative Education, 30(3),* 217–238.

Young, M. (1958). *The Rise of meritocracy, 1870–2033: An essay on education and equality.* London: Penguin.

Young, M. (2001). Down with meritocracy. *The Guardian,* 29 June.

Young, M. (2004). *Government intervention and the problem of knowledge in education.* ESRC Seminar 'Private Sector Participation in Public Sector Education', Institute of Education, University of London, 29 October.

Young, M. (2008). *Bringing knowledge back in: From social constructivism to social realism in the sociology of education.* London: Routledge.

Young, M., & Wilmott, P. (1957). *Family and kinship in East London.* London: Routledge.

Zha, Q. (2009). Diversification or homogenization: How governments and markets have combined to (re)shape Chinese higher education in its recent massification process. *Higher Education, 58(1),* 41–58.

SUBJECT INDEX

NB: *This index picks out main uses of key terms and phrases such as "university," "University of the Future," "the idea of the university," and "knowledge," which are more or less ubiquitous through the volume.* Particularly significant appearances of terms are emboldened.

academic freedom 25, 50, 52, 54, 56, 71, 77, 103, 107, 122
academic identity 150
academic mobility 27, 32, 35
access to higher education 48, 71; *see also* widening participation; inclusion
accountability 51, 55, 57
Africa 9, 28–29, 178–186
alterity 161
anarchism 202, 204
Asia 16–17, 28
attunement 119–120
audit 51, 55
Australia 4–5, **39–49**
Austria 29
authenticity 116

Bangladesh 29
becoming 119
being 7, 8, 113–115, 117, 119, 121–122
Bildung 170
bioengineering 23
Bologna Agreement 19
Brazil 195
bureaucracy 147

capability 146

capital: *see* cultural capital; human capital; social capital
capitalism 64
care 7, 9, **112–122**
chaos 108
cheating 22
China 4–5, **50–58**
church 41
civil society
citizenship 20, 72–73, 115, 158, 168, 182
collaboration 150; *see also* partnerships
Colombia 195
colonialism 62–63
commitment 7
commodification 28
common good 9, **141–151**
commons: *see* intellectual commons
communality 178, 186
community 77, 183–184, 197
competition 33, 70, 143–144, 202
complexity 10
conceptual grammars 34
concern 7
conversation 9
cosmopolitanism 32
Council for National Academic Awards 17
courage 7

creative thinking 27, 98, 189
crisis 26, 45
critical dialogue 5
critical knowledge 4, 34
critical realism 2
critical reason 72
critical spatiality 190
critical thinking 159
critique 81
culture 167, 169–170, 179, 189
cultural capital 194
curriculum 5, 44, 46–47, 67, 71, 148

democracy 5, 10, 45, 48–49, 81, 152–153,
    157–158, 160, 164, 171, 182, 184, 188,
    191
democratisation 28, 30
digitisation 32
disciplines 6, 21, 45–48, 97
diversity 67, 181

economic reason 68, 203
egalitarianism 48, 143
elite higher education 56–58; *see also* mass
    higher education
elites 45, 53, 57, 156
elitism 72
e-learning 22
emancipation 24, 60, 105, 191, 202
empiricism 124, 129; aim-oriented
    empiricism 131
engagement 117–118, 120
England 102
enlightenment 11, 106, 129, 135, 137,
    168–169,
Enlightenment 188
Entertainment 190, 194
entrepreneurialism 33
epistemic fields 63
eros 160
Europe 16, 28
Ethiopia 29
ethical dimensions 121, 143
examinations 17
excellence 165, 167, 177

fluidity 25
fool 8; *see also* university as fool
forgiveness 181
for-profit institutions 21, 145
France 16–17, 21, 102
Freedom 168
Fudan University 56

gender inequalities 30
general education 56, 104, 156–157
geography 136
Germany 15, 19, 24
Ghana 29, 31
good life 9; *see also* the good society
governance 150
global dimensions: global crises 137;
    global economy 63, 67, 142; global
    inequalities 202; globalization 6, 46,
    64, 68, 91, 141; global possibilities 4,
    93; global society 6, 148, 198; global
    spaces 6, 190; global university 197
grade inflation 17

Harvard University 56, 195–198
higher education 1, 16, 18, 25, 47, 49,
    161, 190
history 15, 18
human being 162, 180–181
human capital 165, 167, 170
humanities 6, 23, 96, 103–104, 127, 158,
    160, 163
humanity 103, 126–127, 134, 137, 158, 185
human rights 198
Humboldtian model of university 52, 104
hybridity 64–66, 202
hypermodernity 3, 27, 34

Iceland 29, 31
ideologies of the university 2, 27, 51, 180
imaginaries of the university 26
imagination 2, 97, 100, 121, 203–204
impact 2, 4, 33–34
inclusion 10, 68–69; *see also* widening
    participation
inequality 144–146
inquiry: academic inquiry 125–126, 128–
    129; knowledge inquiry 8, 123–124,
    127, 134–135; social inquiry 127–128,
    133; wisdom inquiry 8, 124, 127,
    134–137
institutional autonomy 25, 50, 52, 54, 73,
    120
instrumentalism 121
intellectual commons 187, 197
intellectuals 184; *see also* public
    intellectuals
internal goods 57
irrationality: *see* rationality
Israel 16
Italy 21, 102
ivory tower 51, 106

Japan 31, 195
Johns Hopkins University 104
Judgement 74

knowledge 8, 19, 24, 35, 40, 46, 59,
    61–62, 72, 75, 78, 89–90, 92, 95,
    112–114, 125–131, 168, 188, 190, 195–
    196, 198; knowledge, authentic 45;
    knowledge capitalism 2, 198, 202–203;
    knowledge, community-based;
    knowledge culture 95, 188; knowledge
    dissemination 215; knowledge
    ecologies 31; knowledge economy 44,
    143, 199; knowledge, esoteric 41;
    knowledge exclusivity 198;
    knowledge generation 20–21; see
    also research; knowledge, geographies
    of 29; knowledge, indigenous 185;
    knowledge inquiry 2; knowledge,
    intellectual 106; knowledge, landscape
    of 99; knowledge markets 67;
    knowledge, profane 40, 47; knowledge
    repositories 98; knowledge, sacred
    39–40, 42, 49; knowledge sharing 193,
    198; knowledge socialism 188,
    198–199; knowledge society 66, 69;
    knowledge, theoretical 39–42, 46–47;
    knowledge, theory of 47; knowledge
    work 32; knowledges 31; knowledge
    socialism 9, 188, 198–199; see also
    critical knowledge

language 163–164
Latin America 4–5, 28, **59–70**
leadership 5, 7, 23, 44, 57
learner 161
learning 61, 71, 113, 115, 121, 147, 149,
    152–153, 155, 160–161, 163, 190–191,
    194; see also open learning
learning economy 190
lectures 109, 171, 173, 174–175; see also
    public lecture
Lesotho 31
liberal education 4, 19–20, 42, 44, 46, 48,
    56, 106, 157; see also general education;
    professional education; vocational
    education
lifelong learning 46
lifeworld of university 53
legitimacy 51
liquid life 56
liminality 7–8, 102, 109–110, 202
literacies, new 32

love 175

Macquarie University 113
Massachusetts Institute of Technology
    (MIT) 192–5
markets 3–4, 15, 18, 43, 46, 50, 54,
    61–65, 143–144, 166; see also for-profit
    institutions
mass higher education 16, 42, 57–58,
    104–105, 171
mediaeval universities 102
mergers 20
meritocracy 39, 144–146
metaphor 87, 96–97, 100, 102
Middle East 15
mind 24
modernity 65–66
modernization 66
modules 18
multiversity 15, 24, 33, 109
mystery 109

neoliberalism 63, 67–68, 199
networks 6, 9, 15, 20, 25, 87, 90, 93, 99,
    101, 108
network society 97
Nigeria 29
nodes 9, 95–96
nomadism 3, 32–33, 98

objectivity 70
on-line learning see e-learning
open access 195–196
open learning 192
openness 9, 187–199
Open University 191–195, 199

partnerships 20
pedaogogical love 161
pedagogy 77–78, 89–90, 155
performativity 4–5, 51, 55, 57–58, 60, 68,
    76, 79, 82
pharmaceutical companies 23
phronesis 147–148
physics 130, 138
plagiarism 22
playfulness 204
postgraduate provision 20
postmodernism 5
postmodernity 51, 62, 68–70, 178
possibilities: see the university: possibilities
    for
private good 46; see also public good

privatisation of universities 16, 28
professional development 76
professional education 19
professional ethics 23
professionalism 5, 48
professions 46, 103–104, 110, 118
professors 170–171, 175
public, a 169, 173–174, 190
public concern 177
public debate 62, 94
public gain 112
public good 10–11, 27, 46, 73, 81, 157,
   188, 198–199, 202; *see also* common good
public intellectuals 27, 55–56, 109
public lecture 172–177
public space 166, 174
public sphere 9–10, 163–164, 168
public thinking 174
publiversity 97

quality 51
quality assurance 17–18, 55

rankings 143
rationality 60–61, 123–128, 159, 182;
   aim-oriented rationality 129; problem-
   solving rationality 124, 126; scientific
   rationality 131, 148
reading 164
reason 70, 72–74, 77, 79, 82, 103, 110,
   112, 114, 125, 147–148, 167, 169, 175,
   177; *see also* economic reason
religion 40
research 9–10, 16, 21, 33, 67, 71–74, 76–
   78, 82, 104–105, 112–113, 115–118,
   120, 123, 161, 177, 183–185, 194
research-led universities 18
responsibility 11, 75, 77–78, 82, 115–116,
   119, 147, 202–203
responsiveness 120
revolution 123
risk 7, 77–79, 83, 121

sacred 177
Saudi Arabia 195
Scandinavia 24
scholars 168
science 6, 19, 130, 132–134, 137–138
service to society 10, 177
skills 43–44, 46, 113–114
social benefits of higher education 150
social capital 30
social class 64–65

social good 11, 29; *see also* public good
social justice 39, 49, 105
social sciences 23, 133
society 6, 9; 'the good society' 9
South Africa 4–5, 29, **71–83, 178**
South Korea 23, 195
Soviet Union 138
Space 176
spaces 91, 93–94, 98–99, 202
Spain 195
spirit of the university 52–53, 166, 203
stakeholders 26
state 53–54, 103, 110, 143
stratification of higher education 40
students 10, 44, 46, 48, 93, 115, 118,
   143, 149, 155, 161–163, 165–167, 170,
   172–173
subjectivities 44
supercomplexity 56
supervision 80–82
surveillance 23

Taiwan 54, 195
Tanzania 29
teaching 9, 21, 71, 113, 117, 152–153,
   155, 159–161, 163–164, 177, 194
techne 148
technology 19, 137
theology 89–90
theoria 148
the university 162; belief in 1; idea
   of 2–3, **50–58**, 59–60, 104, 114; ideas
   of 6–9; possibilities for 2, 7, 118;
   purposes of 117; vision of 155
the democratic university 67–70;
   the ecological university 94; the
   entrepreneurial university 105, 165,
   167–171; the networked university 7,
   87, 95; the postmodern university 15,
   19; University of Culture 106; the
   university as fool 7–8, 101–111;
   University of God 102
the University of the Future 18, 26, 34–35
the University of the Past 26–27
the University of Today 27; *see also*
   publiversity
time 176
transformation 113
Tsinghua University 54
trust 23, 172
truth 5, 70, 78, 89–90, 135, 172, 176

ubuntu 81, 178, 180–182

Uganda 29
uncertainty 19, 170
UNESCO 29, 181
United Kingdom 16–17, 19, 195
United States 16–17, 19–21, 23, 48, 195
universal systems of higher education 42
universality 3, 5, 57
universities 41
University College London 33, 136
University of California 18, 22
University of Cambridge 16, 22, 135–136
University of Central Florida 22
University of Chicago 56, 155
University of Illinois 18
University of Massachusetts 20
University of Michigan 18
University of Oxford 16, 20, 24, 136
University of Peking 52, 54

University of Stellenbosch 80
University of Virginia 18
  see also the university
Unpredictability 69
utilitarianism 74, 77, 82
utopia: feasible utopias 5, 204

values 132, 203
virtues 9
vocational education 4–5, 42, 43–45, 48

web 8, 9, 90, 100; *see also* networks
widening participation 30
wisdom 7–8, 89, 109, 113, **123–38**; *see also* inquiry, wisdom
world-class universities 50, 54–55
world university 94

Zhongshan University 56

NAME INDEX

Agamben, G. 166
Al Mufti, I. 181
Altbach, P. 28, 50, 71
Altman, Bourbon J. 64
Appadurai, A. 30
Archer, M. 41
Ardao, A. 63
Arendt, H. 174–175
Aristotle 147
Aronowitz, S. 106
Asmal, K. 180
Asmal, L. 180
Assie-Lumumba, N. 71
Atcon, R. 65

Balfour, R. 77
Ball, S. 28, 34, 55, 143
Barnett, R. 5, 24, 47, 51, 53, 56, 60–61,
    93–94, 112, 148–149, 203–204
Battle, M. 180
Bauman, Z. 27, 56
Beck, U. 148
Becker, P. 107
Berman, M. 56, 66
Bernstein, B. 39–40, 46, 59
Bevis, T. 52
Besley, T. 197, 199
Bhaskar, R. 2, 45
Biesta, G. 30
Bjarnason, S. 28
Bledstein, B. 104
Bloom, A. 155–156, 160, 163

Bok, D. 143
Boltansky, L. 62
Born, K. 196
Borrero Cabal, A. 60
Bourdieu, P. 200
Bousquet, M. 33–34
Bowker, G. 197
Brabazon, T. 32
Bradbury, M. 153–154
Bradwell, P. 27, 34
Brown, R. 143–144
Brunner, J. 66
Bullen, E. 27
Burik, S. 79

Cai, Y.-P. 56
Cardoso, F. 63
Carr, N. 32
Carson, S. 195
Castells, M. 90–92
Cavell, S. 79, 81–82, 162
Cerney, P. 54
Chen, H.-J. 52
Chen, P.-Y. 52
Chen, S.-Y. 5, 55
Chiapello, E. 62
Chu, Z.-H. 52
Cladis, M. 42
Clark, B. 209
Clark, W. 107
Clegg, S. 32
Coate, K. 112, 148–149

Considine, M. 43
Contreras, N. 66
Cornejo Polar, A. 68
Corredor, C. 66
Crossouard, B. 31
Crozier, G. 30
Currie, J. 52

Dahrendorf, R. 110
Dall'Alba, G. 7, 116
David, M. 29–30, 143
Deem, R. 31
de Certeau, M. 91–92
Delanty, G. 51, 55
Delors, J. 181
De Ridder-Symoens 167
Derrida, J. 5, 59–61, 70, 72–5, 77–79,
    175
Dewey, J. 47, 159
Diamond, D. 200
Diaz Villa, M. 5
Dilthey, W. 96
Douglas, J. 20
Durkheim, E. 39–41

Edelstein, R. 20
Erasmus, D. 110
Exley, S. 34

Faletto, E. 63
Fallis, G. 33
Faust, D. 114, 121
Ferrari, C. 66
Ffrench-Davis, R. 63
Flexner, A. 104, 106
Foucault, M. 169, 174–175
Freire, P. 77
Fuller, S. 110

Gan, Y. 56
Garcia, A. 65
Garcia Canclini, N. 64
Garfield, J. 185
Geiser, S. 211
Gibbons, M. 45
Gietzen, G. 9–10
Giroux, H. 106
Goffman, E. 173
Grewal, D. 90
Grubb, W. 48
Guédon, C. 99
Guri-Rosenblit, S. 22
Gyekye, K. 179, 183

Habermas, J. 66
Hall, Sir P. 21
Harley, D. 22
Hattersley, R. 146
Hayhoe, R. 50, 52
Heath, S. 30
Heidegger, M. 7, 114–116, 118–120
Henriquez Urena, P. 63
Higgs, P. 9–10
Horkheimer, M. 172
Houtondji, P. 179, 183
Hu, J. 52
Huisman, J. 55
Huizinga, J. 108
Humboldt, von W. 176
Huntington, P. 115
Husén, T. 178

Illich, I. 168, 177
Inglis, F. 150

Jackson, B. 146
Jansen, J. 181
Jaspers, K. 61
Judt, T. 9, 141–143, 149

Kaletsky, A. 142
Kant, I. 60, 73, 75, 103, 106, 168–169
Kaphagawani, D. 179, 183
Kavanagh, D. 7–8
Kenjatta, J. 182
Kenway, J. 27, 32
Kerr, C. 15
King, M. 118–119
Kittler, F. 177
Klein, N. 26
Kokotovic, M. 65
Kymlicka, W. 185

Laclau, E. 67
Langley, L. 127
Langmans, S. 97–98
Lastra, A. 62
Latour, B. 175, 177
Lazerson, M. 142, 145
Leathwood, C. 30
Lechner, N. 66
Levinas, E. 162
Levy, D. 28
Li, M. 56
Lienhard, M. 64
Linksruck, N. 165
Lightman, A. 97

Lipovetsky, G. 3, 27, 60–62
Lo, L. 5, 54–55
Lucas, C. 52
Lugg, R. 27
Lynch, C. 197
Lyotard, J.-F. 55

Malherbe, J. 179, 183
Marginson, S. 43, 199
Marx, K. 133
Maskell, D. 24
Masschelein, J. 9–10, 94–95, 98, 174, 177
Maxwell, N. 7–8, 131–133, 135, 138
Mbiti, J. 182
McHenry, L. 138
McKibbin, R. 34, 149
Mei, Y.-Q. 56
Melo, J. 65–66
Menkiti, I. 182
Miedana, J. 32
Mignolo, W. 62–63
Mill, J. 133
Monbiot, G. 29
Moore, R. 41, 61
Morley, L. 3–4, 27, 29–31
Morris, H. 32
Mudimbe, V. 179
Muller, J. 61
Murphy, P. 2, 199, 202

Nietzsche, F. 157, 162
Newman, J. 24–25, 43, 46, 61, 106
Nkwhevha, F. 179
Noddings, N. 114, 116
Nowotny, H. 45
Nixon, J. 9–10
Nussbaum, M. 145, 147–148, 157–161, 163

Oakeshott, M. 181
Ondercin, D. 9–10
Ortega y Gasset 61
Otto, B. 101
Outlaw, L. 179

Parry, G. 112
Passeron, J.-C. 200
Patel, R. 149
Peek, R. 196
Pepper, S. 54
Perry, W. 191
Peters, M. 9–10, 197, 199
Phan, P. 101

Pickett, K. 145
Pityane, N. 180
Popper, Sir K. 129
Pryor, J. 31

Qian, G. 52
Quijano, A. 65

Rama, A. 65
Ramose, M. 180
Ranciere, J. 175
Reay, D. 30, 143
Readings, B. 51, 170
Reeves, R. 33
Rhoades, G. 62
Ricoeur, P. 52
Ritzen, J. 142
Robb, S. 27
Roberts, R. 180
Roberts, S. 87
Robins, K. 61
Robinson, L. 24
Robson, M. 32
Rueda Junguera, F. 64
Rothblatt, S. 3–4, 24

Saunders, M. 34
Schwartz, S. 113, 121
Scott, P. 45
Segal, P. 146
Sennett, R. 69
Shakespeare, W. 101
Shepherd, J. 28
Shumar, W. 143
Simons, M. 9–10, 94–95, 174, 177
Singh, M. 27, 31
Slaughter, S. 62
Smith, A. 106
Smith, D. 127
Socrates 158, 161
Somers, M. 58
Standaert, N. 6, 8, 95
Standish, P. 9–10, 161
Star, S. 107
Stengers, J. 173–174
Stobart, J. 191
Sunkel, O. 63
Sutton Trust 144–145

Teichler, U. 43
Teferra, D. 71
Teffo, L. 179
Thompson, J. 189

Thoreau, H. 163
Tolstoy, L. 25
Touraine, A. 66
Toynbee, P. 145
Trow, M. 16, 39, 42–43, 48–49
Tutu, D. 180

Van Orsdel, L. 196
Vasagar, J. 28, 33
Varghese, V. 28
Veblein, T. 104
Verger, J. 167–168
Verschaffel, B. 91–92, 99
Vest, C. 95, 193
Vidovich, L. 52
Virno, P. 62
Vu, T. 116

Waghid, Y. 5
Waldo Emerson, R. 162
Wallerstein, I. 63
Walker, D. 145
Wang, R.-Q. 53–54

Webster, F. 61, 106
Welsch, W. 61
Weymans, W. 91
Wheelahan, L. 5, 44
White, G. 54
White, H. 52
Wilkinson, G. 145
Williams, G. 143
Wilson, R. 180
Wiredu, K. 184
Wittrock, B. 24
Wyk, B. van 9–10

Xiao, H.-T. 52

Yang, D.-P. 52–53
Yang, R. 52
Yin, Q. 54
Young, M., Lord 146, 191
Young, M. 27, 45, 47
Youdell, D. 28

Zha, Q. 55